THE SIGNIFICANCE OF INFANT OBSERVATIONAL RESEARCH FOR CLINICAL WORK WITH CHILDREN, ADOLESCENTS, AND ADULTS

THE SIGNIFICANCE OF INFANT
OBSERVATIONAL RESEARCH

Workshop Series of the
American Psychoanalytic Association

Workshop Series of the
American Psychoanalytic Association

Monograph 5

THE SIGNIFICANCE OF INFANT OBSERVATIONAL RESEARCH FOR CLINICAL WORK WITH CHILDREN, ADOLESCENTS, AND ADULTS

Edited by

SCOTT DOWLING, M.D.
ARNOLD ROTHSTEIN, M.D.

INTERNATIONAL UNIVERSITIES PRESS, INC.
Madison   Connecticut

Library of Congress Cataloging-in-Publication Data

The Significance of infant observational research for clinical work with
    children, adolescents, and adults/edited by Scott Dowling,
    Arnold Rothstein.
        p. cm.—(Workshop series of the American Psychoanalytic
    Association ; monograph 5)
      Based on a workshop held in New York in 1987.
      Includes bibliographical references.
      ISBN 0-8236-6073-7
      1. Psychoanalysis—Congresses.   2. Infants—Research—Congresses.
    I. Dowling, Scott.   II. Rothstein, Arnold, 1936–   .   III. Series.
      [DNLM: 1. Infant—congresses.   2. Psychoanalysis—congresses.
      3. Research—congresses.   W1 W0848H monograph 5 / WM 460 S578
        1987]
    RC506.S545   1989
    616.89'17—dc20
    DNLM/DLC   89-24454
    for Library of Congress   CIP

Manufactured in the United States of America

Contents

Contributors

George H. Allison, M.D. Clinical Professor of Psychiatry, University of Washington; Training and Supervising Analyst, Seattle Institute for Psychoanalysis; Secretary, Board on Professional Standards, American Psychoanalytic Association

Jacob Arlow, M.D. Past President, American Psychoanalytic Association; Past Editor-in-Chief, *Psychoanalytic Quarterly;* Clinical Professor of Psychiatry, New York University College of Medicine

Harold P. Blum, M.D. Past Editor, *Journal of the American Psychoanalytic Association*; Training Analyst and Clinical Professor of Psychiatry, The Psychoanalytic Institute, New York University Medical Center

Arnold M. Cooper, M.D. Professor of Psychiatry, Department of Psychiatry, New York Hospital–Cornell Medical Center; Supervising and Training Analyst, Columbia University Center for Psychoanalytic Training and Research; Past President, American Psychoanalytic Association

Scott Dowling, M.D. Faculty, Cleveland Psychoanalytic Institute; Associate Clinical Professor of Child Psychiatry, Case Western Reserve University; Editor, *The Psychoanalytic Study of the Child*

Eleanor Galenson, M.D. Clinical Professor of Psychiatry, Mt. Sinai School of Medicine; Past Co-President, World Association for Infant Psychiatry

Jules Glenn, M.D. Clinical Professor of Psychiatry and Training Analyst, The Psychoanalytic Institute, New York University Medical Center; Editor,

Child Analysis and Therapy; Co-editor, *Freud and His Patients* and *Freud and His Self-Analysis*

Joseph D. Lichtenberg, M.D. Editor-in-Chief, *Psychoanalytic Inquiry*; Author, *Psychoanalysis and Infant Research, The Talking Cure*, and *Psychoanalysis and Motivation*; Co-editor, *Reflections on Self Psychology* and *Empathy I and II*

Eugene J. Mahon, M.D. Faculty, Adult and Child Analysis, Columbia University Center for Psychoanalytic Training and Research; Assistant Professor of Psychiatry, Columbia University College of Physicians and Surgeons

Charles A. Mangham, M.D. Clinical Professor of Psychiatry, University of Washington; Training and Supervising Analyst, Seattle Institute for Psychoanalysis

James T. McLaughlin, M.D. Training and Supervising Analyst, Pittsburgh Psychoanalytic Institute; Clinical Associate Professor Emeritus of Psychiatry, School of Medicine, University of Pittsburgh

William W. Meissner, M.D. University Professor of Psychoanalysis, Boston College; Training and Supervising Analyst, Boston Psychoanalytic Institute

Jack Novick, Ph.D. Faculty and Child/Adolescent Supervising Analyst, Michigan Psychoanalytic Institute; Adjunct Associate Professor, University of Michigan and Wayne State University Medical School; Former Supervising Analyst and Faculty, Anna Freud Center

Leo Rangell, M.D. Past President, American and International Psychoanalytic Associations; Clinical Professor of Psychiatry, University of California, Los Angeles; Clinical Professor of Psychiatry (Psychoanalysis), University of California, San Francisco

Arnold Rothstein, M.D. Member, New York Psychoanalytic Society; Editor, Workshop Series of the American Psychoanalytic Association; Author, *The Narcissistic Pursuit of Perfection* and *The Structural Hypothesis: An Evolutionary Perspective*

Melvin A. Scharfman, M.D. Clinical Professor of Psychiatry, New York University Medical Center; Training and Supervising Analyst, The Psychoanalytic Institute, New York University Medical Center

Morton Shane, M.D. Director of Education and Training and Supervising Analyst in Adult and Child Analysis, Los Angeles Psychoanalytic Society and Institute; Associate Clinical Professor of Psychiatry, University of California, Los Angeles

Martin A. Silverman, M.D. Training and Supervising Analyst, Chairman of Child Analysis Section, and Clinical Professor of Psychiatry, The Psychoanalytic Institute, New York University Medical Center; Associate Editor, *Psychoanalytic Quarterly*

Albert J. Solnit, M.D. Sterling Professor of Pediatrics and Psychiatry, School of Medicine and Child Study Center, Yale University; former Director,

Yale Child Study Center; Managing Editor, *The Psychoanalytic Study of the Child*

Rebecca Z. Solomon, M.D. Past President, American Psychoanalytic Association; Clinical Professor of Psychiatry, University of Connecticut School of Medicine

Phyllis Tyson, Ph.D. Assistant Clinical Professor of Psychiatry, University of California, San Diego; Faculty and Supervising Child Analyst, San Diego Psychoanalytic Institute; Geographic Child Supervisor, Denver Institute of Psychoanalysis

Preface

Paul A. Dewald, M.D.

For many people the word *psychoanalysis* refers to a specialized form of treatment for neurotic illness applicable only to a small group of neurotically ill individuals. However, psychoanalysis also refers to a specific and powerful method of observation of the details of conscious and unconscious mental life and to the body of unique observations and theory derived from this method.

As a general theory of the mind, psychoanalysis includes clinical and theoretical formulations which can be helpful to anyone concerned with human behavior. Clinical psychoanalytic theory is applicable to a broad spectrum of phenomena (both healthy and pathological) including clinical situations other than the formal psychoanalytic treatment setting, such as the medical or psychiatric clinic, the public agency, the private offices of psychiatrists, social workers, and psychologists, and the school counselor's office. Psychoanalysis, in this sense, is applicable to the understanding and treatment of the entire spectrum of psychopathology.

In an attempt to demonstrate the usefulness of psychoanalytic thinking to mental health professionals who work in nonpsychoanalytic settings, the American Psychoanalytic Association developed its annual Workshop for Mental Health Professionals. This Workshop has been designed to present psychoanalytic findings and theory and to suggest ways in which psychoanalytic and psychodynamic thinking can be applied to improve the quality and understanding of clinical work.

These Workshops began in 1976 as a project of the Program Committee of the American Psychoanalytic Association with annual meetings presented in New York City. Dr. Arnold Rothstein became the first Chairman of the Workshops in 1981. Since 1985 and 1986, the New York Workshop has been repeated (sometimes with different presenters or discussants) in a second location—San Francisco, New Orleans, Seattle, and Cincinnati—under the co-sponsorship of the local Psychoanalytic Society.

Workshop speakers have been selected from the membership of the American Psychoanalytic Association and have included many of its most senior and experienced analysts. The informal setting has permitted a degree of freedom and candor in expression that has made these conferences lively and educational experiences for analysts and nonanalysts alike.

The success of the Workshops spawned a further development—the publication of an annual monograph, of which this is the fifth. Arnold Rothstein, M.D., has been the driving force, and editor, behind the publication of the monographs. The American Psychoanalytic Association and the readers of the monographs are deeply in his debt for his energetic and devoted work in bringing this project to fruition.

This volume represents a transition. Future Workshops and monographs will be under the direction and editorship of Scott Dowling, M.D.

In recent years, important observations pertinent to psycho-analytic and psychodynamic thinking and theory have been made in settings other than the clinical psychoanalytic situation. New research methodologies and new study populations have led to a clearer model of psychological development in infancy and child-hood, and have sparked intense new interest in developmental theory. This has led to a more accurate and precise delineation of differences between childhood as understood retrospectively through the analysis of adult patients and childhood as it is directly observed. These newer findings have had an impact upon the clinical understanding of the phenomena of adult mental life, and have contributed to new approaches for the treatment of patients with neurotic, characterological, and borderline problems. The current Workshop, "The Significance of Infant Observational Research for Clinical Work with Children, Adolescents, and Adults" reflects this psychoanalytic interest in infant research.

The present monograph contains presentations by child and adult analysts representing different theoretical and clinical persuasions, addressing the issue of how the new data from infant and child observation have impacted upon their approaches to work with patients. The contributors to this volume are among the best known in the field of American psychoanalysis, and all have given significant thought and study to the positions offered here.

Although there is considerable difference of opinion among the individuals participating in the Workshop, and no single conclusive position has been developed, the contents of this monograph are reflective of the stimulation, interest, and new ideas being developed in the field of psychoanalysis. This monograph provides the reader with a sample of the vigor and multiplicity of points of view which are characteristic of American psychoanalysis today.

Paul A. Dewald, M.D.
Chairman, Program Committee
American Psychoanalytic Association

Introduction

Arnold Rothstein, M.D.

The authors of this book explore the question, How do the data of infant observational research influence therapists' work with children, adolescents, and adults? This question inevitably suggests a number of related questions: Is there a resonant relationship between the data, psychoanalytic theory, and derivative interpretations and reconstructions? Do the data influence the practitioner's conception of the clinical situation and process and his active contribution in creating that situation and process?

Although all analytically oriented practitioners value the genetic perspective, there is significant difference of opinion as to the value of the data derived from outside the clinical situation for theory building, for interpretation, and for reconstruction. Some colleagues easily extrapolate emendations of theory and derive reconstructions from the data of infant observational research while other practitioners attempt to restrict their hypothesizing to the data of the clinical situation. Now, it is clear that Freud was fundamentally influenced by his clinical experience. Nevertheless, he employed the serendipitous observations of infants and young children in his theoretical considerations of the development of the ego. In the Project, written in 1895, he emphasized the role of the perception of the hostile object in facilitating the differentiation of the ego. In the highly speculative *Beyond the Pleasure Principle* (1920a), a work that heralded the introduction of the structural hypothesis, Freud employed observations of his nephew's play at the height of the rapprochement subphase to conceptualize the genesis of the ego's proclivity for defensive activity. These considerations have been elaborated and form the basis of our understanding of defensive identifications of the ego. Increasing clinical experience with young children gave greater impetus to the elaboration of genetic propositions. The two most notable early products of this clinical experience were Anna Freud's *The Ego and the Mechanisms of Defense* (1936) and Melanie Klein's revolutionary emendations of conceptions of the development of psychic structures. Although both pioneers worked with young children, they drew radically different theoretical conclusions from their experiences. The reverberations of these theoretical differences are still with us and influence both the content of interpretations and conceptions of mode of therapeutic action of psychoanalysis and psychotherapy.

The post–World War II period witnessed an increased emphasis on child observational research. These efforts were motivated by a desire to elaborate the genetic perspective and to better understand how people become who they are. In 1947, the first article of the first volume of *The Psychoanalytic Study of the Child* was Hartmann and Kris's "The Genetic Approach in Psychoanalysis." In that paper, they noted that psychoanalysts have failed in many respects to take into account the data that child psychology has assembled; an omission that has led to many incongruities. They ended their article by stressing the importance of child observational research in general and in particular with reference to the preverbal stage of child development. They stated, "Psychoanalysis has witnessed the importance of this stage for the future; child observation, however, will have to tell the tale of these eventful years" (p. 29). In the past forty years there has been a significant body of such research data elaborated. Dr. Tyson begins this book with a historical review of the findings of infant observational research.

SECTION I
HISTORICAL REVIEW

Chapter 1

Two Approaches to Infant Research: A Review and Integration

Phyllis Tyson, Ph.D.

In 1910 Sir James Barrie published the story of Peter Pan, a boy who escaped from being human when he was seven days old and flew to the world of fairies in Kensington Gardens. Living a life of pleasure and freedom, when the Queen of fairies promises him anything he wishes, he says he wishes to go back to his mother, but with the right to return to the Gardens if he finds her disappointing. The window to her bedroom being wide open, in he flew. How sweet she looked, but how sad.

> He knew he had but to say "Mother" ever so softly and she would wake up . . . and give such a joyous cry and squeeze him tight. How nice that would be to him, but oh, how exquisitely delicious it would be to her. That, I am afraid, is how Peter regarded it. In returning to his mother he never doubted that he was giving her the greatest treat a woman can have.
>
> But why does Peter sit so long on the rail; why does he not tell his mother that he has come back? I quite shrink from the truth, which is that he sat there in two minds. Sometimes he looked longingly at his mother, and sometimes he looked

longingly at the window. Certainly it would be pleasant to be her boy again, but on the other hand, what times those had been in the Gardens!

He resolved to return to his mother, but at a later time. Months passed until finally he bravely said, "I wish now to go back to mother for ever and always." He had dreamed that his mother was crying, and he knew "that a hug from her splendid Peter would quickly make her smile."

> Oh! he felt sure of it, and so eager was he to be nestling in her arms that he flew straight to the window, which was always open for him. But the window was closed. There were iron bars on it. Peering inside he saw his mother sleeping peacefully with her arm around another little boy! Peter called, "Mother! Mother!" but she heard him not; in vain he beat his little limbs against the iron bars. He had to fly back, sobbing, to the Gardens.

He realized then that for him as well as for most of us, there is no returning. When we try to go back to mother, "it is Lock-out Time. The iron bars are up for life" (pp. 67–76).

One year before Barrie wrote Peter Pan, a story written for and based on his observation of the young sons of one of his closest friends, Freud (1909) published the case of Little Hans, a case history which convincingly demonstrated his highly controversial theory of infantile sexuality (1905). While Barrie captured the narcissism, the omnipotence, and the ambivalent oscillation between autonomy and mother–infant intimate togetherness, Freud described the complicated developmental issues of infantile sexuality and the Oedipus complex.

Barrie's fanciful tale about the inner world of a neonate confirms Freud's (1905) warning that the direct observation of children has the disadvantage of drawing inferences from data which are easily open to being misunderstood. But Freud also thought that an understanding of the early years of life was crucial not only to the theory of psychoanalysis, but to psychoanalytic treatment, where the recreation of early interactional experiences in the transference facilitates the reconstruction of each person's childhood experiences, a reconstruction he regarded as holding the key to unlocking the neurosis. Since Freud also thought that psychoanalytic investigation, reaching back into childhood from a later time, is subject to distortion and to long detours, he suggested that direct observations of infants be made alongside psychoanalytic reconstruction. Then, "by co-operation the two methods can attain a satisfactory degree of certainty in their findings" (p. 201). And so, since its infancy, psychoanalytic research has been two-pronged.

Freud's introduction of his structural model and the greater emphasis on ego psychology led to greater attention being paid to the mother–child unit, with a deeper appreciation of the range of factors influencing development. Whereas Freud's understanding of the dynamics of the interpersonal and intrapsychic world was most explicit, beginning with the Oedipus complex, attention increasingly shifted to the period we now regard as infancy; that is, the first three years of life (although classically infancy referred to the period from birth through the oedipal era). Because this preoedipal period is dominated by preverbal thinking, the classical psychoanalytic approach, even as it was being adapted to children by pioneers such as Anna Freud and Melanie Klein, was largely inapplicable. So the wish to understand infancy and the early development and pathology of psychic life provided an impetus for the increase in developmental research.

In providing a historical review of the data of infant observational research, it is helpful to recognize that two broad currents of endeavor have been converging. One stream, originating from within the framework of psychoanalytic thought, was data gathered largely from the clinical situation or through longitudinal observations in naturalistic or standardized settings. The emphasis in these studies is on the development and differentiation of psychic structures, on the increasing complexity of intrapsychic life, including thought and fantasy, on the origins of psychopathology, and on efforts to find methods of prevention. These studies, which had their origins in efforts to prove or disprove theories which had evolved from reconstruction, have enlarged our knowledge of the many small steps in normal psychic development. Occasionally the infant observations have been subsequently enriched by follow-up data from child psychoanalysis. For example, at the Hampstead Clinic and the Yale Child Study Center, observed infants have become child analytic patients. While there is a strong tendency to attribute pathology to the environment in developmental research studies, some of these longitudinal studies have also illuminated the contribution of the infant's inner world of drives and conflicts in the shaping of emerging object relations and in the eventual manifestations of pathology. Longitudinal research has also demonstrated the resiliency of the infant and the self-righting tendency in the developmental process (Emde, 1981; Harmon, Wagonfeld, and Emde, 1982).

The second current, now multidisciplinary but originating from the tradition of academic psychology, typically proceeds via carefully designed experiments. These are usually carried out in a laboratory setting with babies in a state of quiet alertness, not hungry or in a state of tension. The experiments are usually of brief time duration, and they usually have a more limited objective. These studies usually aim at testing a particular hypothesis, in contrast to longitudinal observational studies, which focus on process. The broad scope of subjects studied has increased our understanding of the range and complexity of infant competence.

Any effort, such as the one I am making, to integrate these two bodies of research data is made difficult because the two approaches often use different concepts and terminology to describe similar phenomena. Developmental researchers use terminology and concepts that can be objectively defined, observed, and measured. Psychoanalytic clinicians–researchers use the terminology and concepts of classical psychoanalysis, which at times means extrapolating from clinical observations to theories about conscious and unconscious mental functioning, or theories about hypothetical structures and systems. While the data and conclusions of these two streams often converge, the differing semantics can and have led to misunderstandings.

Take, for example, the terms *ego* and *self*. Traditionally, psychoanalysts use the term *ego* to refer to a psychic structure of organizing and regulating functions which contribute to the subjective sense of self. Many researchers, however, prefer to use the term *sense of self*, viewing it, as one prominent researcher, Daniel Stern, states, "not encumbered with or confused with issues of the development of the ego or id" (1985, p. 19). However, the same theoretical ambiguities arise with regard to the concept of the self. Some refer to the self as a structure, others refer to an experiential sense of the self, and still others, Sander and Emde, for instance, while not defining the sense in which the concept is used, speak about organizing and self-regulatory processes of the self (Sander, 1962, 1964, 1983; Emde, 1983, 1987) which in their descriptions sound strikingly similar to Freud's (1923, 1926) and Hartmann's (1950) discussions of the organizing, regulating functions of the ego. And when Stern maintains that some senses of the self exist prior to self-awareness and language, his descriptions sound remarkably similar to what analysts speak about as inborn ego functions.

In view of these considerations, I would like to stress at the outset the value of keeping an open mind, and keeping open avenues for dialogue and interchange. Our understanding of infant development is still tentative at best, and we are increasingly confronted with the limitations of our research techniques. As we understand how to ask questions differently, we uncover new and often surprising data. A darker side of the history of this field is the number of times divergent ideas have been criticized, sometimes vehemently so, and the ideas and the individuals holding them, rather than being subjected to open dialogue and further research, have been excluded. A divergent stream is then created, gathers its own followers, and, increasingly, interchange becomes impossible. What is of value in the idea is not integrated with the larger body of knowledge. This contentious attitude partly accounts for the divergency of ideas and directions in the field; contentiousness fosters divergency and discourages synthesis, which can make understanding the data extremely difficult, particularly for the neophyte.

THE HISTORICAL EVOLUTION OF THE DATA

I turn now to the data itself. I am going to broadly survey the best-known data from the most prominent of researchers during roughly the last half-century. In a burgeoning field as confusing as ours, this survey cannot be all-inclusive, so I have confined myself to the studies that seem to have had the widest impact and to primary sources rather than include later integrations and discussions irrespective of the importance of these works.

Anna Freud was a significant pioneer in the field of infant observational research. Convinced of the validity of the theory of infantile sexuality, and of the influence of inner forces on the developmental process, in 1926 she and some colleagues set up a nursery school in Vienna for children undergoing psychoanalytic treatment which was designed to supplement psychoanalytic investigation with observations of environmental influences and of the developmental process. This was the first attempt by psychoanalysts to objectively study the mutual influences of inner and outer forces on the developmental processes. Later, as Anna Freud's colleagues and other Viennese analysts moved to other parts of the world, similar nursery schools were established, providing a wealth of developmental observational data for the psychoanalytic understanding of young children, data which has led to both a confirmation of and to considerable revision of psychoanalytic theory.

In 1940, Anna Freud and Dorothy Burlingham set up, in London, the first wartime center for orphaned and evacuated children, the population of which included very young infants and toddlers. All reactions in the daily routine were carefully observed and recorded. The study soon came to focus on the mother–infant relationship and the reactions to separation and maternal deprivation. Thus, the Hampstead War Nurseries became the first systematic psychoanalytic research project to study the mother–infant relationship.

After a year of study Anna Freud formulated a theoretical model of the unfolding mother–infant relationship and described typical infant reactions to separation at each of the phases (1941). She later (1965) incorporated this model in her concept of a developmental line of object relations. She noted that in the first few months of life, the infant is governed by sensations of need and satisfaction, pleasure and discomfort; its relation to the mother is based on the urgency of bodily needs. By the second half of the first year, the relationship with the mother continues beyond moments of need satisfaction. In other words, the infant's need for affection "becomes as urgent for his psychological satisfaction as the need to be fed and taken care of is for his bodily comfort" (p. 181). In the second year the child's attachment to the mother comes to its full development. All the child's instinctual wishes come to center on the mother, and ambivalence and rivalry emerge, both of which interface with the "happy relationship." Finally Anna Freud described the object-centered phase, characterized by genital primacy and phallic–oedipal fantasies: a wish to possess the parent of the opposite sex and jealousy of and rivalry with the parent of the same sex.

At the same time that Anna Freud was making as systematic observations as possible under the circumstances and given the research methods available, Melanie Klein, also in England, was developing other theories about infant development. Klein's ideas (1928, 1933, 1958) were based on observations made of her own children and on reconstructions made from her clinical experiences, particularly with psychotic children. Klein and Anna Freud disagreed on a number of points. Klein posited an Oedipus complex and archaic superego functioning in the first year—Anna Freud placed these much later. While the two women made some attempts at dialogue, these led to heated debates with little resolution—and now each is represented by their respective followers in an administratively united, theoretically divided British Psychoanalytic Society. Klein's hypotheses continue to spark interest, but none of her ideas has been subjected to systematic study, and therefore few revisions to the theory have been made.

John Bowlby, beginning as an associate of Anna Freud in her separation studies, and later influenced by the theories of Klein and also by ethological research, has become one of the most influential figures in research on infant attachment. He proposed that the propensity for attachment is a biologically based motivational system, activated by certain maternal behaviors, which are in turn activated by certain infant behaviors (crying and smiling). This propensity for attachment, Bowlby maintained, is an instinctual response system which is as important a motivator of infant behavior as is drive satisfaction. Analysts viewed Bowlby's questioning of the primacy of Freud's dual drive theory with great disfavor, and heated debates followed (A. Freud, 1960; Schur, 1960; Spitz, 1960). The psychoanalytic position maintained that the instinctual systems to which Bowlby referred should not be compared with the psychoanalytic concept of libidinal drive, for the latter refers to psychological experiences and mental representations. While innate response patterns may trigger the first psychological processes and thus underlie both libidinal drives and object relations, essentially biological and mechanical response patterns should not be confused with psychological processes. The debate continues to the present with Bowlby's attachment theory (1958, 1969, 1973, 1980) finding favor largely among developmental psychologists. Ainsworth and her colleagues, for example (Ainsworth, Blehar, Waters, and Wall, 1978), designed the strange-situation experiment, which attempts to discern the quality of attachment on the basis of the infant's affective reactions to separations. Ainsworth has found that optimally attached infants approach their mothers eagerly, but the ambivalently attached, or avoidantly attached infants may show little or no distress on separation, avoid eye contact, and make no approach gestures on reunion, although they display anxious behavior at home. Recently, Sroufe (1983) has extended Ainsworth's work to study the implications of early attachment for the preschool child's social competence. Consideration of the implications of faulty attachment led others (Broussard and Hartner, 1970; Massie and Campbell, 1983; Broussard, 1984) to develop assessment techniques to discover infants at risk for attachment disorders. Still others (Fraiberg, 1980) developed principles for intervening in situations of pathological attachment syndromes, which were sometimes life threatening.

Winnicott, another member of the British Psychoanalytic Society who was influenced by the ideas of A. Freud and Klein, derived many of his ideas from clinical work as a pediatrician. His famous aphorism, "there is no such thing as a baby" (1953 p. 99), emphasized that considerations of infant attachment must be balanced by considerations of the "good enough" mother's emotional investment in her baby. He further thought that optimal development of self-esteem depended on the mother's capacity for affective "mirroring" (1967); when a mother is depressed or otherwise unable to reflect her delight and pleasure in her infant back to the infant, the infant's development may be influenced in a variety of pathological ways. Winnicott's calling attention to the importance of and role of the good enough mother led others, Klaus and Kennell (1976), to investigate the conditions necessary for optimal maternal attachment and parenting behavior. They hypothesized that the events in the first minutes and hours after delivery might affect the mother's or father's later attachment or "bonding," which, in turn, might affect their later interest, affection, and attention to their infant. While the exact conditions for optimal "bonding" may be hard to delineate, a number of studies have documented the reciprocal interaction between the development of the infant's stability, adaptation, and attachment to the parent and early parent–infant interaction (deChateau and Wiberg, 1984). Clinicians such as Kohut (1971, 1977) and his colleagues have made extensive use of the mirroring concept in pinpointing the dynamics of the early mother–infant interaction; disturbances of this interaction may possibly account for adult pathology. Winnicott (1953) was also interested in the way in which the infant used the good enough mother to facilitate independent functioning, and he introduced the idea of transitional phenomena. He thought the baby used a transitional object as a symbol, associated as it was with pleasurable interactions with the mother. The favorite blanket helped to soothe the infant and provided a bridge between the "me and not-me" world as he was becoming aware of separation. The concept of transitional phenomena has been elaborated upon by many authors, and figures especially prominently in discussions of creativity.

René Spitz was a prominent figure in early studies of the mother–child relationship. Shortly after World War II he undertook a series of observational studies of infants in institutions and foundling homes where, although the infants were physically cared for, they were given little stimulation or affection in interaction with a constant caretaker. The visual evidence in Spitz's films of starving, developmentally delayed babies staring vacantly at the camera, dramatically illustrated the destructive effect of maternal deprivation on infant development. Not only did he document the resulting disturbance in object relations, he demonstrated deficits in ego, cognitive, and motor development and how, in extreme cases, maternal deprivation leads to infant death (Spitz, 1946a,b).

In subsequent reports, Spitz (1962) and Spitz and Wolf (1949) described how early genital masturbation or play, which he observed to be present in all infants with a sufficiently good mother–child relationship, tended to be replaced with atypical, self-stimulating, autoerotic activities when the relationship was a problematic one, and tended to disappear altogether when the mother was absent, as in the foundling home. Spitz concluded that the amount of and kinds of stimulation available were as important to optimal development as was food itself.

Spitz (1962) introduced the idea of mother–infant reciprocity in a discussion of Harlow's work with infant monkeys who were raised with inanimate surrogate mothers (stuffed towels). Spitz recognized that the affective reciprocity established between the mother and infant stimulates and allows the infant to explore; this facilitates his expanding motor activity, his cognitive processes and thought, and his growing capacity for integration and mastery. Mother–infant reciprocity, focusing on the two-way affective dialogue, not just the infant's attachment or the impact of the mother's behavior, therefore seemed essential for healthy ego development. Spitz (1963) wished to emphasize that reciprocity was a complex and meaningful nonverbal process which influenced both the mother and infant. He stressed (Spitz and Cobliner, 1965) that reciprocal feedback within the dyad is asymmetric, since what the mother contributes is different from what the baby contributes. "Each of them is the complement of the other, and while the mother provides what the baby needs, in his turn (though this is less generally acknowledged) the baby provides what the mother needs" (p. 96), an awareness reflected in Barrie's description of Peter Pan.

The concept of affective reciprocity has dominated the

emerging field of infant research. Emde, a follower of Spitz, has been particularly active in this area. He has shown, for example (1983), that from earliest infancy, mothers respond to what they perceive as the infant's expression of emotion. By the second half of the first year, the infant's behavior appears to be based, in part, on the mother's emotional expression. Emde and his colleagues gathered material suggesting that the infant utilizes perceptions of the mother's emotional expressions as a clue about the safety of a new toy or strange situation and gauges responses accordingly in what has been called "social referencing" (Emde and Scorce, 1983).

The ways in which infants seem to be "tuned" to read the mother's emotions also has received attention from pediatrician Brazelton and his colleagues (Brazelton, Tronick, Adamson, Als, and Wise, 1975; Brazelton, Koslowski, and Main, 1974). They think that the infant's behavior toward the mother suggests that the infant anticipates affective interaction. While normally the infant responds to the mother's face with a smile and expectant body gestures, if the mother has been coached to become unresponsive and "still-faced" in the middle of an exchange, as early as three months of age the infant becomes upset, withdraws, then tries to reengage her (Tronick, Als, Adamson, Wise, and Brazelton, 1978). Utilizing observations of the infant's affective responsiveness as well as his competence, Brazelton (1973) developed a scale for assessing the neonate. Brazelton maintains that this assessment tool can be a means of providing information to parents about their infant, and as such can help to prevent attachment disorders or can be used as an effective intervention tool in situations of pathological reciprocity (Brazelton, 1984; Als, 1984).

Stern (1984, 1985) describes another concept related to mother–infant reciprocity as "affect attunement." "Affect attunement" refers to the capacity of the mother to behave in a way that matches the pace, intensity, and inner emotional state of the infant. Mismatching, or misattunement, results in observable disruptions in the infant's state or play. The importance for favorable development, Stern believes, is that the experience of attunement makes it possible for the infant to realize that "internal feeling states are forms of human experience that are shareable with other humans" (p. 151), and because attunement operates by way of nonverbal metaphor and analogue, it represents a necessary step in the use of symbols and, therefore, language (see Call [1980, 1984] for a similar idea).

Freud's (1926) final theory of affect set the stage for the current emphasis on affect theory. Freud made it clear that from very early in life the infant's unpleasurable distress and his pleasurable sensations of gratification in connection with drive tension or drive discharge were object related. In addition, he stressed that under optimal conditions ego maturation brings the ability to anticipate being overwhelmed by emotions so that affects come to be used as signals and anticipatory responses can be developed. Affects were therefore seen as highly complex structures, inseparable from cognition, which function to monitor and organize activity, thought, defenses, and symptoms; and that therefore they have a regulatory role in maintaining psychic equilibrium. An outcome of Freud's signal theory of anxiety was that it led not only to greater recognition of the role of mother–infant interaction and the significance of early infantile experience for later healthy personality functioning, but also that affects came increasingly to be seen as having a decisive role in motivation.

In this connection, Greenacre (1941) suggested that later ego functioning might reflect the nature of affective experiences in early life. On the basis of casual observation of children and reconstruction from adult analyses, Greenacre suggested that severe traumata, overstimulation, long-term exposure to frustration, and unrelieved organismic distress all undermine emerging ego functioning. Neurophysiologic patterning may be affected, producing a special sensitivity to physiologic anxiety responses (i.e., a "predisposition to anxiety"). She thought such a predisposition, when combined with constitutional factors, might increase the severity of neurotic disorders and that subsequently early environmental factors could not be distinguished from constitutional factors. More recently, Weil (1970, 1978) offered evidence from longitudinal studies of the wide-ranging deficiencies in ego functioning that can result from noxious or depriving early affective climates. Brody (1956) and Brody and Axelrad (1970) have also documented the relation between maternal behavior and the emotional and cognitive development of infants in the first year of life.

Increasingly, attention has been directed less to the effect of single traumatic events and more toward the strain and stress placed on the child by cumulative experiences and the affective climate in which they occur (Khan, 1963; Spitz, 1947). Emde (1987) suggests that what may be formative about cumulative experiences is not individual coping styles and behavioral patterns per se, but rather that *relationship* patterns become set in an enduring way. Styles and patterns of early relationships become internalized (Sroufe and Fleeson, 1985; Stern, 1985) and it is these *patterns* that are reactivated in later relationships throughout life. Sandler has written in a similar vein (1976, 1981).

Much of this recent interest in relationship patterns can be traced to the work of Margaret Mahler and her colleagues. She began her work by observing the pathology of object relations in autistic and psychotic children, and then undertook (originally with Gosliner [1955]) longitudinal studies of average mothers with normal babies to try to determine the ways in which the evolving relationship with the mother influences psychic structure formation and functioning. Her research design, utilizing a naturalistic setting, unobtrusive observational techniques, as well as participant observers, became a model for psychoanalytic longitudinal research studies. The data resulting from this longitudinal observational research enabled Mahler and her colleagues to conceptualize the developmental progression in what she called the separation–individuation process. She thought progressive steps in the development of relationships with objects imply a gradual buildup of mental representations of the object and of the self; these mental representations underlie ego structuralization and superego formation. While the very young infant is able to make primitive cognitive (perceptual) distinctions between various aspects of the outer world, only gradually is he able to forge a unique and stable sense of himself as functioning distinctly and separately from his primary love objects in what Mahler calls the "psychological birth of the human infant" (Mahler, Pine, and Bergman, 1975).

Throughout her studies, Mahler emphasizes the expansion of

psychic systems that accompanies increasing complexity in interpersonal relations. She describes those aspects in the mother–
infant relationship which contribute to the establishment of
libidinal object constancy wherein the sense of security, comfort,
and love endures in the absence of the mother's actual presence.
She thought that establishing libidinal object constancy would
facilitate independent ego functioning. Mahler (1971) also describes implications for pathological ego functioning when there is
a disturbance in the mother–infant relationship. McDevitt (1975)
discusses the reciprocity between aggression, conflict resolution,
libidinal object constancy, and psychic-structure formation.

Of particular importance in Mahler's work is her making
explicit that it is the emotional availability of the caregiver and the
affective interchange between mother and infant that seems to be
the important central feature in promoting optimal growth. Although increasing knowledge of the details of infant development
may lead to some modification or change in emphasis of her
theory, Mahler's attention to the details of the affective interchange has promoted enormous research efforts not only related
to the mother–child relationship but also to the father–child
relationship (Abelin, 1971; Cath, Gurwitt, and Ross, 1982; Pruett,
1983, 1985). These studies have increased our knowledge about
normal development as well as our appreciation of the emergence
and prevention of pathology. While Mahler's work has implications for clinical work, she was concerned lest her theories be
uncritically and mistakenly applied to the adult clinical situation
without regard to the intervening steps that occur later in development.

Mahler (1975) also made inferences about superego development. Although Freud's discussion of the superego leads one to
conclude that this psychic structure emerges as a precipitate of the
Oedipus complex, Mahler's findings suggest the existence of
precursors to the superego. The study of the superego, its
formation and functioning, is indeed another area in which
observational research, has "cooperated" with psychoanalytic reconstruction to contribute to a better understanding of the psychic
system. Spitz, in his direct observation of infants, described how
the learning of prohibitions and commands, as early steps in

superego formation, "parallels the unfolding of object relations . . . and is inextricably intertwined with them" (1958, p. 379). Furer (1967) discusses the way in which a mother's empathic consistency in setting and enforcing rules contributes to consistent superego functioning, and McDevitt (1979) describes the interaction between resolution of rapprochement conflict and superego internalization. Emde (1987) describes laboratory experiments investigating the affective climate of the mother–infant relationship and the emergence of what he calls "moral emotions" during the years one to three; these findings largely support psychoanalytic propositions on the early development of the superego.

Mahler consistently emphasized the interaction between emerging object relations and psychic-structure formation. In this regard she may have been influenced by the work of Hartmann. For, although not a child analyst or infant researcher, Hartmann's contributions to the theory of ego psychology (1939, 1952, 1953) have had a profound influence on infant researchers, both directly and indirectly. He believed that the nature of the mother–infant relationship influenced ego growth in subtle and important ways. He also thought that certain innate cognitive, perceptual, and motor functions are present from birth; the infant is "preadapted," to what he called an "average expectable environment." He was explicit that Piaget's work on cognition parallels Freud's work on emotion, that the two must be considered together. The combination of psychoanalytic understanding, particularly of mother–infant affective reciprocity, with Piaget's work on the evolution of the child's thinking, especially his explication of sensorimotor modes of thinking, provided a basis for much of today's research into the range of infant competence.

Papousek and Papousek (1979, 1984), for example, emphasize the reciprocity between parent–infant bonding, infant cognitive competence, and intellectual development. Elaborating Bowlby's psychobiological view of mother–infant attachment, they describe ways in which the caregiver's interaction with the infant provides the context for building memories of action patterns. While memories of events in the preverbal period may not be subject to recall later, action patterns and "how to" memories persist and contribute to expanding areas of competence (see also Lichtenberg [1987]).

Focusing particularly on the infant's cognitive competence, on the ways in which this competence facilitates the affective dialogue and interactive patterns between infant and caregiver, Stern (1985) postulates that affective interpersonal experiences are the basis of memory, and that preverbal representations of interactions become the basis of an organized self-experience. Indeed, he suggests that the sense of self, rather than the ego, is the primary organizer, and he focuses particular attention on the emergence of the sense of self. Stern's interest reflects another contemporary trend in developmental research, a concern with the establishment of the sense of self. Perhaps influenced by the growing emphasis on the self in psychoanalytic theory, a number of studies focus on the emergence of the sense of self, while paying increasingly less attention to the structures of the tripartite model.

This trend, together with the growing tendency toward viewing affects as having a more decisive role than drives as motivators of behavior, has led some to question the utility of the classical psychoanalytic theory of drives (Stern, 1985; Emde, 1987). Stern maintains that a number of motivational systems are operative in early infancy which eventually become hierarchically organized. Gaensbauer (1982), one of Emde's collaborators, comments that while the dual instinct theory has proven to be of theoretical and clinical usefulness, it is a mistake to look for direct manifestations of instincts in the infancy period. Rather, instinctual drives become defined through mother–infant affective interaction. Loewald (1971) similarly considers that the neonate's reflex activities become organized into instincts which assume aims and direction as they become associated with environmental responses that engender pleasure.

This dispute stems partly from the debate over Bowlby's work questioning the primacy of the dual drive theory, and partly because of the long argument, originating in Freud's theorizing, over whether expressions of pleasure and unpleasure should be viewed as the earliest evidence of drive differentiation, or as early affective expressions (Emde, Gaensbauer, and Harmon, 1976). The most we can say is that drives and affects seem to be related as indicated by the effects of developmental disturbances. Weil (1978) has pointed out that frustration of oral stimulation or

delays in satisfaction of hunger undermine primitive ego synthe-
sizing processes, lead to early and exaggerated expressions of
aggression, and set the stage for anxiety readiness, with anxiety
and rage primitively intertwined.

Data from observational research convincingly suggest motivational influences of somatic origins. In addition to the observations by Spitz, described earlier, where maternal deprivation
influenced the form of libidinal expression, Dowling (1977) studied the relation of gratification of hunger to infant–mother
reciprocal interchange. In a nice model of the way in which
psychoanalytic theory and developmental research can be combined, Dowling observed that in infants with esophageal atresia,
where the infant is tube-fed so feeding is unrelated to sucking, a
pattern of motor, affective, and social retardation appeared. He
was able to prevent these consequences, in some cases, by arranging for the mother to bottle-feed the child while gastric tube
feeding was in progress; the milk ingested by the infant's sucking
drained out via a surgically fashioned fistula. In these infants not
only was sucking stimulated, but sucking was associated with
hunger satiation. Though many variables are involved, Dowling
concluded that normal development requires, in addition to
adequate mothering, the support and elaboration of innate oral
reflexes which come to be associated with ingestion of food and
also with pleasure.

The emergence of nonhostile aggression as well as specific
object-directed anger and the role of the father in facilitating
control and modulation of aggressive drives has been the subject
of other infant observational studies (Spitz, 1953; Parens, 1979;
Herzog, 1982; McDevitt, 1983). Galenson (1986) has recently
studied situations of child abuse and noticed that when mothers
are unduly aggressive toward their infants, distortions in aggressive drive development result, accompanied by disturbances in
object relations and distortions in ego functioning.

Roiphe and Galenson (1981), in a longitudinal study of
seventy toddlers during the second year of life, found behaviors
which indicated anal drive derivatives and they found that interspersed with anal libidinal activities were genital activities. Their
description of what they term the "early genital phase" and their

reports on the origins of gender identity merit consideration in the context of other research in this area, including that of Anna Freud (1941), Kohlberg (1966), Kleeman (1976), and Stoller (1976, 1979), all of which indicate that sexuality and aggression have an important influence in infant development.

Recognizing the interrelatedness of affects, drives, object relations, and ego and superego functions in the process of development, Spitz (1959) became dissatisfied with the classical model of development based on the unfolding stages of the libidinal drive. He proposed a model that emphasized not so much the unfolding of functions in one system or another but rather the progressive integration and organization of functions. He observed that rather than being continuous, the developmental process was characterized by major shifts, at which time new affects and behaviors emerged. He understood these shifts to indicate progressive integration of functions and progressive organization within the ego. He therefore suggested that ego development be conceptualized according to these shifts, where the appearance of a new phenomenon (the social smile, eight-month distress, or "no" gesture) indicates that a new level of organization had been reached.

Approaching the subject with the aim of finding a context within which to evaluate normality or pathology, Anna Freud (1963, 1965) also proposed a revision in the developmental model, using the familiar metaphor of developmental line. Emphasizing that behavior represented the interaction of psychic structures and environmental influences she thought that the child's personality could be described in terms of a series of predictable, interlocking, overlapping, and unfolding developmental lines.

More recently, Sander (1983), being one among many influenced by the growing emphasis on systems theory (von Bertalanffy, 1968), suggested that our conceptualization of personality development should be based on generalizable principles that characterize living systems. This would include organizational complexities at biological, behavioral, and psychological levels. Sander also stressed that polarity, paradox, coherence, and uncertainty characterize development.

Increasingly, the data of infant observational research have led to an emphasis on the complexity of the developmental process (Lichtenberg, 1983). While the introduction of the structural model (Freud, 1923) made possible an appreciation of the range of factors which influence development, the implicit if not explicit supremacy of drive theory has gradually yielded to a broad organizational model. Such a model is characterized by change and plasticity, and the activity of the infant is also stressed, not the view that the infant is a passive recipient of maturational determinants and environmental forces. Development, according to this kind of model, can be viewed as the product of a complex, interactional system which is constantly changing, integrating, transforming, and moving to more complex organizational levels. In such a model many points of view about the infant can be accommodated, since drives, ego, self, superego, object relations, gender identity, affects, and cognition can all be viewed as systems simultaneously evolving and interacting, with no one of these being considered as more important or superordinate to another. In such a model no one phase or stage is viewed as decisive; every issue, be it a libidinal impulse, an object-related wish, or a conflict, may emerge within one particular stage, but it may also be elaborated over time and is always a potential influence. The infant, in this model, is seen as moving in multiple, interrelated ways toward greater psychological complexity, increasingly gaining a sense of his own personal reality; "reality" is not a "given" to which the infant must passively adapt, but is something he actively constructs (Emde, 1983).

CONCLUSION: THEN AND NOW

Over the years there have been changes in the techniques of infancy research. In *its* infancy, observational research was done by a few investigators and was limited to macro-observation of a limited number of subjects. Piaget used his own children and carefully wrote down their responses; Anna Freud took detailed notes about the daily life of the handful of children in the war nurseries. Then, film making became possible; large, noisy cam-

eras, difficult lighting situations, and somewhat artificial conditions, such as Spitz in his white coat, or the Hampstead nursery
staff looking self-conscious and awkward, characterized these
early efforts. Yet the influence of those early films was enormous.
The data became available to educators, doctors, and hospital
staffs. The visual evidence of the starving, retarded, dying children filmed by Spitz had a very different impact as compared with
written or spoken words. The data could no longer be ignored.
The films of James Robertson (1952, 1958, 1968, 1969, 1971) and
later in collaboration with Joyce Robertson (1967, 1971), showed
the effects of hospital procedures on young children and documented the infant's dramatic responses to separation. These films
led to a more penetrating examination of the impact of the adult
world on infant development. Treatment facilities such as child
guidance clinics were established to help children who had experienced various early traumata. This increased the demand for
child psychotherapists, which led to more demands for training.
Better training led to more interest in research. Mahler's longitudinal project was used as a model for numerous psychoanalytically
based naturalistic observational studies. Spitz and his followers
became one group among many to use and develop laboratory
techniques. Research methods grew increasingly sophisticated as
the need grew, interest grew, and money became available.

Today, thanks to the electronic revolution, the picture is very
different from what it was in the early 1940s. Video monitors
permit nonintrusive, naturalistic observations to be made under a
variety of circumstances. New methods of reviewing data reveal
subtle complexities that could never be observed or recognized by
the naked eye; Condon and Sandler (1974), for instance, demonstrated that neonate movement is synchronized with adult speech.
With videotapes, Stern (1977) can convince us that the "games"
shared between the four-month-old and the caregiver are complex
indeed.

Finally, we might observe the differences in subjects studied.
Freud began with oedipal little Hans. Anna Freud began with
preschoolers; later she included babies. Mahler concentrated on
toddlers. Barrie spun a fanciful tale about seven-day-old Peter
Pan, but researchers are now using sophisticated techniques to

study those seven-day-old infants. While they do not seem to find evidence for the range of colorful fantasies imagined by Barrie, their research has brought home to us the scope and the complexity of the developmental process.

As infant researchers continue to pursue a variety of issues, analysts and psychotherapists are increasingly drawn to their studies. Both researchers and analysts appreciate the complexity of development; both groups recognize that there are few, if any, one-to-one equations between early development and later psychopathology. As a result, analysts vary in their sense of the usefulness of infant research in their day to day work. Still, few would disagree that this data has forced a fuller appreciation of the complexity of the developmental process and hence of the therapeutic process.

SECTION II
THE WORKSHOP PAPERS

Chapter 2

How Does Infant Research Affect Our Clinical Work with Adolescents? A Case Report

Jack Novick, Ph.D.

What is the relevance of infant observation to work with adolescents? To many of us, infant observation is so integral to our history, our training, and our work that it is like asking what is the relevance of breathing to work as a therapist. In his introduction to this monograph, Dr. Rothstein pointed out that Freud used infant observational data as early as 1895. Others, however, influenced perhaps by Jones's tendentious statement that Freud had "inhibitions" about getting at too close quarters with the child's mind (1955, p. 261), tend to deny or ignore the degree to which Freud's work and theorizing were influenced by his extensive and intensive experience with children. It is understandable that any history of the development of psychoanalysis would focus on the period Freud spent in Paris with Charcot, but few writers go on to describe his subsequent trip to Berlin to study the diseases of children at Adolf Baginsky's clinic. He had done so because he had been offered the directorship of the neurological department in a public institute for children's diseases in Vienna headed by Dr. Kassowitz. Freud worked at that clinic for several hours a day, three times a week, from 1886 to 1893.

Concurrent with his beginning papers on psychoanalysis,

Freud published numerous works on neurology based on this experience with children. Through his book on aphasia, and nine further papers, Freud became and is still known as an expert on paralysis in children. He told his wife Martha that the work provided him with a rich source of clinical material, and, from the number of personally observed cases cited in his research papers, the experience with children at that time was indeed vast. So, at a time when Freud was struggling with his first dynamic formulations and was about to enter the period of great psychoanalytic discoveries, his professional life involved extensive contact with children.

His personal life at that time also brought him close to children. Between 1887 and 1895 the Freuds had six children, three boys and three girls. Freud worked at home and, as he said in a letter to Fliess, his life was spent in either the consulting room or the nursery upstairs. His letters to Fliess are full of details of the children's sayings and deeds and it is clear that Freud was intimately involved with all aspects of the growth and development of his six children. Not only was Freud involved with children in both his personal and professional life, but he also had the remarkable capacity and bravery to be open to his own childhood experiences. In 1897 he undertook his self-analysis, a truly revolutionary achievement, and what he discovered and recaptured were memories of childhood.

It is not surprising then, that throughout his work, Freud revealed an empathy with and a creative use of the experiences of childhood for the development of his theories. The interest in childhood continued when he began to gather followers: the early psychoanalysts were encouraged to observe and discuss observations of their own children. In 1908 Freud undertook the first psychoanalysis of a child; this was done through the father, a member of the Wednesday evening group (Freud, 1909).

James Anthony (1986) documents Freud's consistently positive views regarding the contribution child analysis makes to psychoanalytic theory. In *Moses and Monotheism* (1939), written near the end of his life, Freud stated that "the analytic study of the mental life of children has provided an unexpected wealth of material for filling the gaps in our knowledge of the earliest times"

(p. 84). Freud's continued interest in and use of infant and child observation also is evident in Ruth Mack Brunswick's seminal paper, "The Preoedipal Phase of the Libido Development" (1940). According to the author, this paper was written in collaboration with Freud and is clearly influenced by observations of children. Anna Freud's introduction to Volume 1 of her writings explicitly places the development of child psychoanalysis in the context of a Vienna which "had at that time also become a fertile ground for the analytic study of normal child development . . ." (1974, p. viii). Inspired by Siegfried Bernfeld's "Kinderheim Baumgarten," a camp school for 300 displaced children, Anna Freud started her own "experimental day nursery for toddlers." This led directly to the wartime Hampstead Nurseries, a residential nursery for up to ninety babies and children set up in England in October 1940 during the first phase of the German air raids. In all a total of 190 babies and children found shelter in the five years of its existence and, as Anna Freud said, the nurseries "incidentally provided an unprecedented and unending source of observational material for all of us who shared in the care of them" (1974, p. x). Following the war, Anna Freud and many who worked with her or supported the Hampstead War Nurseries turned their attention to the harrowing and seemingly impossible task of helping the child survivors of Tereszin and Auschwitz. These reparative nurseries and homes set up at Bulldog Banks and Lingfield provided, again, a rich source of "observational material," some of which was described by Anna Freud in "An Experiment in Group Upbringing" (1951). When the Hampstead Child Therapy training in child analysis was established in 1947 it was natural that opportunities for infant and child observation would be included in clinical training. The tradition of integrating infant and child observation with clinical work is so strong that in many training institutes (at least in Europe) candidates in adult analysis do a year of infant observation as their first course. I have tried to show that observational experience with infants and children is so integral to our history and our training that it is difficult to demonstrate its particular significance in our current work with any age group. However, it would seem that the term *infant observational research* refers to the body of data accumulating exponentially in the last ten years following what Stern (1985) called "a revolution in infancy research" (p. 38). As in any vital area of research, the field is in ferment, there are major areas of controversy, and one should, as Virginia Demos (1985) suggests, avoid premature closure. However, recent summaries of current findings by Lichtenberg (1983), Stern (1985), and others reveal important commonalities. There are many who claim that with the new data the Mahlerian scheme of development is "utterly refuted" (Gedo, 1985, p. 612; Stern, 1985; Demos 1985), as have been the views of Kernberg, Melanie Klein, and the classical Freudian image of the infant as a passive receiver of oral supplies.[1] The image of the infant which emerges from this vast array of data is of a highly competent, active organism who can do much more, much sooner than most people, including infant researchers, ever thought. Through vivid descriptions and video presentations we now view the neonate as having an inborn capacity to elicit preprogrammed empathic responses from the caretaking person and set in motion a complex infant–mother transactional system in which attachment is fostered by "contingent responding by the caregiver" (Demos, 1985, p. 556; Silver, 1985). How does this new view affect our clinical work? What if we take our cue from infant researchers and the ingenious way in which they have turned questions around? How would I respond if asked what my work was like before I knew anything about current infant observational research? I will attempt to answer that question by presenting a summary of the psychoanalytic treatment of a boy seen five times a week from July 1966 to March 1973.

Dave is the second of three boys. The case was referred to me when he was eleven and a half and terminated almost seven years later, soon after Dave's eighteenth birthday. He was referred because of severe obsessional rituals which had intruded into every part of his life; the initial diagnosis was neurotic disorder. It soon became apparent that Dave's atypical ego development and functioning warranted changing the diagnosis to borderline pathology.

---

[1] See Kaplan (1987) who accepts the body of research but points out the flaws in Stern's "excessive" interpretations of his data "and his misinterpretations of traditional psychoanalytic views of infancy" (p. 431).

The range of symptomatology raised questions as to the intensity of anxiety and adequacy of his defense system. Most ominous were the obsessional defenses which existed side by side with direct drive expression. Death wishes were conscious, and aggressive attacks frequent; the expected shift of cathexis from the body to the mental sphere was not evident in Dave. There was an intense preoccupation with his body and body products and frequent undefended expressions of anal wishes. Reaction formation seemed nonexistent as he talked of smelling bottoms, touching bottoms; he frequently passed flatus in the sessions, and expressed the wish "to do a poo" in the room. He would eat his snot, blow his nose into his handkerchief and lick the snot, smell his finger after defecating and lick it. The most apparent area of deviation could been seen in his pervasive confusion between self and object representations. Higher level, more adaptive defenses were not available and he used primitive denial, projection, and external-ization. In the sessions he accused me of wanting to kill him, and these projections would alternate with externalization of a frightened, helpless Dave. He would call me fat, ugly, stupid, idiot, all of which represented feelings about himself. There were rapid shifts between feelings of magical omnipotence and abject worthlessness. It became evident that his obsessive mechanisms were not directed primarily against drive expression but were desperate efforts to stave off fears of annihilation and disintegra-tion. Drive material emerged in a mixture of all levels of develop-ment and he frequently said that he would die, that the water at the Clinic was poisoned, and the ladies of the Clinic were out to get him. His pleasurable sexual fantasies consisted of thoughts of watching naked girls, being seen naked, smelling bottoms, wiping bottoms, kissing fish and meat, and "fucking standing up."

Within a few weeks I was faced with a severe management problem. Direct pregenital drive expression emerged in full force. His behavior became wild and uncontrolled, and there were long periods when I could make no contact with him. He would, for example, charge into the room with a BB gun shouting "All right, Novicks! I'm going to kill you" and fire the pellets at me. One moment he could be lying on the table licking his snot, telling me he had no friends, and at the next moment he would shout at me "You fat pig, you'll die for this!" The playthings were scattered over the room, broken, thrown at me, thrown down the stairs or out the window. Dave would write on the wall, try to force open the files and lockers in the room, and generally attempt to destroy the place. He would shout, laugh hysterically, use a variety of noises, and go through a rapidly shifting series of imitations. Interspersed with the wild behavior were peremptory demands for need satisfaction. The slightest real or imagined hesitation on my part was taken as a total rejection. The management problem was handled by first focusing on his wishes for immediate gratification and his narcissistic depletion when frustrated. I interpreted that my not meeting his wishes led to the painful feeling that I did not like him. I described the wild behavior as an externalization of his own feelings of helplessness and rejection; he was making me feel what he felt. My continued focus on his externalization led to the emergence of his painful feelings of sadness and emptiness. For example, at the end of the hour his wild behavior would be preceded by frantic nose-picking and statements such as, "I feel you're throwing me out. I know why you have to go. You have a son and he's one year old today." Increasingly the transference seemed to reflect a severe impairment in the early mother–child relationship. I said to Dave that when he was feeling so unloved, uncared for, and unresponded to, he was letting us know what he had felt when he had been a little boy. His mother, I said, had been depressed and preoccupied. He had been too little to understand why she hadn't come right away and he had probably felt that this was because she didn't love him. The effect of this reconstruction was to take the sting out of his aggression and break the increasing spiral of rage, projected rage, panic, and further defensive aggression.

His intense distrust decreased and for the first time he could talk about his current problems in school and with friends. There were still frequent periods when I would completely lose contact with him and our work focused on his defensive merging with his objects. I interpreted the merging as a defense against intense feelings of self-devaluation. When I said that he was running away from himself because he didn't like himself, he collapsed on the floor and said in a subdued voice, "What do you mean I don't like myself? How do you know? Do you think other people know?" He held a chair in front of his face and mumbled that he didn't like what I had said. He felt like running home. He hid under the desk, said I couldn't see him, that I would never see him, and then became immersed in a story about having switched names with his elder brother. I took the devaluation as an internalized feeling, one going back to his early experience of feeling unloved and devalued by mother. I added that in reality there were many things to like about him, but since he tried so hard to pretend to be someone else, he couldn't see these nice qualities in himself. This eventually led to his recalling early memories of experiences with a black maid who had been available until he was two. Increasingly, in the transference, he saw me as his maid; he would lie on the desk, his face close to mine, frequently touching me with his leg or hand. Even his nose-picking became more object directed, as he would now do so while gazing into my face with the look of a child being fed by his mother. The name-calling had a soft, loving quality. He said he wanted a secret language. He wanted us to sing and play together. The material centered on his love for the maid, his anticipation of loss, and his passive to active reversals in which he would leave or reject me before I would do so to him. The sessions became calmer, and increasingly Dave was able to spend the whole time talking or playing games. Through this the intensity and pervasiveness of his masochistic behavior became apparent and remained a central feature of the analysis. His central fantasy was that by being the messy, damaged, anal child he would maintain a preoedipal tie to his mother, he would defend his mother against his own sadistic wishes, and he would participate in the sadomasochistic sexual relationship of his parents.

The work in the first three years of analysis enabled him, at fourteen, to make a relatively normal move into adolescence. He started to improve significantly in school, to have somewhat more adaptive peer relationships, and to join in appropriate activities. With the increase in structuralization and concomitant decrease in immediate discharge in action, Dave could develop, maintain, and find discharge via conscious fantasies. At this point he began to

develop beating fantasies. A typical fantasy was as follows: while
masturbating he first thought of undressing a girl in his class. The
girl then changed to an older woman, and then, as his excitement
mounted, the image changed to that of his mother. As he reached
a climax the content of the fantasy changed to his father walking
in, holding him down, and beating him on the buttocks. By this
time Dave was as tall as his father and he felt that his father was "a
Hitler" capable of killing him. He not only wished to replace his
father, but also thought that his mother wanted him to do so. He
was convinced that he could do anything he wanted and no one
could stop him. The beating fantasy and the underlying masochism functioned, in part, in lieu of a superego, as a way of stopping
him from gratifying his omnipotent wishes.

Dave passed his ordinary level high school exams, was a
member in some youth groups, was studying for his advanced
exams, and planned to go to university. Change was taking place
on all fronts, yet at the same time there was a desperate clinging to
the old sadomasochistic relationship with his parents and with me
in the transference. Any achievement or appropriate pleasure
with peers was immediately followed by masochistic submission to
me or to his parents. For example, he had become a tall, handsome
young man with an active social life. On one occasion he said that
he realized that women are attracted to tall men. He appeared
very pleased, then suddenly clutched his chest, choked, said he
couldn't breathe and rolled off the couch writhing in pain. He got
up, walked back to the couch and was confused, forgetting what he
had been talking about.

By the time he was seventeen years old he was actively doing
much of the analytic work. Despite evidence of continuing borderline tendencies it was felt that further analysis might do him
more harm than good. Prior to his summer holiday, in the context
of his need to maintain the old masochistic tie to his mother, I
contrasted his obvious changes with his attempt to keep things
unchanged. I interpreted his fantasy that analysis would go on
forever and said that this could not be, and in fact could be
harmful. He reacted to this with a burst of independent functioning, taking my statement as permission to separate and function
on his own. After working through his usual regression following

a vacation, the theme of termination could once more be taken up. He had avoided picking a termination date, and then, when he finally did so, he wanted to stop in two weeks time. We eventually agreed on a date almost four months later and began to work toward this.

During this period there was repetition of masochistic behavior and enactment of his beating fantasy in relation to termination. He felt termination was something I was sadistically imposing on him. He had a dream in which he hurt himself because I rushed him out of the session and he went to my wife for comfort. From the dream and his current behavior we pieced together and verbalized the current beating fantasy: I am bad to him, it is all my fault, his life is miserable; my wife, on hearing this, is angry at me, rejects me, and out of pity for Dave goes to him. In the last session he spoke about always having had the problem of "being himself." He realized that he could not be himself until he allowed others to be themselves. He said, "If I can't see you as a real person then I can't see myself as a real person." He spoke realistically about his plans for the future, showed me his drawings, and then, at the end of the session, stood up, threw his shoulders back, and thanked me for all I had done for him, all that we had done together, he emphasized.

How would my technique and understanding of this case differ were I to see him now? Further, what is the significance of infant observational research for the changes in my technical approach to this case? I think the relation between infant observations and clinical work remains the same as it was in 1905 when Freud said that "by cooperation, the two methods can attain a satisfactory degree of certainty in their findings" (p. 201). Infant observations can refine, limit or expand clinical reconstructions, and this adds to the sense of conviction with which we make our interventions. Were I to see Dave now I would hold more firmly to the view that his addiction to pain started in infancy and led to a persistent "delusion of omnipotence" (Novick and Novick, 1987). His beating fantasy encapsulated the magical delusion that wishes from all levels of development can be gratified through pain. The image presented in recent research of the competent, active, and effective normal mother and baby highlights what was missing in

Dave's transactions with his mother. Instead of the sensitive mutual repair of inevitable mismatches between infant and mother seen in the infant research work, Dave and his mother were locked in a frustrating system of escalating failures in which mother blamed him for her own sense of inadequacy. His own inborn capacities to elicit an empathic response failed and the persistence of this failure led to the creation of a magical omnipotent system in which pain rather than a smile or a laugh brought a reinforcing response from mother. I first felt this in the raging, painful, and frustrating interaction with Dave. My reconstruction was confirmed not only by Dave's response but also by mother's and father's memories of his early development. Current infant research provides further confirmation of the clinical hypothesis that a transference consisting almost entirely of pain, rage, and helplessness can reflect a severe impairment in the early pleasure–pain economy in mother–infant transactions. Especially relevant are those studies where the focus has shifted from the normal mother–infant dyad to a microanalysis of failure to repair a mismatch in dyads with a depressed, or otherwise disturbed, caretaker (Fraiberg, 1980; Demos, 1982; Beebe and Sloate, 1982; Gaensbauer, 1982, 1985; Mintzer, Als, Tronick, and Brazelton, 1984; Blos, 1985; Tronick and Gianino, 1986). In an ongoing study of teenage mothers and their infants we have been able to observe the onset and sequelae to such mismatches, as for example in our film of mother feeding Nicole before four months (Novick and Novick, 1987). The infant attempted to engage her mother in social interactions between bites. After each bite Nicole's mother literally scraped the smile off Nicole's face with the spoon, until the sixth bite was followed by a frown.[2]

If I were to analyze Dave now, I would not have terminated until we had made further headway into his addiction to pain. The consistent experience of frustration and pain in working with such patients, reported by many, can represent a recreation in the

---

[2] This case is selected from an ongoing study of adolescent mothers and their babies. I am grateful to the other members of the study group, Drs. Kay and Linn Campbell, Connie Silver, A.M.L.S., Don Silver, M.D., and Kerry Kelly Novick; the views presented here are my own and do not necessarily represent those of the group.

therapeutic relationship of painful early mother–infant interactions. The technique of dealing with such a primary addiction is a clinical challenge for psychoanalysis, while the question of how a mother becomes associated with pain is an intellectual challenge for the infancy researcher.

Chapter 3

Gender Disturbance in a Three-and-One-Half-Year-Old Boy

*Eleanor Galenson, M.D., and
Barbara Fields, M.S.W.*

In a recent review of their clinical experience with more than five hundred gender-disturbed patients, Meyer and Dupkin (1985) examined their clinical observations with regard to the three major etiological hypotheses concerning gender disturbance: (1) biological influences; (2) nonconflictual identification; and (3) conflict leading to defense formation. The biological-imprint hypothesis awaits verification from future research. The nonconflictual identity hypothesis proposed by Stoller (1968) is predicated on an extended blissful symbiosis with a covertly bisexual mother who has intense penis envy, and an absent or uninvolved father. Finally, the conflict–defense hypothesis proposes the occurrence of trauma in early childhood, with distortion in object relationships and separation–individuation, and subsequent oedipal conflict.

All of these hypotheses agree in one respect, namely, they propose that the origins of gender disturbance lie early in life. With this in mind, Meyer and Dupkin examined their data on twelve children from their ongoing study of gender disturbances—ten boys and two girls ranging in age from five to thirteen years at the time of initial contact. All patients satisfied the criteria for childhood gender disturbance (Meyer and Dupkin, 1985): the childhood onset of consistent cross dressing, the stated wish to be of the opposite sex, and the reversal of sex-typical roles in their imaginative play, games, and playmate preferences, criteria which were also satisfied by Green's (1974) sample.

None of the children described by Meyer and Dupkin had a history of blissful symbiosis, unlike Stoller's small group, but many had experienced multiple separations from parents, paternal absence or abandonment, and maternal bisexuality. Furthermore, precipitating factors included traumatic sexual overstimulation, repeated separation traumata, and maternal psychosis connected with childbirth. Subtle influences of parental psychopathology were also in evidence in the group, and none had any physical or psychological abnormalities. The presence of early traumata in the history of this group supports the conflict–defense hypothesis.

As Meyer and Dupkin emphasized, gender identity is now believed to normally emerge during the later preverbal and early verbal periods, and is clearly demarcated by two years of age (Hampson and Hampson, 1961; Money and Ehrhardt, 1972; Galenson and Roiphe, 1974; Mahler, Pine, and Bergman, 1975). Furthermore, the onset of fetishistic, transvestite, and gender-disturbed behavior in children less than two years old has been described by a number of authors (Sperling, 1963; Greenson, 1966; Green, Newman, and Stoller, 1972; Galenson, Vogel, Blau, and Roiphe, 1975; and Stoller, 1975, 1978). With this in mind, Meyer and Dupkin have tentatively concluded that the ten children they reported appeared to have been relatively fixated in their development near or at the phallic–narcissistic state; that is, at about two to three-and-a-half years of age, and a number of their cases suggested an even earlier onset of developmental deviations. Their pathology is consistent with and best understood in terms of the conflict–defense hypothesis. It can also be understood as a pathological elaboration of the developmental issues of the phallic–narcissistic phase which emerges in the early part of the third year of life.

Galenson and Roiphe (1971, 1974, 1980) postulated that there is an early genital phase of body–genital schematization which emerges between eighteen and twenty months of age, a postulate which is critical for understanding both the early dynamics of normal gender formation and the early and subsequent psychopathology of gender disorders. In their view, children are vulnerable to profound disturbance and equally profound defensive measures at the time of gender formation. This takes place precisely because of the heightened sexual drives of the early genital phase, the incomplete discrimination of self and object, and the anal phase with its heightened aggression and ambivalence.

Galenson and Roiphe (1980) described three boys from their series who apparently resemble the children studied by Meyer and Dupkin (1985) in demonstrating severe disturbances in body–genital schematization during their second year. Difficulties in the early relationship with their mothers included heightened aggressive ambivalence toward the mother, and unusually intense identification with her. These three boys played with dolls extensively in a rigid, repetitive, and compulsive manner, and preferred to wear their mothers' clothing and jewelry.

The early genital phase, as proposed by Galenson and Roiphe, is a developmental sequence which may be viewed as a "psychic organizer," in that the psychic system is restructured on a higher level of complexity. Through self-induced genital stimulation, the infant can now *actively* achieve the pleasure previously associated with passive maternal contact, and also the pleasure previously derived from a fantasy of the mother's presence. This shift in the passive–active balance would undoubtedly aid in consolidating differentiation of self from object, so that the act of masturbation and its accompanying fantasy state not only provide a feeling of closeness to the mother, but simultaneously enhance differentiation from her, specifically around the supremacy of genitality. In addition, masturbation and its fantasies provide something equivalent to trial action, offering specific satisfaction at the genital level and possibly facilitating repression of regressive prephallic fantasies of merging with the nonsexual mother of early infancy.

In the case of gender disturbance we will present, the diagnostic assessment and form of treatment were designed on the basis of gender identity formulations derived from the research data described above. While the details of the child's early development and his parents' response during treatment provide an unusual opportunity to understand the dynamics of the gender disturbance of this particular child, we do not postulate that all gender disturbances share these dynamic features, nor do we maintain that the trauma he sustained would eventuate in gender disturbances in all boys. However, the combination of circumstances this boy experienced were very similar to those postulated from our research data. In this case, they did indeed lead to a gender disturbance of profound severity.

Ben, a pleasant, obedient, intelligent boy of three-and-one-half years when we first saw him, had begun to attach his girl playmates' hair barrettes to his own hair at two years eight months, during a vacation with his parents and in the absence of the housekeeper who usually cared for him. Soon thereafter he began to wear his mother's jewelry, her scarves, and her t-shirts and insisted on wearing only pink or purple clothing. Simultaneously, he stated for the first time that he wanted to be a girl. A stutter which had appeared briefly at eighteen months now returned, and Ben began to be very fearful of his mother's even mild disapproval, constantly inquiring whether she still loved him.

By three years and three months, Ben was even more insistent on wearing pink or purple socks and shirts, and wore paper bracelets and necklaces which he made himself. He draped t-shirts or other clothing about his waist as a make-believe skirt and draped clothing over his head as "pretend" long hair. The "little purple pony," a feminine-looking horse with a long silky mane, and a doll with long hair became his favorite toys. At the same time, he said he wanted to kill people with guns and he had cut a swatch of his hair in order to look "like the Indians who attack their enemies." He would stroke and fuss with his mother's hair for as long as she tolerated it, and had become fascinated by the stories of Cinderella, Snow White, and Sleeping Beauty. Always playing the parts of Cinderella and Sleeping Beauty in these fairy tales, he would elaborate on his fear of the witches and the stepmother in these stories, yet insisted on hearing and playing them out, fearful yet obviously excited as well.

Ben had been an unplanned first and only child whose delivery was long and painful; he was separated from his mother in the hospital for the first three postpartum days because of her physical debility. His mother thought him an ugly baby when she saw him, and had stated again that she had wanted a girl. But she did nurse him for two months and then returned to her previous full-time professional work which required long hours away from home. Ben's first full-time nurse left abruptly during Ben's four-teenth month; the two weeks that followed were marked by his incessant crying whenever either parent left him, the first time he showed distress on separation from them. However, he quickly became attached to the second housekeeper as soon as she arrived, stopped crying when his parents left to go to work, and in fact often appeared to ignore them altogether. He gave up his bottles at two years ten months without difficulty (about two months after his cross dressing began) and he toilet trained himself by the end of his third year.

Linguistically advanced for his age, Ben was an obedient little boy who socialized well at the prenursery school he began to attend shortly before his third birthday. There, although he preferred to play in the girls' corner, his behavior was not considered aberrant, and neither his fears of witches, his stutter, nor a sleep problem which had slowly worsened after his cross dressing began, caused concern on his parents' part. However, the mother's friend, a psychotherapist, urged the parents to seek consultation because of his concern over Ben's wish to be a girl.

Significant in the parents' background was the mother's life-long ambivalent relationship with her mother, a woman who berated her daughter constantly, and the maternal grandfather's rages which had terrorized the family. Also, Ben's mother de-scribed her own life-long fear of overt aggression, her severe anorexia from early childhood on, and bouts of anxiety which had led her to seek treatment for herself. Yet, despite these psycho-logical problems, she had maintained a successful business career before Ben's birth and continued to do so afterwards.

The paternal grandparents were chronically ill and depressed people. Despite this background, Ben's father had been successful in building up his own business and had no serious psychological complaints. However, he described himself as overconscientious and a worrier. It was he who tended to Ben's needs and wants on many occasions, as well as during the housekeeper's brief absences. The father described no homosexual fantasies or homosexual activities of any kind. The parents had been close to one another during the ten years of their marriage preceding Ben's birth, and still continued to enjoy their life together, despite Ben's difficulties.

When we saw Ben for the first time, he was a boyish, handsome, highly articulate child who made excellent social contact. However, Ben fluttered from one toy to another, simultaneously relating a story about "my little pony" which he had seen on television. A very bad witch had come from "the gloom," he said; she ate spiders and also melted "my little ponies" and ate them. (This theme of being the victim of attacking witches or bad queens was to be played out in endless varieties over the next few months of Ben's treatment.) Ben said he wanted to be a girl in answer to my query about his gender preference, and then immediately placed a toy pipe between his legs. Going to our playroom "little pony," he brushed the long silky mane with obvious and intense pleasure. Noting the anatomical dolls, he made no comment but quickly wrapped them up in blankets and pretended to feed them and put them to sleep. He asked for "Sheera"—a female figure not in the playroom—saying he planned to dress as Sheera for Halloween. He then pulled apart the legs of a doll, he called a stuffed dragon a "fairy," and drew "two monster spiders."

His second session was equally revealing. He brought his own doll, "Sheera," to the session and called our attention to her blonde hair which, he said, he loved to wash. He told us she was powerful and had a sword which he had not brought with him. In contrast to the first visit, Ben now appeared anxious and much more stimulated. He pretended to cook, handled and played with play dough briefly, and then anxiously washed his hands. This was followed by regressive play in which he pretended to be a baby girl while his mother took care of him. Other toys were touched very briefly in passing. These initial sessions proved prognostic of what was to come.

The treatment plan was as follows: Ben and his mother were to attend two sessions each week together and his father would accompany him for the third session. Both parents would gradually become actively engaged in the treatment process with therapist B.F. Both parents would also attend separate weekly sessions with the second therapist, E.G. (This type of intensive conjoint treatment of children and their parents has been evolved gradually and has proved extremely effective in dealing with psychopathological disorders of many young children (Galenson and Fields, unpublished). Based on the premise that the child–parent relationship is already deeply disturbed, treatment is aimed at therapeutic dyadic and triadic restructuring of the entire family.

As treatment proceeded, it became evident that Ben's play was unusually literal and concrete in that he appeared unable to accept semisymbolic substitutes. Thus, he would enact the part of the heroine of his stories and insisted that his therapist or one of his parents enact the other parts, rather than pretending to play. These enactments had a limited and repetitive quality, unusual in a child with such an excellent verbal capacity. Metaphor was unacceptable; he literally "became" the whole pony, for example, rather than identifying with partial aspects or qualities of the pony. This difficulty in substituting "the part for the whole" interfered with Ben's development in going from concrete to abstract thought, particularly in regard to matters pertaining to identity. His defensive feminine identification had, in essence, invaded and distorted a specific aspect of his symbolic development (i.e., wherever body imagery was involved). This type of behavior (i.e., the enactment of a character or event) frequently characterizes patients with gender disturbances. They perform puppet play, as well as dramatic presentations, in which they "act out" their conflict over gender identity—using a female voice, body movements, and body decorations in a massive denial of their maleness.

It soon became evident that Ben's severe separation anxiety had been defended against by his feminine identification. As this defense was challenged by his therapist, Ben began to cling to his parents in our playroom and also feared the end of each session when he had to part with his therapist.

Our impression concerning the dynamics of Ben's psychopathology was as follows: the absence of an active autonomy push during his second year indicated a serious distortion in his separation–individuation process, a consequence of the trauma he incurred with the sudden loss of his first housekeeper at fourteen months and the concomitant emotional unavailability of his mother. Although he seemed able to substitute the second house-keeper almost immediately, we postulate that an unusual degree of hostile aggression had been provoked by this sudden loss, partic-ularly in view of his tenuous attachment to his mother. The witches and other "bad" fantasy female characters in the fairy tales probably represented his split-off and projected anger at his nurse and mother, as he attempted to hold on to the "good" mother. When Ben's behavior indicated a beginning awareness of his genital sensations and the male–female genital differences—somewhere between sixteen and nineteen months—he tried to become as much like his mother as possible in bodily appearance and particularly in genitality. He thereby surrendered his phallic sexuality when it first began to emerge; he did this as a defense against the threat of separation from her which disidentification would entail. Every boy is faced with the need to acknowledge the genital difference between himself and his mother during the latter part of the second year, an acknowledgment which normally intensifies separation anxiety. Ben's props—the barrettes, skirts, and other adornments—served as phallic supports as well as substitutes in the unusually severe dilemma of reconciling his self-representation with that of his mother. He appeared to have adopted the defensive strategy of becoming the "phallic woman," partially preserving his masculinity, albeit in a fetishistic form.

We were also concerned with Ben's mother's psychopathology. Her exposure to her father's rages had made her intolerant from her earliest years of the expression of aggression in any form, either in herself or in those about her. This inhibition of aggres-sion laid the ground work for her highly ambivalent relationship with her mother, setting the stage for her serious chronic depres-sion. The depression intensified with the birth of her son—a male like her father and therefore a potential aggressive threat.

We have postulated that Ben, an unplanned and unwanted male, aroused unbearable hostility in the mother, with infanticidal wishes against which she struggled by distancing herself emotionally from him. Ben's father, whose family constellation had required considerable repression of his own hostile aggression, had not actually surrendered his masculinity, but his basically passive attitude became evident as we got to know him. Yet, despite all these parental conflicts, Ben steadfastly maintained that he did not think he *was* a girl, but only that he *wanted to* and *pretended* to be a girl. Furthermore, his good ego development as shown by his firm reality testing in general and his excellent language development support our view that despite the serious traumata he had sustained and despite his partial renunciation of his masculinity, a solid early relationship with his primary object, the first housekeeper, had been established. Furthermore, his father appeared capable of participating actively in Ben's treatment, although he too had hitherto maintained an emotional distance from his son.

Treatment included all three family members precisely because of both parents' severe intolerance of hostile aggression in themselves and in others. As we began treatment, the mother had asked my "advice," as she put it, regarding her move from a full-time job to a part-time one. The mother's increased availability was enormously helpful, as it turned out. We agreed that the housekeeper would remain for the time being, but would slowly retreat as Ben's primary caretaker as the mother took over this role. We agreed that no new feminine "props"—pink and purple clothing, dolls, or other feminine equipment—would be purchased for Ben, but the current ones were to remain in place lest Ben be forced to use his "props" in secret.

During the first three months of treatment, Ben was encouraged to regress both at home and in his sessions. This was accomplished by responding to the many subtle signals he gave us: he wanted to be fed and cuddled by his mother, he spoke more babyishly, he fed and cuddled dolls, and began to want sweets incessantly. Only very gradually was his mother able to participate in this level of relationship with her son, one which she now realized had been denied to both of them during his infancy; her guilt over her earlier absences would often seriously depress her. Along with his regression, Ben began to challenge his parents with open anger and oppositionalism in every form. Temper tantrums, slapping and hitting, biting, deliberately urinating on the carpets, and so on turned Ben from the quiet passive boy of the first few months of treatment into a hellion whenever he was with his parents. His housekeeper, however, remained free from his attacks for the time being, and his school behavior was unchanged.

But even as Ben attacked his parents, he also clung to them; he now began to imitate his father both by wearing his clothing and in many of his actions. Rough-and-tumble play became a regular and mutually enjoyable activity between them. At the onset of treatment Ben said he disliked his penile erections and questioned his mother apprehensively about whether his penis was in danger of getting longer. Now Ben anxiously noted small cuts and bruises on his body, and his handling of his penis became almost incessant. Some phallic derivative play with guns and Superman emerged now and then during his sessions, but at home he still continued to "style" his mother's hair. It was interesting that his feminine play did not upset her nearly as much as his overt anger and oppositionalism and his newly emergent demands for sweets. The dynamics which had impeded Ben's phallic development were becoming more evident.

During the fourth month of treatment, Ben began to play out and verbalize fantasies of magically transforming himself into a girl ballerina by adding a scarf to his head or a t-shirt about his waist. The dynamic connection between Ben's anger at his mother, his fear lest this anger lead to separation from her, and his defensive use of female identification with a phallic mother in the face of this conflict now became even more evident. While interpretations of these connections seemed to be rejected as Ben seemed to ignore them, some effect was evident in that Ben began to cautiously explore female bodies. He tried to touch his mother's and his housekeeper's breasts, commenting on the "big nipples," and he said to his mother, "You don't have a penis, do you?"

Both parents often expressed their discouragement with Ben's treatment. His mother was increasingly anxious and intolerant of Ben's insatiable demands for sweets, fearing he would "damage his teeth and body" and that he would choke on the candies he demanded. This fear of choking, the husband now remembered, had plagued her from Ben's earliest months. Ben's father was much more upset by the cross dressing and refused to participate in the fairy tale enactments during the therapeutic sessions.

By the fifth month of treatment, Ben began to articulate his fear of going to sleep because of the witches and robbers in his dreams which corresponded to the witches in his fairy tale enactments. His behavior during the day began to show both masculine and feminine trends; while he continued to imitate and rough-house with his father and for the first time touched his father's pubic hair and penis in the shower as if to explore them, he also made believe that he had lost a leg, all this while saying he would always have "a boy's head and a girl's other parts." His fury still emerged periodically as he hit and provoked his mother in particular, but he would still dissolve in tears at her slightest reaction.

Gradually a new theme emerged at home and in his sessions: Ben began to question his mother about having a brother or sister, saying, "What if you have a baby and she's a girl?" He wanted to know how babies were born and where they came from, and he spoke of marrying his five-year-old girlfriend. Yet, as his fourth birthday passed, his tantrums, oppositionalism, and food demands once more became more intense and his feminine behavior increased as if he had expected a magic birthday present which had not materialized. At the same time, however, he played he was a baby, looking for his old baby clothes and carrying a newfound transitional object, his "blankie." Although he was disconsolate *after* his birthday and obviously disappointed in all his gifts, he shortly thereafter asked his mother what a vagina was like and told her she would feel better if she had a penis.

After this birthday upheaval Ben's play slowly began to change in a fundamental way: he began to *pretend,* and for the first time was satisfied to use a variety of symbolic substitutes in his fairy tale plays. His imitations of both parents in their various activities increased, and he began to draw and make puppets with which he would then play out some of his fairy tales. Clearly the shift to defensive femininity appeared to be less urgent as a protection against the anxiety of separation.

Ben began to note that his father's arms were very big and

asked if his own would someday match them in size. His enuresis and clinging behavior slowly decreased, and he was now jealous of sharing his mother's attention with others. For the first time, he refused to go out with his maternal grandmother, saying that his mother could protect him better—a statement to which the mother responded with tears of relief as well as guilt over his "lost infancy."

His current status is best described in his mother's own words:

These last three years have been the worst in my life; at first I felt I had no son at all, then I felt so guilty at what I had done to him, and now I am half a mother, but not very good at it yet, as I'm not good at my work either. As for Ben—while passing a stool recently, he said, "I don't really want to be a girl—I know I'm a boy, but sometimes my mind tells me something else."

And on a recent visit to a friend's house where there were many dolls and purple ponies, Ben played with these toys but he left without a backward glance at them—an almost unbelievable change from his behavior six months previously.

DISCUSSION

Ben is certainly not yet free of his defensive femininity, nor of the severe castration and separation anxieties which we believe led to this defensive elaboration. However, his relationship with his mother has a distinctly different quality—a mutual tenderness and a playfulness which had previously been entirely absent, and a tolerance of a moderate degree of hostile aggression on both sides. Although Ben's shelves had been lined with toys, as had our own playroom, Ben did not play with them for many months (although he immediately noted anything that had been changed). He had not been able to experiment with the world of toys since they were not "the real thing," and he required the concrete object, rather than even a partially representative one. The defensive genital reconstruction whereby he had endowed his mother with a penis, while he partially castrated himself psychologically to conform with her, had severely inhibited the development of abstract thinking in this quite intelligent child.

We were particularly impressed by the emergence of intense hostile aggression as his fetishism was gradually challenged—rage which we assume had reached unusually severe proportions after the first traumatic separation from his housekeeper at fourteen months, leaving him with a barely viable, fragile maternal relationship. This maternal relationship had to be protected by projecting his hostility in the form of the witches and other females supplied by the fairy tales his parents told him. His oral rage was unusually intense and was an important aspect of his symptomatology. It appeared to be dynamically connected with his mother's severe intolerance of hostile aggression. We do not yet know whether it was Ben's *maleness* which was a particularly powerful stimulant for the reemergence of the mother's preoedipal psychopathology, or whether the reawakening of her own oral experiences played an important role in her pathological reaction to Ben. But we are convinced that the joint treatment sessions during which Ben's anger and regression were acted out in a hundred different forms not only stimulated painful memories and affects in the mother, but were indeed essential for the formation of a positive tie of sufficient depth and strength to balance Ben's primitive rage at this same mother. This took place without the major splitting of the object which we assume had occurred during Ben's second and third years (Galenson, 1986).

It is likely that Ben would have maintained his perverse femininity had intensive treatment not been instituted at this age. While we are not yet certain of the outcome, we do not think Ben will become an acting-out homosexual, although some feminine wishes may well remain. We believe we have uncovered in this child the major aspects in the genesis of *one* type of homosexuality, and the dynamics of a perversion in formation. The conflict–defense hypothesis of gender disturbance is supported by the dynamic constellations uncovered during the treatment of this child.

Chapter 4

The Therapeutic Dyad in the Light of Infant Observational Research

Melvin A. Scharfman, M.D.

As someone trained in child analysis, for a long time I had incorporated observational research and other data obtained from nonclinical areas as a natural part of both my theoretical and clinical thinking. In spite of this, I found myself uncertain about how to approach the topic of infant observational research. How does one define infancy? Was this to be limited to a traditional dictionary definition of infancy which would focus on the child before language development, namely the first year of life, or should it be more broadly taken as referring to the infant in the psychoanalytic sense which stresses the infantile neurosis and therefore refers to early childhood? I will attempt to separate these two areas; there is a vast volume of research, both recent and ongoing, that relates to children in the first year of life which I will separate from the observations of somewhat older children in the second and third years of life by Mahler, her coworkers, and many others.

It may also be useful to consider observations of preverbal children separately from observations of children who have begun to verbalize, for psychoanalysis and psychotherapy are primarily verbal therapies. Certainly the verbalizations of both patient and therapist have been more a focus of study than the nonverbal interactions which are inevitably present in all therapy. These nonverbal communications play an important, sometimes a central, role in therapy, although they have often been neglected and are not always utilized to their best advantage. It remains to be seen whether some nonverbal communications, such as the position of the patient's body, the nature of the patient's eye contact, facial expressions, and so on, provide clues to a better understanding of the preverbal child.

I would like to turn to some of what we do know about the preverbal child, and its potential significance for clinical work, specifically with latency-age children. There has been an explosion of research on the preverbal period, whether one chooses to define that as birth to fifteen months, eighteen months, or even later, by both developmental researchers from an analytic background and by others from a variety of nonanalytic backgrounds. It is impossible to do justice to the many who have contributed. Drawing on the work that began thirty or more years ago by Spitz (1945a,b, 1966), Fries and Woolf (1953), Benjamin (1961), Bridger (1962), Escalona (1963, 1968), Korner (1964), Wolff (1965, 1966), Brazelton and Als (1979), major contributions have been made by Sander (1975, 1985), Sameroff (1978), Greenspan (1979), Emde (1980, 1983, 1988), and Stern (1985). Many of these contributions interface well with analytic theory; in other instances, analytic theory has been challenged and changed. Still other contributions have not yet been used to test analytic theory. Since our focus is on clinical work, I will mention a few of the contributions that are potentially applicable to our work with patients.

Infant observational research leads to a very different picture of an infant than that which was held a few decades ago. The infant is not passive, nor is its only function to reduce tension to an optimal level. The infant is born with a variety of developmental apparatuses or functions that require stimulation. These biological systems or apparatuses become active in what Hartmann (1939) called "the average expectable environment" (p. 23). The best studied apparatus in this regard is the visual system, which is relatively mature at birth. Haith (1977), Fantz (1958, 1961), and many others have established that the infant's visual activity is spontaneous, stimuli are searched for, and selective discrimination occurs, both in looking at different stimuli and in a preference for looking at the human face.

Infants have also been found to respond selectively to the sound of their mother's voice, to the smell of her milk, and so on. Many researchers conclude that these discriminations clearly demonstrate an active engagement with the environment and substantiate what Emde (1988) and others have called a basic motive of activity, something akin to drives. These discriminatory activities take place even during the first two months of life, the time that has been described by Sander (1975) as one of physiological regulation and by Greenspan (1979) as homeostasis. Interactions between mother and child vary during these two months. In addition to establishing physiological regulation, the infant fixes its gaze in response to the mother's talking, singing, smiling, and so on, and the mother, in turn, responds to the infant's crying, fretting, or gazing. Some researchers, including Stern (1977), call these mother–child interactions "early social interactions." Stern (1977) also questions the use of terms such as *autistic phase* and questions the concept of a stimulus barrier.

A host of other observational experimental studies also indicate that the infant has more ability to actively respond to the environment, to discriminate and selectively react than we had previously known. While all of this research will undoubtedly lead to modifications of analytic theory regarding early development, I personally do not see their clinical application for psychotherapy at this time. However, applications are undoubtedly possible in early preventive education, especially in the education of caretakers of very young infants.

Another aspect of early infant research has been a focus on questions of "match" or "fit" between mother and infant; that is, questions concerning how well a given infant's biologically determined systems match the expectations of the mother. Does the mother want a child who is awake much of the time, or does she want one who sleeps? Will she stimulate the sleepy child or try to feed the awake child to get it to go back to sleep? Such early interactions appear to modify biological givens within a specific range. There are still other related issues. The mother's affective state clearly influences the infant's early affective manifestations, a process which Emde (1988) calls affective monitoring. Infants, even in the first year of life, recognize and respond to the facial patterns of basic emotions, such as joy, anger, fear, sadness, disgust, and surprise. The emotional signals between infant and caregiver provide the basis for communicating needs, tensions, and satisfactions. These signals communicate meaning and motivations and provide a guide, not only for need satisfaction, but for learning, loving, and exploring.

Emde further states that the emotional availability of the caregiver during infancy seems to be the most important growth-promoting feature of the infant's environment. The infant looks to the mother's face or voice when it is trying to make sense of a situation that is otherwise ambiguous or uncertain and thereby regulates its behavior. He describes social referencing beginning during the first year of life and becoming prominent in the second year. His research also indicates that positive expressions of emotion, such as interest, joy, and surprise, are particularly important in the early caregiving relationships. Such positive emotions contribute to the infant's pleasure in life and generate an interest in the expanding world. They also encourage the development of sociability.

All infants recognize and express the facial patterns of basic emotions in the first year of life (Emde, 1988), a finding that implies a strong biological preparedness. The sharing of such common affective expressions is an activator of these affects in the infant. This activation occurs in the context of the social interaction and social referencing between infant and caretaker and is the basis of an affective core of self. Thus, the infant develops an affective core of self that includes recognition of oneself in the context of the other. Self does not develop except in relationship to the caretaker. Such a view obviously concurs with Winnicott's statement that "there is no such thing as a baby, only baby with mother" (1953). Where there is a lack of emotional availability of the early caregiver there will be a restriction of experience and some disturbance in the development of the self system.

The early patterns of interaction between caretaker and infant become internalized and are the basis for a continuing pattern of interaction throughout childhood and into adulthood. It is within the early interactive relationship with the mother or other caretaker that the infant comes to recognize and be aware of the self and of the other. Emde, Sander, and Stern (who uses a somewhat different terminology) all focus on a core sense of self as it develops in the relationship with the mother. They postulate an interdependence of connectedness and autonomy in the child's increasing sense of self and of other; Stern's view is perhaps the most far-reaching. These authors agree that early infancy research will lead to a reformulation of psychoanalytic theory and may profoundly influence clinical work.

Emphasizing, as it does, an object relations viewpoint, all of this work suggests that there is a need to look more closely at the therapeutic dyad. The implication is that there is the possibility of "making up" for early deficits in emotional availability within the therapeutic dyad and, consequently, the possibility of therapeutically restructuring the self and the "self with others." This viewpoint emphasizes the opportunities for a corrective emotional experience within the therapeutic relationship.

This is the central issue we are discussing today. We should consider if and how to use such a formulation as it applies to work with children, adolescents, or adults. We are only beginning to look at these possibilities in detail; it will take much future work to determine their effectiveness. We must ask whether or not certain early patterns of affective relationship are reversible, and if so, to what degree. Is there a point beyond which the introduction of what was deficient will be too late to permit new development? To put it in another way, the emotional availability of a caretaker can be demonstrated to be part of the "average expectable environment" that is necessary to unlock certain developmental processes. It has been implied that if it is subsequently provided, the emotional availability of a caretaker–therapist will unlock these same developmental processes. There are reasons to question this formulation. Developmental processes are time related. Research in other fields has indicated that even basic innate reflexes require stimulation within a given time frame or they cease to function. The sucking reflex, for example, will cease if there is no stimulus for sucking. When an infant animal is fed only by surgical tube, there is a critical time period beyond which the infant loses the capacity to suck (Schneirla, 1956). Such data may relate to human infants. It may be many years before we know how much later experience can make up for deficiencies in earlier experiences; it is an interesting and challenging question.

At this point we have a series of clues about the possible directions in which clinical work might be led by these formulations. One area thrown into particular focus is the role of the therapist's emotional availability and of the therapist's range of expressed emotion. If the child, adolescent, or adult maintains the same kind of social referencing used in infancy, what will happen when he is confronted with the therapist's different range of emotional availability as compared to that of the primary caretaker? Such questions lead to a whole series of provocative ideas. An infant's social referencing occurs primarily through the visual sense; he sees himself reflected in the emotional responses of another person. With children in treatment there is a good deal of visual contact. Child patients search for familiar responses and react to any affective response by the therapist. I will return to this subject shortly.

What are the implications for work with adults or older adolescents? Are some patients who have disturbances in their self systems better treated face to face? Should the therapist be free to indicate a range of emotional responses, not necessarily role-playing, but allowing a full range of spontaneous demonstrated responses? Given their importance in early development, positive responses by the therapist may be a major factor in the therapeutic process.

What are the possible implications of the research done on "match" or "fit" of child to caretaker? We all know that there are times when this is an important or crucial factor in therapy, but we do not know much about how to take it into account, how to assess whether or not a given therapist is a good enough fit with a given patient. This is an area of interest for clinical research, although not easy to accomplish.

Let us turn to the more ordinary, everyday questions of technique and therapeutic stance. A paper presented at the American Psychoanalytic meeting in December 1987 was titled,

"Developmental Psychology and Psychoanalysis: I. The Context for a Contemporary Revolution in Psychoanalysis" (Leichtman, 1987). I do not see the likelihood of any revolution, but I do see a gradual integration of new data through a process of evolution. Much infant research is consistent with self psychology and/or object relations theory. My own impression is that these orientations have been effecting slow, subtle changes in a majority of psychoanalysts. At the very least, they lead the clinician to look at some aspects of technique in a different light, bringing changes in style of interpretation or reconstruction. Over time, most of us probably change the nature of some of our interventions, testing in our own way the efficacy of any theory. Some of the research done in infancy has made me more aware of the probable nature of a child's earlier experience. If I say to Donny, an eight-year-old boy, as I recently did, "I see how hard it is for you to decide what you want to do; I know you look at me to try to understand what I feel about it," this can certainly be seen as a transference manifestation in the realm of very early social referencing. He looks to me for an affirmation of himself that he did not often get from his mother.

However, it is unlikely that any reconstruction I make with this boy would go back to the first year and a half of life. For one thing, I don't think he would relate to such a reconstruction, being far more concerned with his everyday functioning. For another, his behavior in the session is part of his ordinary functioning. He has sufficient ego development, observing ego, and sense of self to be able to become aware of the behavior when it is pointed out to him and is able to begin to try to figure out why he behaves as he does.

What would be the mode of therapeutic action in treating this boy? At eight he is shy, anxious, and uncertain in new situations, finds it difficult to make friends, and functions close to his level of ability in school only when he has a particularly warm and responsive teacher. He is preoccupied with imagined physical ailments, lacks confidence in himself, and is unable to continue to work on any task unless it comes easily to him. He rarely seems happy, spontaneous, or excited by anything. He views the world as an uncertain, and at times frightening, place. When interviewed, his mother shows very little open emotion, and seems somewhat depressed; we must consider the possibility that, very early in life, he may have experienced a deficit of emotional responses from his mother. How will therapy change this? How much will he be able to change if this formulation is correct?

There is more information to support the idea that this might be a reasonable reconstruction of something that occurred during Donny's first year. Early in the therapy, he constantly looked at my face to see how I was reacting. An important part of the work at that time was to help him identify his own affects, to name them. When he talked about something exciting he didn't look excited. When he was unable to solve a game he was playing, he would not appear terribly frustrated or angry. He looked to see how I would show my feelings or how I would suggest he must be feeling. The inhibitions in his affective responses changed very gradually and it was a long time before he could really share any kind of emotional response. When his dog died he came in to ask me if I would cry when my dog died. On another occasion, when he witnessed a rabbit giving birth, he wanted to know if that would be an exciting thing. All of this, of course, sounds quite compatible with a young infant's search for an emotional response from his mother and for the importance of reinforcement in identifying and allowing his own emotional responses. But Donny was not an infant, and his emotional responses were much more complicated and overdetermined by later influences in his life. Donny was almost four when a younger brother was born. On that occasion his mother became depressed for five or six months. During that time Donny stopped playing with his friends at school, was difficult to involve in activities, and eventually insisted on staying home rather than continuing with the nursery program. During this time, he was overtly hostile toward his younger brother as well as toward his mother. After a time of trying competitively to engage his mother in some interaction he seemed to give up. As the mother's depression gradually lifted, Donny's mood changed as well. He became more cheerful and outgoing. He was even able to engage his baby brother in play and particularly enjoyed playing peek-a-boo. When he was five, it was time to start kindergarten, which he seemed to do without any difficulty.

Almost six months later, Donny had to have surgery to repair an inguinal hernia which had begun to cause problems. While the parents were reluctant for him to have the surgery at this age, the surgeon felt that there was a definite danger of an incarceration of the bowel. The surgery was done over a school vacation period. The parents had done everything they could to inform Donny about the procedure and to allay his obvious anxieties. In spite of this preparation, the parents became aware that Donny's personality changed considerably following the surgery. He began to have nightmares and was difficult to reassure. In school he avoided any kind of play with other boys, clearly afraid that he would be injured. A teacher described him as daydreaming a great deal. At home he was subdued and cried easily. He was extremely upset when his parents left him for any reason, even though he stayed with a grandmother he knew quite well. But he showed little overt indication of these emotions. A month later he wet his bed several times in conjunction with dreams—something that had not happened for almost two years.

These are just a few aspects of Donny's history, all of which emerged during his treatment. His treatment demonstrated the complex interplay whereby any given developmental phase influences the subsequent developmental phase and is, in turn, retrospectively influenced as it is mentally represented. This is particularly so when any kind of trauma occurs. I believe that Donny's experience as an infant made him more vulnerable to the events surrounding the birth of his brother. That occurrence, in turn, influenced whatever early mental representations of the mother existed. Probably helped by his oedipal organization, he seemed to bounce back when he started kindergarten. Once again, a trauma intervened. Lacking in a sound sense of himself and of what Erickson called "basic trust" and after having this vulnerability intensified by his brother's birth and his mother's depression, Donny was more easily hurt by the oedipal trauma. The oedipal trauma, in turn, retrospectively made the previous experiences more traumatic. He had become a boy who did not basically trust the world around him, one who now posed a much more complex therapeutic task.

Donny had developed a phobic neurosis and the beginnings

of a phobic character. These problems were organized around the oedipal level of organization and were related to both conflict and trauma. There were other characterological difficulties that originated in his early infancy and in preoedipal difficulties. Phobic symptoms, including their transformation into characterological patterns, are very much conflict-related in the traditional sense, and, for the most part, can be resolved in treatment by interpretation. Neurotic disturbances have long been viewed as responding best to analytic treatment. Much of what has dominated the psychoanalytic literature in recent years pertains to other kinds of disturbance. This is the area where most questions arise about whether or not different orientations need to be considered, orientations such as object relations, self psychology, and other approaches, all of which differ, in varying degrees, from the traditional model of intrapsychic conflict.

In my own view, all of these approaches shift away from interpretation within the transference neurosis as the central factor in assessing the mode of therapeutic action. Their focus is essentially on an early disturbance in the object relationship, primarily with the mother. In that sense, they make a very real contribution to furthering our understanding of the origin of certain characterological disturbances. That, it seems to me, is one of the essential clinical contributions of early infancy research. It supplies a background for more specific understanding of global patterns of the individual's responses, of the individual's basic means of relating and of coping. Many of these global patterns are not accessible to change by interpretation. The new approaches emphasize those aspects of the therapeutic situation that have been considered a "real object relationship" or "corrective emotional experience."

Unfortunately, the term *corrective emotional experience* took on a negative connotation years ago when used as part of an attempt to shorten the process of psychoanalysis (Alexander and French, 1946). A multitude of papers and panels in recent years has included discussion of this factor (Escoll, 1983). If every psychoanalytic treatment involves elements of a new kind of object relationship, and I believe it does, a better understanding of very early childhood can help us understand exactly what use can potentially be made of that object relationship. In the future, infant research may help us to understand more about the extent to which the patient–analyst relationship is a factor in treatment and will influence our decisions about what kind of therapist is optimal for a given person. This, of course, assumes that we will be able to get enough data about an individual to suspect certain patterns in their early relationships, something that is not easy to do. This whole area can be illuminated by prospective, long-range studies which will allow us to determine the early infant experiences which contribute to later patterns of functioning.

I will return to Donny to illustrate some of these ideas. Donny seemed, by virtue of his mother's depression and constricted affective responses, to be a boy who had grown up uncertain of his own affects and with a definite need to "check out" any new situation or person, a need to know how they were responding to him. If, knowing this, the analyst is more open in his emotional responses, he can provide a better milieu for modification of that mode of functioning.

I anticipate that some people will see this as a suggestion to role-play. I don't believe I am referring to that. A therapist who does not allow emotional responses can be seen as playing a role, in this case, the role of a caricature of a psychoanalyst. No analyst should try to be what he is not, yet I think this sometimes happens. During many years of observing psychiatric residents and psychoanalytic candidates go through training, I have frequently known them to believe they have to play a role. They become uncomfortable with some of their normal responses, such as the extent to which they display affect. This is not a desirable situation; people whose style tends to be more constricted should not try to express themselves in a more open fashion. The analyst or therapist allows the patient to use him in a variety of ways. I am emphasizing that there are times when the reality of the analyst's personality influences, in some way, how the patient experiences and uses him. This is certainly a tricky and controversial area.

From my perspective, Donny used me as a new object, one who was responsive and helped him get in touch with his feelings. At times this occurred by his identifying with the way I might feel; in finding it easier to "read" me, he became more able to "read" himself. Where such an element operates in analysis, it is not by virtue of interpretation. It is an element of a new object relationship, a corrective one, if you will, that becomes internalized. For the most part, this process operates as a relatively silent part of the treatment and occurs fortuitously. Child analysts, in particular, have emphasized the new object relationship as a factor in the psychoanalytic process, but it has also been discussed as operating during adolescence and in early adulthood (Casuso, 1965).

To return to a point I made earlier, the extent to which such an approach will modify pathology consequent to early deficiencies in the interaction of a mother and her infant or child is as yet unclear. Observational research has taught us a great deal about the many factors that influence an infant's development, and we will learn a great deal more in the years ahead. The extent to which we will be able to apply that knowledge clinically will undoubtedly continue to be discussed as more information becomes available.

Chapter 5

The Significance of Infant Observational Research for Clinical Work with Prelatency Children

Jules Glenn, M.D.

My views on the significance of infant observational research for insight-oriented psychotherapy are based on observations of prelatency children in treatment. Such treatment, which depends on the patient's verbal expression and on his nonverbal expression in activity (e.g., in play and art), is rarely undertaken with a child under three. I will not discuss treatment of families in which one tries to alter the environment, including the parent–child interaction. For instance, the treatment of infants who fail to thrive due to insufficiencies in the mother–child relationship will not be included. In the first section, I will concentrate on one case, a child in psychoanalysis, to illustrate the issues. The direct observational data I will discuss will include Mahler's observations on symbiosis and separation–individuation.

In the second section I will propose some generalizations about the role of infant observations in clinical work with prelatency children. I will also caution the reader about certain faulty conclusions that have been reached on the basis of infant observation.

Jan was three and a half years old when I saw her in consultation. She had been a difficult child before, but the troubles intensified after her brother Max was born two and a half months before the consultation. In the months just before we met she had more temper tantrums than previously and her mother, who became more and more furious, had greater difficulty controlling the little girl. For instance, mother took Jan to Toys-R-Us to get a swing set and something small—a doll set. Jan became very upset, cried, screamed, and kicked because they only had father and mother dolls, not a complete set. Mother had to take her out of the store forcibly as people watched the struggle. On another occasion, when mother tried to prevent Jan from throwing a ball in the house, Jan pulled mother's hair and threw a tennis ball at her. Although father could handle Jan better than mother, he had difficulty also.

Jan's trouble antedated her brother's birth. At two years of age, she frequently fell and sometimes rolled her eyes; a physician was concerned that she might be having petit mal seizures and ordered an EEG. After these events she became quite anxious, had increased trouble sleeping, and cried and screamed more. However, the EEG and neurological evaluation were normal. After the sequence of episodes just described, although her parents let her cry for a few nights, they generally gave in to her demands. Jan clung to her mother. At day camp she didn't want her mother to leave and cried for her.

Additional relevant parts of the history included difficulty with toilet training. While her mother was pregnant with Max, Jan wanted to be a baby and didn't want to be toilet trained. At the time of the consultation, she had become toilet trained for urination although not for bowel movements, but, when the treatment started, the reverse was true. Jan was then BM trained but wet at times. After toilet training was partially accomplished Jan masturbated more, though when she started masturbating is not clear. Significant evidence that Jan was preoccupied with oedipal fantasies appeared in the history. Her parents told me that weddings fascinated her, even the Smurfs' marriage on TV when she was three. Jan play-acted being a bride and recently said she would marry her father.

The history and diagnostic interviews suggested a frightened child struggling with separation issues as she entered the oedipal stage.

After a short period of psychotherapy Jan started analysis. I will present a few sessions of the analysis which illustrate the issues that arise when one tries to apply knowledge from infant observation to an almost five-year-old child. I have selected this segment of the analysis because it involves separation issues that *seem* like those observed in smaller children, but actually are more complicated and advanced.

Jan had been a reasonably productive child in analysis, playing games that indicated both separation and oedipal problems, but the analysis was dominated by her clinging to her mother. Often either mother would have to come into the consulting room with Jan, or Jan would be seen in the waiting room with mother present. At some sessions Jan would hide behind mother or sit in her lap. Interpretations were often made about Jan's clinging to mother; for example, because of her love for mother, because of her need for protection against the dangerous analyst, to keep mother from staying alone with brother, and as a defense against being angry or anxious.

Shortly before Jan's fifth birthday, both she and her mother seemed ready for separation. Mrs. A. brought Max to the session that day. She wanted to take him for a walk but hesitated to do so unless Jan explicitly gave her permission. Mother observed Jan's reaction and decided that she had probably approved her leaving with Max. She was about to leave, but first asked the analyst if Max could look into the consultation room. The analyst replied that this was Jan's special place, so he'd have to ask Jan about it. Mother took this to be a refusal. Apparently her sensitivity to rejection and her reluctance to have Jan become autonomous appeared in the transference to her child's analyst. In any case, she left with Max. Jan was alone in the office with the analyst for one of the first times.

She said she was angry that the therapist did not let her brother look in, but then settled down, making birthday presents for the baby doll, an activity she had pursued before. At the end of the session, when mother and Max returned, Jan invited her brother into the consultation room. He looked about until the analyst said time was up. Jan lingered very briefly before leaving.

In the next session Jan continued to deal with separation problems. She brought Ken and Barbie type dolls dressed for attending nightclub and theater, and played at excluding the analyst from the threesome. She sat in the analyst's chair, turned so that he could not see her as she played, and drew. The analyst pointed out that Jan was leaving him out, and Jan told him not to peek. When he asked her what to do, she refused to tell him. "It's not a game," she added.

Then Jan said that a friend of hers had died because she put her nose into a can and was killed by it. The dolls played silently, but brother doll and the analyst were not allowed to see what was going on. The analyst stated that Jan knew how it feels to be excluded and tried to make him feel that way also.

These are interesting sessions which can be understood in a number of ways. Jan is trying to give up her clinging to her mother and to allow her mother to be with her brother. She is trying to become autonomous, but the autonomy is painful. She becomes angry because she feels left out, and becomes anxious about the anger. She defends against these affects by becoming the leaver, the excluder of the analyst, a displacement object who represents mother. She also played a variant of the peek-a-boo game, hiding behind the chair so the analyst could not see her, but the analyst did not respond, refusing to play the game with her. In the second session he partially interpreted her need for control, to turn the tables and to make him feel the painful affect. If she could accomplish these goals she would not feel so bad. Jan's strategy seemed to work. She could allow her brother into the room, partly because she identified with him, partly out of altruism and love for him. There are also indications of a more complex relationship with the analyst—a desire to have him put his nose into her business, a desire that she would thwart because it is too dangerous.

Jan's behavior does remind one of an infant's. In some ways she *appears* to be arrested at the symbiotic stage (Mahler, Pine, and Bergman, 1975). The clinging to mother, sitting on her lap, and hiding behind her skirt bring this to mind. At times she *looked* as if she were one with her mother. Mother also had separation difficulties and I assume she communicated her wish for Jan to be with her. We are limited in our understanding of Mrs. A. because she did not accept previous recommendations to enter therapy. Mrs. A. commented that her older sister was her mother's child and she was her father's child. But her father, with whom she had been very close, had a heart attack when Mrs. A. was six and died when she was twelve. Mrs. A.'s mother started dating when Mrs. A. was in high school and then married. She was away a great deal and Mrs. A. missed her. One response was to take drugs for a period, although she "wasn't that kind of person." She had to return from college during her freshman year because of anxiety attacks which lasted a year. A few months of psychotherapy the next year enabled her to settle down, finish school, work, and get married. During her pregnancy with Jan she became anxious again when the doctor told her that she might have a placenta previa, but her anxiety ended when a sonogram proved all was well. Mrs. A. identified closely with Jan and worried that Jan was, like her, an anxious person.

Although the history suggested that Jan and mother were tied in a symbiotic union, Jan's communications in the analytic sessions made it obvious that the symbioticlike states were not the same as the symbiosis of the two- to five-month-old. We may note that symbioticlike states and fantasies occur throughout life and should be differentiated from the symbiotic stage. Mahler (1975) has stated that symbiosis per se occurs during the period from two to five months and that a feeling of the mother's powerful and protective presence continues beyond that time. For instance, a child of the practicing subphase of separation–individuation is buoyant because he feels a fantasied union with his mother, and a child of the rapprochement subphase becomes deeply disturbed when he feels his mother is not about.

Stern (1985) has challenged Mahler's observations on symbiosis. He notes that mother and child are attuned, "in sync," prior to, during, and after the "symbiotic stage," but he does not call this mother–child harmony symbiosis. Stern observes that caretakers and infants "mutually create chains and sequences of reciprocal behaviors that make up their social dialogue" during the first nine months and that the mother almost always works in the same modality as the infant. After nine months affect attunement occurs between different modes. For instance, mother may move in the same rhythm as the child or for the same duration that the child makes a sound. The attunement is noted by the child who reciprocates by continuing his activity. I take these attunements to be evidence of "symbiotic states" between parent and child rather than evidence for a symbiotic stage.

Further, Stern notes that the mother may communicate her fears and needs for closeness to her child through a selective attunement in which the mother responds to one of the several feelings the infant experiences. In this way she may encourage the child to accentuate certain emotional reactions. Or the mother may communicate an affect that the child did not originally display and thus impose that affect on the child. Either way, child and mother come to share affects. Later, fantasies too can be shared.

Clearly, Jan and her mother demonstrate the closeness that occurs at a more mature level than the two- to five-month period.

Now, let us compare Jan's behavior with that of children in the differentiation and rapprochement subphases. Again we will see that Jan's behavior is more advanced.

The child of the differentiation subphase—from about five to ten months—starts to play peek-a-boo games which the mother initiates. The parent covers her own face or the baby's face so that mother seems to disappear, only to happily reappear when the cover is removed. Child and mother smile happily. Later, during the practicing and rapprochement subphases of separation–individuation the child can initiate these separation and mastery games. Latency children play a more complicated version of hide-and-seek. Jan's game, in which she turned the chair about and thus was out of the analyst's view, derived from the earlier games but is more complex. It included an invitation for the analyst to intrude. The need for the mother is more complicated insofar as the mother is now the protector against oedipal desires, not just the primary love object and protector against general dangers from the external world.

Jan's behavior reminds one of the rapprochement subphase child of fifteen to twenty months; she is attempting to achieve autonomy, but is upset by the attempts. The rapprochement child tries to break away from mother, but becomes angry and panicky when this occurs. He feels as though mother has deserted him, that he is alone. He becomes furious and frightened, then starts to cling again. He initiates defenses such as splitting to guard against these dangerous affects.

Although in some way she *looks* like a rapprochement child, Jan is a five-year-old trying to guard against oedipal feelings. Her behavior contains and transforms earlier, infantile reactions to her attempts at separation and autonomy; they are not unmodified repetitions of the original patterns of response. She strives for autonomy by taking control of the situation, being the deserter and being the seducer, threatening injury and death if the analyst succumbs to the seduction.

As the child undergoing separation–individuation becomes more autonomous and achieves object constancy, oedipal wishes emerge. In Jan's case oedipal wishes have appeared in the past. Now she seeks closeness to her mother for protection. Mother, for her own reasons, has cooperated with Jan to achieve this aim. In treatment, as defenses were interpreted and Jan felt ready to give them up to a degree, she was able to express her oedipal desires more clearly. Let us resume the description of the analysis at this point.

The analytic material shifted to oedipal, primal scene, and sibling rivalry themes. When Jan's teacher married, Jan became preoccupied once more with issues of marriage, an interest previously described by Jan's parents when they provided the history. She enacted and had the analyst draw scenes of the wedding which Jan claimed she had actually attended in Hawaii. She talked of her own wishes to be married in a local catering establishment.

The drawings of the wedding included the bride's dressing for the occasion and the ceremony itself, the exchange of rings, and the lifting of the couple on chairs. Jan hinted at other mysterious, exciting parts of the wedding. Intermeshed with these pictures and stories Jan described violent scenes: grown-up dinosaurs ate baby dinosaurs. The analyst was directed to draw blood on the teeth of the dinosaurs; marriage was pictured as a fight. It

appeared to lead to aggressive sex with the birth of babies which
were rivals. In the play a brother was buried by the lava.

Associations, at this point mostly verbal descriptions of current events and feelings, indicated the relation of the babies and
brother to the patient's brother. When her mother locked Jan and
her brother in a car to go shopping, Jan became terrified; the two
children were helpless allies for the moment. Also, Max's birthday
was coming up and Jan anticipated a party and gifts for him.
When the analyst suggested that Jan was angry at her brother, she
denied it, saying she loved and hated him. The conflict of love and
hate was interpreted. She did love her brother and at times this
masked her love for her father. Her anger at her mother for
taking brother with her also contained anger at her mother for
having father.

From the experience with Jan, I will suggest some generalizations about the role of infant observational research in the
treatment of similar children.

A knowledge of what infants are like can enable the therapist
to develop an understanding of the preoedipal determinants that
have led to the patient's present, more mature, personality structure and conflicts. In Jan's case the mother's early clinging to the
patient made it difficult for the little girl to become appropriately
independent and facilitated her defensive use of the close relationship with her mother.

A knowledge of what infants are like enables the therapist to
acquire a *feel* for the developmental level of a child he is treating,
and for its degree of stability. The therapist can also get a sense of
the preoedipal components that have entered into and have been
transformed by oedipal development, and he can judge how these
preoedipal components affect the texture of the oedipal complex.
This will enable him to make interpretations in accordance with
the patient's psychic organization.

There is a danger that the therapist will make interpretations
on the wrong level. For instance, Jan, like most three-year-olds
capable of analytically oriented therapy, has entered the oedipal
stage, but preoedipal contributions to her oedipal development
are self-evident. If the preoedipal precursors are interpreted
without reference to the oedipal present, the insight suggested will

be erroneous. The patient, I might add, may save the day by misunderstanding the therapist; that is, she may interpret his interpretation in accordance with the correct level of interpretation. Frequently the therapist will offer an open-ended or ambiguous explanation to the child that the patient can understand in accordance with his own perception of the facts.

Prelatency children generally do not benefit from detailed reconstructions. Hence, explaining to a child what the preoedipal experiences were that led to the current conflicts often falls flat. Attempts at reconstruction often fail at this age because of the limited cognitive capabilities of the child and because of the child's lack of interest in the past and in how it affects the present. The child is generally interested in and focuses on the present, the here and now, not on past events or future occurrences.

Although the primary therapeutic instrument of child analysis is interpretation and the primary means of psychoanalytic therapeutic action is insight, there are other means of therapeutic action which can be effective (Glenn, 1978). As Anna Freud has said (1965), analysis offers the child a smorgasbord from which he can choose. The child, she says, "selects for therapeutic use, [from] . . . the full range of possibilities that are contained in child analysis" (p. 229). In borderline children, she adds, "therapy is served . . . by verbalization and clarification of internal and external dangers and frightening affects which are perceived preconsciously but which his weak and helpless ego, left to itself, cannot integrate and bring under secondary process dominance" (p. 230).

Children with libido defects . . . due to severe early deprivation in object relations . . . may answer to the intimacy of the analyst–patient relationship, which is favorable for the proliferation of libidinal attachment because of the frequency and long duration of contact, the lack of interruptions, the exclusion of disturbing rivals, etc. [p. 231].

The therapeutic element in intellectually retarded children consists of the analyst's reassuring role.

In analytically oriented therapy the smorgasbord includes

fewer dishes of insight than in psychoanalysis. It is important that the therapist be aware of how the child is using the treatment. Does the child use it to acquire oedipal gratification, actual or fantasied parental protection, or actual or fantasied parental presence? Does he use it to reinforce his capacity to control himself and the outer world, to complete a fantasied incompleteness by mirroring or attunement, or as a source of information about how defenses can be used or drives modulated? The very fact that the therapist understands the child or "reads his mind" may have gratifying and often therapeutic effect. However, the analyst's empathy is more complicated than a mother's affect attunement (Stern, 1985).

To develop satisfactorily, children require actual adults, real objects, as a base on which they may build representations. An adult may not be available to the child at home or, if a grown-up is present, the child, for internal reasons, may be unable to use him or her as a libidinal object or as a benign recipient of aggression. A child may then further his development by using the therapist as a real object. The therapist may also serve as a transference object or a displacement object (Neubauer, 1971).

In order to make correct interpretations as well as to avoid interference with development by inappropriate activity, the therapist must be able to assess his patient's verbalization and behavior and the significance to the child of the therapist's own activity. He must know the child's developmental level and the nature of the patient's representations of the therapist. In Jan's case the therapist enabled the child to achieve autonomy and independence in the analytic situation, but was available, if needed, as a protector. He was available as an oedipal object to be loved or hated without realistic fear of punishment. Eventually he could interpret her affection, antagonism, and fear, thus using insight to help her. As treatment progressed the child could also use his presence to achieve developmental stability. If he had erroneously interpreted her attachment as that of a small infant, he might have discouraged her from retaining the maturity she had achieved. She might have interpreted his incorrect evaluation as a wish on his part, and might have compliantly responded with regression.

An oedipal child's nonverbal communications, expressions,

and interactions with his therapist may appear to be preoedipal in nature. Sometimes, especially in younger three-year-olds, preoedipal meanings will predominate. A child may attempt to attain libidinal object constancy (usually reached by three years of age) by playing games in which he identifies with grown-ups (Mahler, Pine, and Bergman 1975). Mahler has described children during the subphase she labeled "to object constancy." They may imitate adult behavior in games—driving buses and automobiles or caring for babies, for instance. Through such play they identify with and internalize adults so they can tolerate loss by feeling their parents are with them even when they are not.

Further, other types of preoedipal mastery may be achieved through repetitive play during therapy. A child who has not been fully toilet trained may practice that task or may impose it on the adult therapist in play. The little patient becomes the aggressor who forces his will on the parent substitute rather than submit as the passive recipient of training. Similarly, children who have undergone operative or other shock trauma during the preoedipal years may attempt mastery through reenactment. They may, for instance, become the surgeons who cut and repair (Freud, 1920a; A. Freud, 1936). Interpretation of such games often adds stability to the therapeutic effect of nonverbal play.

For the most part the oedipal child has incorporated preoedipal manifestations into the oedipal organization and should not be treated as purely preoedipal. The case of Jan illustrates this.

Infant observational research is extremely valuable in helping us understand normal development and in helping us to know where a patient's development stands in relation to earlier developmental stages. However, we must recognize the limitations of such research. The very small child's verbalization is limited, and hence the content of his thoughts and the quality of his emotions often have to be guessed. An example of this uncertainty was brought to my attention at the May 1987 Mahler Symposium. Both Henri Parens and Anni Bergman remarked that it is often difficult to decide whether a certain behavior is rapprochement or oedipal. For instance at one-and-one-half years of age triadic behavior appears that may not be oedipal. Abelin (1975, 1977) has written about this early triangulation in which the toddler identifies with the rival father's wish for mother. From his description a strong drive element is present. Blum (1977) has pointed out that certain cognitive capacities are required for a full-blown oedipal triangulation; this differentiates it from preoedipal triangulation. Jan was advanced cognitively, as her play indicates, and was dealing with oedipal conflicts.

In addition, one is in danger of underestimating the importance of drives when research is carried out under conditions when drives are ordinarily subdued. Some infant researchers (Stern, 1985) have concluded that drives do not exist or that their influence is minimal. It should be noted that in order to do certain experiments the researcher must be sure that the infant is in the inactive alert state that facilitates perception of the external world. When he feeds the child to produce optimal conditions, the researcher diminishes the observable influence of drives. He then may decide, incorrectly, that drives do not exist (Galenson, personal communication).

Many researchers, including Dowling (1977), A. Freud (1922, 1980), Mahler, Pine, and Bergman (1975), Parens (1979), and Roiphe and Galenson (1981) have made observations under other conditions and have concluded that drives exist and are potent in influencing behavior and development.

We must also recognize the danger of simplistically applying knowledge about infants to later stages of development as if transformations do not occur as the child matures. The observer of an infant may make the unwarranted inference that the child's characteristics will continue to manifest themselves relatively unchanged in later childhood and even adulthood. Since the infantile state does not include the internal conflicts that the older child, adolescent, and grown-up experience, the conclusion may be reached erroneously that such conflict does not become characteristic of or important for the developing child. The case of Jan demonstrates, as did Freud's case of Hans (Freud, 1909) and countless others, that unconscious conflict invariably appears in childhood and especially in the oedipal period.

SUMMARY

Infant observational research is invaluable in helping us understand normal development, but its application to insight-oriented psychotherapy of conflicted prelatency children is limited. It does help us understand where our patients stand in relation to earlier stages in their development. However, we must also recognize that a child of the oedipal period and thereafter does not display preoedipal manifestations in their original form. The oedipal child has transformed the preoedipal configurations and has incorporated them into the oedipal organization. Interpretations should be made in accordance with the child's developmental level and therefore must take these later transformations into account.

Chapter 6

Infant Research and Adult Psychoanalysis

Arnold M. Cooper, M.D.

A nalysts generally agree that the primary psychoanalytic task is the understanding of the patient's psychic reality, rather than his material reality, and that, ultimately, we are interested in the genetic point of view, not the developmental one. Analytically, the past that the patient has internalized, rather than some "realistic" past, is the past that is relevant to his present. For example, a toddler who has just been spoken to sharply by his mother runs to his father and says "Mommy pushed me down and bit me." The discrepancy of fact and report is clear, but the child may internalize his fantasied version rather than the realistic one, since at the moment a feeling of overwhelming injustice done to him is more satisfying to his injured narcissism than an admission of being a bad boy who is too small and helpless to ward off punishment. It is that genetic past—the past as experienced, including the distorting defenses that make experience tolerable even at the expense of some observable truth—that his future analyst will attempt to unravel.

The question of the role of infant research in adult analysis can be approached by asking how the analyst brings himself to the task of understanding psychic reality, including the genetic past. We know that none of us is naively open-minded. Thousands of years of naive open-mindedness did not lead to the discovery of psychoanalysis. Rather, each of us approaches the patient with a limited array of mental templates that predetermine the shape that we give to the communications we receive from the patient. While being psychoanalysts will impose some uniformity upon our approaches to listening and understanding, there are broad areas of differences among analysts that are relevant to our question.

Even though it may be obvious, I want to emphasize that we have never derived our data solely from our patients. Freud, while creating the genetic and developmental points of view for understanding the patterns and details of adult life, patterned the patient's associations according to his own inner vision of the infant's early life, as have all analysts since Freud. We now know those visions vary enormously, but all of them are limited. Freud, discovering the Oedipus complex within himself, looked for corroboration from developmental observation of children (Freud, 1905). The two pioneers of child analysis, Melanie Klein and Anna Freud, "observed" very different children; neither was able to make a theory-free observation. The Freudian baby, driven and frightened, is quite different from the Kleinian baby, rageful, paranoid, and depressed, who is, in turn, very distinct from the Kohutian baby, ambitious and relatively content. Significantly, the intent of the early child analysts was quite dissimilar from the aims of the developmentalists during the past few decades. The earlier analysts were interested in extending and expanding an existing theory of the meanings and origins of adult psychological function; the newer baby-watchers, on the other hand, have been doing their best to find out what babies actually do, unencumbered by immediate therapeutic aims, and trying hard to put aside accepted theory. This scientific effort has now accumulated a vast amount of data, some of it well-known to analysts, and some of it still quite obscure. Bowlby's recent review (Bowlby, 1988) is essential for an understanding of the issues. I believe that the science of infant observation had done three things for psychoanalysts of adult patients: (1) it has challenged and changed some of our core theories in important ways that influence our therapeutic endeavors; (2) it has opened the way for us to hold a far richer and more varied vision of baby life, thus changing the way we listen to our patients' associations and providing more interpretive possibilities than were previously available; and (3) it has placed relative limits and regularities on possibilities, so that we know that certain adult psychic constellations probably do not appear without accompanying childhood circumstances. Buckley (1986), in his recent volume on object relations, says:

> Direct observation of young children and their mothers by Margaret Mahler and her colleagues has resulted in a body of "objective" behavioral data upon which a developmental model of the infant's psychological separation from the mother has been built, a model which has major implications for object relations theory and for therapy, since some clinicians now emphasize pre-oedipal mother–child dyadic issues in their work with patients and trace transference back to early mother–child interactions [p. xii].

Buckley is, I believe, correct in deriving these changes in our practice from Mahler's observations on children. I would add only that Mahler is one of a number of researchers who have brought this newer perspective to analytic work. David Levy, Bowlby, Stern, Emde, Sanders, Ainsworth, Greenspan, and others have enriched our visions of the baby and his activities, while demonstrating the profound effects of the vicissitudes of the early dyadic relationships on later life. I think the case can be made that the growth of object relations theory in this country and our increased focus on preoedipal constellations have been enormously reinforced by what we have learned from infant and child development. Not only has that work led many people away from instinctual motivational theories toward object relational ones but, more importantly, that work has altered the narrative possibilities, the plot paradigms of growth and development, that the analyst is inevitably creating with his patient as he hears his or her story.

As much as we try to keep our focus on the patient's experience with us, that experience will always be, to some significant degree, more complex than we can comfortably contain. Therefore, in our inevitable attempt to impose some intellectual and affective order on the unfolding life story, we call upon the familiar pictures in our mind of the circumstances of pain and suffering that we imagine might engender our patients' neurotic patterns, and that make our empathic responses possible. The modern analyst has a number of experiences that, I believe, indelibly imprint his intellectual and affective psychoanalytic world. For example, seeing Harry Harlow's movies of maternally deprived infant monkeys (Harlow, 1959, 1960), or George Engel's movies of his patient Monica (Engel, 1953), or James Robertson's movies of children going to the hospital (Robertson, 1951–1952, 1959) conveys a sense of the child's experience of loss that will inevitably color the way the analyst hears his patient speak of experiences of helpless loss and disappointment in love. Similarly, our knowledge of the infant's extraordinary communicative and attachment repertoire and range of affective and cognitive capacities has changed our sense of the "personhood" of the baby. It is inevitable that our listening and interpreting will be somewhat reductionistic, but we want it to be as minimally reductionistic as we can manage; a goal that requires our openness to many versions of both the current narrative that the patient unfolds with us and its possible precursors in the past. As a result of child development research, the newer versions of patient life stories that we weave have a much greater role for mother, and a much more active infant, eagerly seeking experience, responding not only to his instinctual needs, but developing his needs in accord with the interaction he experiences with his mother.

Freud was explicit (Freud, 1920b) in claiming that no prediction could be made from the past. The direct prospective study of development, however, shows us not only how difficult it is to understand the detailed present out of the past, but also how much can, in fact, be predicted from a knowledge of the past. Prospective work in temperament (Thomas, Chess, and Birch, 1968) and Engel's work with Monica and her children (Engel et al., 1985) show that some predictions can be made, and that some patterns laid down very early are extraordinarily enduring. Monica, a child with an esophageal fistula, was fed lying flat on her back with a feeding tube inserted into a gastrostomy. Later, as an adult, she fed her own infant child in the same position, and that child was observed feeding her dolls in the same fashion (Engel et al., 1985). I think we would probably agree that something so basic as the feeding pattern between mother and child will have powerful and lasting effects on later developmental stages. Bowlby's recent review (Bowlby, 1988) stresses that we must assess personality structure and its attendant personal vulnerability and resilience, rather than current functioning alone. He states that while there are important discontinuities in development, there is a solid basis for predicting that:

> Given affectionate and responsive parents who throughout infancy, childhood and adolescence provide a boy or girl with a secure base from which to explore the world and to which to return when in difficulty, it is more than likely that a child will grow up to be a cheerful, socially cooperative, and effective citizen and to be unlikely to break down in adversity. Furthermore, such persons are far more likely than those who come from less stable and supportive homes to make stable marriages and to provide their children with the same favorable conditions for healthy development that they enjoyed themselves. These, of course, are age-old truths, but they are now underpinned by far more solid evidence than ever before [p. 9].

While it remains true that the individual outcome is an unpredictable resultant of genes and environment, we know the actual effects of developmental vicissitudes on later function far better than we once did. It is likely to matter in the course of analytic work whether we are dealing with an individual whose temperament or genetic makeup is such that only the most skillful and sensitive handling could avoid traumatizing him during childhood, or whether we are dealing with someone whose temperament or genetic makeup allows him to respond healthily to a broad range of environments, and for whom only gross failure of parenting will cause damage. Analytic outcome may be heavily dependent on this variable, which may be assessable in the course of treatment. Our knowledge of the infant, derived from infant research and from direct observation, has contributed to a major intellectual shift in psychoanalysis. Infant research now provides the biological underpinning for modern analytic work, replacing the theory of instincts which served this role in the earlier period of psychoanalysis. This research provides new insights into the interpersonal world of the infant as well as a more detailed and precise set of inferences concerning the infant's experiential world; together these will provide the boundaries for the narrative or hermeneutic reconstructions which many today believe are the core of analytic clinical effort.

Direct empathic child observation also permits us a sense of the kinds of child environmental interactions and maturational events that may directly contribute to certain affective and object relational constellations. With knowledge of these we are in a better position to recognize the ways in which our patients' stories may be defensive, disguising other constructions. The Sandlers' concept of past unconscious and present unconscious is useful in this regard (Sandler and Sandler, 1987), pointing to the layering of the narrative. Developmental knowledge helps us to help the patient sort out differences between experience as he now perceives it, influenced by all the defensive aspects of development, and experience as it may once have been. The better our knowledge of actual plots of early interpersonal life, the more likely we will be to enable our patients to relive those plots within the transference. It is equally true that child observation may set limits to the genetic narratives that can be reasonably entertained; if a patient's story contradicts our knowledge from direct observation, it will be listened to very differently from one consonant with the data of observation. Sometimes a patient will tell us an unfamiliar story that will open up a developmental possibility that can now be sought in direct observation. More likely, the patient's story alerts us to a new inventiveness of defenses and screens, and directs us to look beyond the tale as told. We know that there are some reports of developmental patterns which cannot be developmentally true. The patient who reports that he was never held or touched by his mother and yet has grown up to be a functioning human being, is, in all likelihood, reporting a fantasy. This is important in itself, but the importance is tempered in the analyst's mind by the conviction that the fantasy is serving defensive needs. As analysts, we question the source of the discrepancy between the developmental and genetic histories. In this sense, one may view infant observation as refining and redefining our ideas of infantile trauma. The newer views will not only alert us to a different order of traumatizing conditions, but they will emphasize developmental pathways rather than fixations.

All of us looking back at our own analytic material, or reviewing reports of others, have little difficulty detecting instances in which the analyst, believing that he was helping the patient to understand his own experience, was, in fact, forcing the patient to a view of the experience which was determined by the analyst's view of what that experience must have been. The analyst's limitation in envisioning possible plots stems not only from countertransferential blind spots but also from the analyst's failure to recognize important story lines other than the ones which he has already learned. When Freud discovered the oedipal plot it was not self-evident that it must be true or universal, as indeed it seems to be. Our task is to be on the alert for all of the variants of that plot, since it is those variations that are important for our interpretive purposes. But, even more, our task is to look for other basic plots. Empathic observation of infant maturation and development is helping us achieve that task; our vision has been extended by knowledge of the early infant.

I shall present some clinical material indicating how the knowledge of infant observation influences my clinical work. I am powerfully influenced by the work of Stern and Emde on the early interactive nature of a child's relationship to its mother; by the work of Greenspan showing the profound effects on child behavior of alterations of the mother's psychic state, and her attitude toward the child; by the work of Bowlby on the effects on the infant of separation from its mother; and by Harlow's work with baby monkeys. I take away from each of these workers a conviction of the profound effects of early mothering on the developing self and on the defensive attitudes and activities that are set in motion in the effort to maintain well-being under less than optimal circumstances. It also seems to me that many of these characterologic attitudes, strongly entrenched before the oedipal phase, are readily expressed in the transference, often in nonverbal aspects of the relationship, and can be worked with.

• • •

A thirty-five-year-old professional woman explains that all her life she has been fearful of new activities; she has never learned to swim or ride a bike. Anorexic during early adolescence, she has felt unattractive and sexually inhibited. She has been successful in her scholarly pursuits, but is lonely, with few friends. She is polite, reserved, precise in her speech, plainly dressed, as if hiding her sexuality, and looks sad. In fact, at times during our initial interviews, her facial expression was that of a sad child as we have come to know it from child researchers; the anxious look, the down-turned eyebrows, the pinched facies. She describes her father as an artistic genius, who was attentive to her and very interested in her development. Her mother was a "nice person" who was content to serve and idolize the father. For reasons she cannot imagine, since she believes she had good parents who loved her, she recalls being a terribly unhappy child, school phobic, and only moderately comfortable at the side of one of her parents. During our first interview, she also described a previous therapy during which the therapist made affectionate advances toward her, and she was concerned that I, too, would find her sexually attractive and make an advance.

In the analysis she was also unhappy, convinced that any activity on my part, whether an effort to probe a bit of her past, or to understand her current feelings toward me or toward herself, could only succeed in making her more unhappy by forcing her to see things that were even more unpleasant than the things she knew. An attempt to understand this conviction brought the same response. How does one listen to this story?

Although some believe that we should listen without memory or desire, presumably theory-free, I believe, for the reasons I have already indicated, that such a mode of listening is inherently impossible and, therefore, I think it desirable to be aware of all that we bring to the story that is told. As I hear her tale, I have several reactions. I think it most unlikely that her parents could have been as supportive as she describes. I base this belief partly on her conviction of my pernicious intent, which I take to be a manifestation of her expectations of caretakers. But I think it also, and perhaps primarily, because the data of child development do not support the idea of the development of such a glaring lack of self-esteem and such fearfulness in a loving and sympathetic atmosphere. One can, of course, construct numerous oedipal dynamic constellations that could help to explain the phenomena, but as I read the data of child observation, it is extremely unlikely that such an extensive sabotage of self-esteem could occur without important early precursors. Again I emphasize that I am not imposing a foreign theory on the patient, but I am doing what every analyst inevitably does, both consciously and unconsciously, when ordering the story in accord with an analytic world view. As the analysis proceeds, it becomes apparent that the father was a severely narcissistic character, interested in the daughter only to the extent that she admired and imitated him; the one positive aspect of her identification with him was her capacity for scholarly work. On the other hand, he was devoid of affection, and spoiled all her attempts at independent play or pleasure by demanding her attention for himself.

Another aspect of her behavior has become increasingly apparent as the treatment proceeds. She often speaks in the tremulous, fearful, sad voice of a three-year-old, a voice one might expect of a child who has been left alone by its parents and is fighting not to show tears. When asked about this she begins to describe her mother in more detail. Her mother had only one aim in her life—not to anger the father. This meant that no one in the family was allowed to display any anger, or make a fuss of any kind; everyone's needs were secondary to those of the father. The children were dressed as the father wanted, and the food on the table was what suited the father. At about age five, the patient recalls, she was often left home to "look after" her demented grandmother while her mother accompanied her father to an art event. No matter what was happening, the mother insisted that everything was fine, and under no circumstances was the child allowed to be angry, nor did she ever receive sympathy for her unhappiness; her mother simply denied the possibility of unhappiness. The picture of the mother that emerged over time was of an emotionally severely limited woman who had been brought up in a foster home, and who was determined to avoid all affective display, and do nothing that would jeopardize her role as the person who allowed nothing to interfere with the father's serenity, the source of her own safety. The patient, eager to avoid any semblance of criticism or conflict with her parents, needed great encouragement, and persistent focus in the transference upon her negative expectations for this material to emerge. The issue, while conflictual, is more importantly one of understanding the background of affectivity, the capacity for tension regulation, and the experience of safety. Unless this is addressed, all later conflictual issues can be resolved only within the limits set by these convictions or anticipations.

I think that several decades ago, without the impact of object relations theory and the data of the interactiveness of early childhood, one might have seen this patient differently, focusing on her obvious oedipal attachment to the father, and her guilty self-denigration and avoidance of self-assertion as penance for her oedipal desires. That is not a false story; rather it is a later story, easier for her to cope with. In fact, she thrusts it forward at the first session, but it fails to deal with the recoverable earlier origins of her difficulties. I do not want to be misunderstood; what we see in the adult is not a simple reproduction of childhood. Development has occurred, and the persistence of early patterns has undergone numerous epigenetic alterations of form and meaning in different developmental stages. For example, the sadness seen in this adult patient is not just a continuation of her childhood feelings; rather, that sadness now reflects her masochistic attachment to those feelings, a desire to expose her bad parents by demonstrating her suffering, a demand for reparations for her suffering before she will relinquish it. However, the knowledge from child observation of the responses of the child to the parent during the early years, and the emphasis on affective interaction rather than on instinctual satisfaction were important in helping to sort out her current defenses.

In summary, the increasingly precise and emotionally compelling data of infant observational research must exert an influence, both conscious and unconscious, on the form and content of the plots that we construct with our patients in our continuing struggle to make sense of our patients' life stories. Child observation has alerted us to a variety of infant behaviors, interactions, and potentialities that are part of the background of psychological development; their derivatives may appear in adult mental life. The closer our reconstructions within the transference are to the patient's developmental experience, the more likely it is that our interventions will be genuinely empathic and effective, eliciting more associations and loosening rigid defenses.

Chapter 7

Model Scenes, Motivation, and Personality

Joseph D. Lichtenberg, M.D.

Since Freud was first forced by the associations of his patients to reconstruct the sources of adult psychoneuroses through an understanding of childhood, all psychoanalysts have worked with what I call "model scenes" of infancy (Lichtenberg, 1989a,b). These include the presumed "oral bliss" of the nursing infant, the presumed "autistic" or "narcissistic isolation" or "solipsistic" state of the neonate, the conflict of the toilet-training toddler caught between retention and expulsion, and all the variants of the oedipal child's sexual pursuits and rivalries. These initial efforts to conceptualize the early infantile past of the adult are, by contemporary consensus, inadequate and, especially for the first two years of life, inaccurate. My premise is that research and direct observation of children provides us with a set of model scenes closer to the lived experience of the child and that these normal and pathologic prototypes facilitate the analytic process. To illustrate I will present an analysis of a patient with many peculiar and puzzling personality traits. I have selected this type of case because without an understanding of normal infancy and the factors that lead to distortion in the development of the self, I believe analysts are apt to experience themselves as handicapped in their efforts to be empathically perceptive with this type of patient.

My case presentation also provides me with an opportunity to illustrate and apply my approach to the organization of motivation. I believe five motivational systems form in infancy and continue to function and develop throughout life (Lichtenberg, 1989a,b; Stern, 1985). Each motivational system is built around a specific need: the need for the psychic regulation of physiological requirements, the need for intimacy and later affiliation, the need for exploration and assertion, the need to react aversively through antagonism and/or withdrawal, and the need to seek sensual enjoyment and sexual excitement. At any moment, one or more of the motivational systems (Sameroff, 1983) may be dominant while the others are subordinate. In each motivational system, affects amplify all the experiences, serve as signals to caregivers and to the self, and serve as goals for the self as it attempts to recreate past situations in order to reexperience the affect state. *Self* as I use the term (Lichtenberg, 1989a,b) refers to an independent center for initiating, organizing, and integrating motivation. A sense of self arises from experiencing that initiation, organization, and integration. Experiencing has an active (agent) and a passive (receptor) mode.

All of this may seem abstract in a clinical presentation without relating it to the psychoanalytic method. The therapeutic process consists of a frame of familiar arrangements and procedures performed by a trustworthy, consistent, caring individual—the analyst. Within that frame I, as analyst, attempt as consistently and persistently as possible to make empathic entry into the state of mind of the analysand, especially as his or her associations reveal an overt and latent perception of me—the transference. When I believe that I understand what the analysand is attempting to communicate to me, I share my understanding through interpretation. The success I have in understanding and sharing creates an empathic ambience that in itself promotes self-cohesion and self-righting. Most importantly, however, my failures, especially partial failures, promote a back and forth consideration of the source of the failure and its effect on self-cohesion. The interpretive sequence doubles back on itself, creating, recognizing, exploring, and explaining the nature and effect of empathic successes and failures (Lichtenberg, 1983; Schlesinger, 1988; Friedman, 1988).

The effort by both analyst and analysand to find meaning in the analysand's affects, associations, attitudes, and behaviors activates symbolic representations in the form of current experiences, memories, and transference reenactments. Reorganizing of the symbolic representations then occurs in the *analyst*, facilitating his or her understanding and interpreting, and in the *analysand*, facilitating his or her restructuring of motivations and functioning. If my view of the analytic process is accepted, then the significance of increasingly accurate model scenes for making relatively correct empathic entry into the intersubjective experience of unfolding transference will also be accepted. Humankind had all the perceptual data about the shape of the world; but until someone conceptualized that the world might be round and not flat, the data was without meaning.

I shall now present some perplexing data from Mr. Roseman's analysis and offer explanations I came to as a result of matching the experience he and I had with model scenes derived from the five motivational systems.

Mr. Robert Roseman, a dour-looking structural engineer specializing in the construction of tunnels, began his seven-year analysis when he was in his early thirties. Analysis had been suggested by his cousin's husband, a psychoanalyst in another city. Mr. R. stated in the initial interview that he was coming because of irritability and depression. He was concerned that his wife was troubled by his moods. I inquired about his own reaction and he answered he only knew of his mood being altered when his wife told him so. In telling about his childhood he gave a relatively clear picture of a household with a frequently depressed mother and a controlling, obsessional, but phobic father. The grandmother, a silent woman, dominated. His cousin, Marge, a few years older, lived nearby; she was a frequent sleep-over guest. When I asked about his feelings regarding his mother's depression, he answered that he had no memory of it. He had spoken with Marge and was simply repeating what she had told him. In fact, he added, he didn't remember anything about his past. Both his statement about not recognizing his feelings and about having no memory of his childhood were made in a matter-of-fact manner. He evidenced no reaction to the unusualness of these statements or to my surprise.

In his first hours, Mr. R. reported that he had a dream in which he felt the need to yell and scream out but could not do so. He was frustrated and awoke making a sound that woke his wife. He added that he didn't awake in terror. His desire was to get someone's attention.

During the course of the analysis, Mr. R. never yelled or screamed. His motto was, "Don't get mad, get even." He sulked, he pouted, he missed hours—generally one for one that I had missed. He never experienced terror except in dreams. He mainly signaled distress by yawning. After yawning, he would generally fall silent and remain so for extended periods. When I inquired about his experience during his silence, he would report in an affectless tone that he was reviewing his day's schedule and planning the work he had to do. What we were talking about when he turned off was entirely obliterated from his memory. When I would remind him of the issue from which he withdrew, he would acknowledge the content, and speculate on the emotion it might have triggered, such as anxiety, anger, or sexual arousal—all equally unwelcome. And then he would yawn again. He began many hours acknowledging he had not thought of what we had talked about or he had a dream but didn't remember it. Whether content of the previous hour or unremembered dream, he expected *me* to know what it was and to tell him.

Lest I convey too one-sided a picture of his "peculiarities," I should mention he lived a quite ordinary married life, had attended prestigious schools from which he received his doctorate, and was highly skilled and valued in his field.

I will now make the unorthodox step in a case presentation and leap ahead to the last weeks of the analysis and report in our own words what Mr. R. and I had learned about him in the intervening seven years.

EXCERPT A—2 WEEKS BEFORE THE END

Mr. R.: I have a disinclination to do anything for myself. I was reading about what gives a child confidence. My natural way is to do the opposite. To say to my children, "I told you *not* to do that." Being told not to has made me scared to do for myself. I wait to be shown. Even academically, where I am at my best, I'm insecure.

Dr. L.: If you try on your own, you could wind up with a chorus saying, "I told you not to do that."

Mr. R.: Yeah. I took the chorus in and now I tell myself not to.

Dr. L.: Ah, yes.

Mr. R.: And I play that out with you because I've learned to do it so well! Because I see you the same as my family. You're like them telling me what to do and what not to do. I don't like that. I'll show you—the back-door way to get power—out of *spite*. If I were confident, I'd stand up for myself more. I'd say: "Screw you. I'll do what I want." My way costs me more than if I took the risk, said "No!" and made you mad. But I don't change.

Dr. L.: With your sense of accumulated hurts from me, is it hard for you to want to do business with me outside of spite?

Mr. R.: With Alice [his wife] too. I don't say let's talk it over and settle it. Why don't I say: "This is driving me crazy. I have to change." I do try with Jane [his daughter], but it's so hard. I wanted to take her to the pool. She said, "No, I want Mommy." I felt hurt. I tried to joke. Jane was saying: "Nobody will play with me." I said: "What am I, chopped liver?" It's foolish that I should be hurt over a kid wanting her mommy. But she's not reaching out to me. I say, "okay, fine. You want her, you stay by yourself until she's free."

Dr. L.: When we consider that Jane is one of the few people you look to to stir your joy and who sometimes reaches to you for her joy, we can understand your hurt when she doesn't reach out.

Mr. R.: Yeah. It gets back to my parents. The pleasure I get out of being spiteful is a poor attempt to replace the pleasure I'm missing. Being deprived. If they won't reach out to me the only pleasure left is being spiteful and that's better than nothing. But I end up skeptical

and suspicious. The next person comes along. I wait
until I can see if I can count on you. I'm expecting it, so
with the first disappointment, I react, "See, I told you
so."
(Pause)

Dr. L.: And you fall silent.

Mr. R.: That's being spiteful.
(Pause)

Dr. L.: Then you wait to see if I will come after you?

Mr. R.: Yeah.

Dr. L.: And if I don't, you say that's what you expected.

Mr. R.: You met my expectation. You failed my test. And I
lapse into, "I'll get back at you."

EXCERPT B—2 WEEKS BEFORE THE END

Mr. R.: It occurs to me that what we talked about—the analysis
in retrospect has had a pessimistic tone. What might
have been. (Wistful) When I wanted to stop last year I
was upbeat. "I can do this on my own." Unrealistic,
possibly euphoric. Or I'm being unduly critical now. I
realize that because analysis ends it doesn't mean the
process for me ends. If I'm going to continue, the value
is knowing when I've had trouble before. I see the value
in going over things. I still have a sense of regret. Had
I known then what I know now. I'll use it as a stimulus
or sink back into a negative defeatist attitude.

Dr. L.: You're wondering: What will you choose when you get
to that fork?

Mr. R.: I usually chose the pessimism of my parents. No good
will come of it. Now maybe I'm more likely to resist it.

Dr. L.: Were you saying to me implicitly why didn't I let you
leave when you were in an optimistic state? Why didn't
I match your optimism with mine?

Mr. R.: I hadn't thought of it. But yes. Wouldn't I have been
better off?

Dr. L.: You could look at me as a pessimist. I'm saying I don't believe your optimism?

Mr. R.: I know you were saying: "Stay. Be optimistic. We can get something more done." But you were also saying: "Don't go!" Doubting. An echo of my parents. "Be careful crossing the street." Even when I knew how and could.

Dr. L.: Your parents would, say, inhibit long before you got to the edge of your potential.

Mr. R.: (excitedly) That's what I do here!

Dr. L.: Umph.

Mr. R.: I could go on but I stop. The quicker we get moving, the quicker I am to turn it off. The net effect is I'm not capable. Don't build self-esteem. I can't go on my own. You encourage me. Say go on. But that kind of encouragement isn't strong enough. I need to be shown, not told. A kid wants to go beyond the end of the block with his bike. I got the feeling of being beaten down. Told "don't" so many times. "Don't, it's dangerous." A kid loses interest in going further. I became convinced they were right. I lost my curiosity to go beyond. (Yawn) I need you not only to undo my parents' command, but to reinstate my curiosity. (Yawn)

Dr. L.: Do you sense yourself waiting now for me to stimulate your interest, reinstate your curiosity?

Mr. R.: And my enthusiasm. I know what to do and I know successes I've had—the recent special area I went to Europe to learn. But I used to go on believing I'd fail and at the first hint of failure—it's, "I told you so." Go back to never initiate.

Dr. L.: Then you set up a test that is stacked against you.

Mr. R.: Bound to fail. People are unlikely to express interest in me if I don't offer something first.

Dr. L.: A very ebullient person like your cousin Marge might ride right past that subtle testing and get you going?

Mr. R.: Yeah. When Jane is enthusiastic she overwhelms that. Gets to me before I have time to consider.

Dr. L.: And that feels good and makes you want it again.

Mr. R.: Yeah. But let down if I don't get it.

Dr. L.: And helpless. Your approach left you feeling you had no resources of your own.

Mr. R.: I hadn't internalized the spark to be able to generate it myself.

Dr. L.: And that's what you have to do now—do what you can to do that.

Mr. R.: It's easier because you haven't been as ebullient as my cousin and Jane. I've *had* to do more for myself.

EXCERPT—1 WEEK BEFORE THE END

Mr. R.: Yesterday I was despairing. Never be able to change.

Dr. L.: We don't know how locked in you may feel to unrealized expectations with me or how free you may feel when you are no longer fighting that battle with me.

Mr. R.: That makes sense but it's something I don't want to see. Spiting you is difficult to accept. That I am fighting.

Dr. L.: At the end of yesterday's hour, you said you know how to initiate. You did it with your course. I agreed and you countered. "But it wasn't fun."

Mr. R.: Fun is not sanctioned.

Dr. L.: You know it is by me—you are aware obliquely of my swimming pool, and of my interest in sailing and art. Still you are fighting the old battles.

Mr. R.: I assiduously avoided using you. I don't allow myself. Your way is not sanctioned. You couldn't be a good parent.

Later in the Hour

Dr. L.: You feel you gave me an opening and I didn't follow an exact channel.

Mr. R.: I can't accept anything that deviates from the script. Get it and I go on. If I don't, the whole thing falls apart. I can't adapt to a different response. (Yawn)

Dr. L.: Or it's hard for you to; it makes you anxious?

Mr. R.: Yeah. My father's inflexibility. Avoiding anything that's new. The model for the script here is that it's open-ended. Each statement opens the potential for going off in all directions. That makes me anxious. Like you going off in all directions. I want you right here! Not going off sailing or playing tennis.

EXCERPT—LAST HOUR

Mr. R.: I kept feeling that I should quit. Get out of the trap. Is the hour up?

Dr. L.: You devoted a lot of feeling toward the idea you could escape your trapped feeling by escaping from analysis.

Mr. R.: *Or I could escape my trapped feeling by escaping from feelings.* Which obviously didn't—doesn't—work. I'm anxious about ending. Will I be able to put into practice what I've learned? Do more for myself and enjoy the positive reinforcement. I'm reminded at the end of *Portnoy's Complaint*—the last line: "Now we can begin."

From what I have described I believe it is clear that Mr. R.'s personality or self was organized pathologically around aversive motivation and that his adaptational strength centered on his exploratory–assertive motivation in his professional life with the narrow channeling tunnels. This was not, regrettably, equally so in his analysis with the open-endedness of associations. Therefore, I must describe the normal development of the aversive motivational system and contrast it with our reconstruction of Mr. R.'s infancy. Ideally, aversive responses of withdrawal, distress, and antagonism serve as *signals* in each of the other motivational systems, calling for a response from the caregiver. For example: an infant signals the need to stop feeding when satiety has been reached by pushing the nipple out, or signals his distress when too long an interruption occurs during a pleasurable social exchange by averting his eyes. The model for secure attachment is an infant whose dominant lived experiences are those of positive affective states and whose positive affective states are quickly restored after an aversive signal. The distress signals may be vigorous as long as the caregiver has the skill and concern to relieve, and the infant the capacity for being calmed and soothed. When this ideal is approximated during the neonatal and young infant periods, the aversive system does not become fully organized as a system dominating motivation through antagonism and/or withdrawal.

Toward the end of the first year and during the first half of the second year, the organizing and stabilizing of the aversive motivational system take place around three separate tasks. The first is the older infant's learning the instrumental power of anger to augment exploration and assertion in overcoming obstacles. A model scene is a crawling infant intently pushing a toy car across the floor. He is stopped by a rug, pushes again without success, then more in frustration than intention, gives the toy a whack, sending it flying over the obstacle to his surprise and delight. The second task is learning to be aversive where danger would be *un*recognized. Parents may help in the mastery of this task by a sensitive combination of flat "don'ts " mixed with "not that way, but this." The third task is to learn how to conduct controversy. With the older infants and toddlers vigorously practicing "intention-ality" in their choice of foods, areas to explore, people and times to be intimate, and body parts to be fondled and stroked, endless opportunities exist for agendas to conflict. Children must feel their intentions fully, and yet put together a repertoire of methods for resolving differences by using their developing subjective awareness, their empathy for the hurts of others, and their altruistic tendencies.

Now where did Mr. Roseman stand in all this? Starting in early infancy how well were his signals of aversion recognized and responded to? In the motivational system involving the need for regulation of physiological requirements, evidence emerged that his mother failed to read his signals of satiety in feeding and overstuffed him into a borderline obese child. His mother, herself overweight, organized her own martyred, slavish existence around feeding her family and cleaning up. The combination of over-weight and having his signals of satiety overridden encouraged sluggishness and passivity. Mr. R. resisted both and, as a preteen-ager, he associated his lack of friends with his weight. He then rebelled against his family's feeding and instituted an iron-willed restrictiveness. While he never recognized his depression and irritability as such, the signal he used to alert himself was eating compulsively and having insomnia.

In the attachment motivational system, Mr. R.'s aversive responses to the violation of positive expectancies of reciprocal social smiling and playful exchanges more often than not went unanswered because of his mother's depression. He knew what a smile was and retained some capacity for intimacy pleasure. However, he was so entrenched in expecting a flat expressionless response that he gave the signals for it; and when he elicited nothing more, the disappointment fed his defeatism. With me he established a pattern of two greetings—a flat perfunctory nod in the waiting room, and an eye-to-eye glance with a faint smile on entering the consulting room. While the depth of his mother's depression did not seem to have been serious, the impact of her lack of delight in her baby was intensified by the dreary ambience of the home. Mr. R.'s father mixed occasional frightening out-bursts of temper and argumentativeness with a general withdrawal into obsessive activities. On his father's return home, Mr. R. was never allowed to engage him until his father did his daily accounts and read the paper. Mr. R.'s grandmother was like a silent gray eminence and his grandfather a subdued shell until her death when, as if liberated, he became a lively social being, interested in his grandson's progress. It was the dour ambience of the home that Mr. R. hung like a dark cloud over the analysis, his employees, and, at times, his wife.

In contrast to the discouragement he received for his interest in social relatedness and exuberant affects of any sort, his bur-dened mother was delighted to have him disengage from her and involve himself in play with toys. In the analysis, after failures in communication and intimacy with me, he would disengage from contact with me. In the solitude of his mind he would explore his day calendar and assert his intelligence and mastery at a task from which he could derive competence satisfaction if not pleasure. What he could not do was "play" with me in our mutual task or share with me much about his work interests. As we understood it, his burdened mother had little or no play in her, and father was too worried and fastidious to play. But everyone in the family appreciated indications of his intelligence and the A grades he was to achieve. In this respect the analysis was a double disappointment. He couldn't do it well because of his restrictive use of secondary process and his fear of primary process. Thus, he didn't earn A's and his engineering skills couldn't bring him applause from me. Play was the crucial developmental step he missed, although not entirely. Play had come to him special delivery in the form of his effervescent cousin and might disappear just as quickly, leaving him with a taste for exuberant pleasure and no belief he could self-create it. He never successfully took the steps that lead from an infant's social and toy play to an older toddler's symbolic play and to later play as a hobby and recreation, as well as to study and work, with each successfully completed step providing both efficacy and competence pleasure. He learned to accept a burdened life of chores and obligations, and he hoped with pessimistic defeatism that exuberance in play someday again would be delivered to him.

Play bridges into sensuality and sexuality. The ordinary activities of feeding, cuddling, changing, bathing, powdering, and eliminating stimulate sensation-rich mucous membranes, skin, and genitals. Soothing is itself sensual with great overlap in the rhythms. Excitement from any source easily spreads to the genitals as attested to by how often aroused, joyous toddlers will reach for their genitals. In Mr. R.'s situation, where intimacy pleasure was subdued and colorless, the sensual–sexual motivational system was equally lacking in self-sustaining vigor, and was easily subdued by shaming and disapproval. With the asexual tone in the home, the sleep-over visits of his cousin, during which they shared the same room, were excitement states both welcome and bewildering to the little boy. Puzzlement and embarrassment reoccurred in the analysis when he remembered and talked about occasional highly erotic dreams in which his penis might be fondled. Their exciting play did not serve him as a bridge to masculine sexual seeking although he remembered wanting to play a game with her in which he was a cowboy. She insisted they play "house" and he be a doll she cared for, a game that further encouraged his passivity.

His sensual–sexual motivational system became organized

around two core relational approaches. In one he eschewed sensuality, developing into something of an effete person, actively aversive to sexuality. He remembered with disgust his mother's body and genital smell and recalled putting a pillow over his head to get to sleep when he heard sounds from his parents' bedroom. In the other approach, he hoped to be discovered by an ebullient woman who would seek him out and stir him up to sexual excitement and potency. When he met Alice, she was a vivacious redhead, eager for exploration. Rather than lose this dream come true, a revenant of his cousin, he vigorously fought off his family's disapproval, standing firm against his father for the first and, possibly, only time in his life. What he didn't know consciously was that Alice had her own potential for depression. Burdened by his sulking and draining expectations of cheer from her, and by raising Jane at the expense of her career hopes, Alice no longer was able to "create" a sexual life for the two of them. He felt powerless to cheer her and her appeals to him to be more romantic only exposed him to the humiliation of his feeling that he couldn't be.

Now we are ready to return to delineating the pathological orientation of Mr. R.'s aversive motivational system. The model scene I envisioned from his associations and, especially, from the transference and my responses, is of a mother–infant pair in which an ordinarily robust infant is dealt with relatively consistently by a conscientious mother. The problem was that Mr. R.'s mother responded to his aversive signals of distress in a ritualistic and desultory manner, leaving him chronically frustrated. He was tended and done for, but with no room for the pleasure of intimacy to develop. A memory from later conveyed the feeling of the early scene. Mother would prepare dinner slavishly, serve it perfunctorily, and before anyone could relax after eating, she would start clearing the table. Of the two forms of aversive responses (antagonism and withdrawal), withdrawal was implicitly encouraged by a burdened woman, probably pleased to be left alone. Antagonism in all its forms was explicitly discouraged. Mr. R. was reported to have had tantrums but, according to family lore, by the time he was a preschooler, he had become the superficially compliant good boy he was to remain. Thus, as in his initial dream, he could not yell or scream or even be fearful. What was sanctioned was his passive acceptance and his withdrawal. During latency, when frustrated he would retreat to his room where he would sulk and wait for someone to seek him out and redress his hurt feelings. More often than not, no one did; his silence and absence were misread as without meaning. Anger as an instrument for pressing on with curiosity and assertive intentionality was largely lost to him.

In contrast, the second task, learning the caregivers' assessments of danger, was all too well absorbed. Not only was playful exploration and assertion regarded as dangerous by each family member, but also sexuality and all expressions of feeling. He was tamped down as if he had to maintain the decorum of a mausoleum, grandmother's silent controlling providing both a model of manners and of secret power. In his initial dream he not only couldn't yell or scream, he had to deny his terror. Fear itself was treated as dangerous. He often complained of a trapped feeling that he tried ineffectually to escape. The trapped feeling referred primarily to his affectless rut, but it was also symbolized in a dream as a pit of depression. He craved joy but it had to be brought to him, aggressively sparked off in him. With exploration and assertiveness restricted to work, he built a rut of seeking A's. Without anger as an instrumental power, he could not initiate forceful opposition to his rut. One solution he dreamed of was mercifully killing a wounded soldier who kept slogging along. By killing him he could put the complainer, whether himself, his mother, his father, or me, out of his or her misery. With danger inculcated as omnipresent, he was frightened of initiating, of disturbing the status quo with the slightest *open* expression of aversion to it. Here the collusion of male and female adults in two generations, all sending the same signal: "Don't," was almost overpowering to the developing self.

Thus, Mr. R. was unsuccessful in the first two tasks of developing an organized aversive motivational system. He was left without an experience of the instrumentality of direct anger, and an appropriately selective sense of danger. Consequently, Mr. R. was handicapped in achieving mastery of the task of learning to handle controversy. Throughout his life he attempted to avoid controversy by restricting his exploratory and assertive motives to intellectual and mechanical endeavors. In the toddler period he learned to blunt the vigorous expression of "I want" and "I don't want" that characterize a child's contributions to most controversies. Probably "I don't want" was more present, if diffuse, except in the reported, never remembered, tantrums. The effect, as we could observe it, was a smoldering persistent resentment rather than a clear assertion augmented by anger. Normally children are encouraged both to express and constrain their intentions and anger during controversies. Adaptive constraint of antagonism during controversy is facilitated by the awareness of the potentially hurtful impact by the child on others, combined with a toddler's innate altruistic tendencies (Zahn-Waxler and Radke-Yarrow, 1982). Altruism has a double appeal: first it is accompanied by a sense of the power to effect positive change in another person, and second, after the aggressiveness inherent in controversy, it allows the child to restore the pleasure of intimacy.

But with Mr. R., his experience with his depressed mother had already failed to assure an awareness of his being able to exert a positive influence. This important forerunner of altruism arises during social exchanges when a child is able to elicit smiles and to restore a momentarily distracted mother's interest in the fun of playful conversational runs (Stern, 1985). For an infant, child, or adult to be without the sense of being able to positively influence those that he or she cares about is a depressing experience indeed, one all therapists often have to live with. For Mr. R. as an infant it probably contributed appreciably to a sense of finding contact with his mother desultory and unrewarding—the reward being sought, as Kohut (1971, 1977, 1984) put it, is the glint in the mirroring mother's eye. As a toddler Mr. R. could not engage in controversies in lively manner because of the blunting of his positive assertion and reinforcing anger. Neither could controversies be ended by empathic sensitivity to the other's feelings and altruistic gestures restoring intimacy pleasure. Empathic sensitivity neither forms nor maintains well in states of chronic depressive sameness. To become encouraged and valued, altruism must be responded to positively.

In later life, controversies for Mr. R. had no beginnings or endings he could recognize. He lived in a state of chronic low-keyed resentment, punctuated by spiteful actions. During the time of his parents' illnesses and deaths, he performed perfunctorily, but felt no real sense of loss. In comparison, during the illness of his cousin's mother, who was a cheerful, venturesome person, he was emotionally moved and he mourned her loss. We learned in the analysis that the significant fact was not only that she could and would make him smile, but that he could bring cheer to her. The reciprocity of joy in intimacy that had begun so well with Alice was lost when his excessive needs for her to take the initiative and focus her attention on him overwhelmed her. He was able to rekindle the joy of reciprocal intimacy with his daughter. When the child wanted her mommy, not him, to cheer her, he was hurt. The analysis itself constituted a rekindling of Mr. R.'s major narcissistic injury in the requirement that he be an initiator. He responded to the hurt he experienced with his version of narcissistic rage—spite. "Don't get mad, get even." He wouldn't use the cheer or model of me available to him, except to get a second greeting from me, a smile close at hand.

The analysis of adults is not designed to be an exchange of cheer, although it is a most desirable adjunct pleasure and sustainer when it occurs. The aim of the analysis of adults is to restore cohesion to the self as an independent center for initiating, organizing, and integrating motivation. A restored self will seek and create the pleasure of physiological regulation, intimacy, competence, power, sensuality, and sexuality according to its own "design," to paraphrase Kohut (1984). Analysis does this in two ways: through self-righting, an inherent capacity observable beginning in infancy, and through the later developed capacity for symbolic representation and reorganization. Self-righting is facilitated by the ambience of the analysis in which deficits and distortions of development in the presymbolic period become activated and a new experience with new expectancies and consistencies occurs. The work of the analysis—free association, interpretation, and working through—facilitates reorganization of symbolic representations. The model scenes of Mr. R.'s infancy provide the depressed, uncheerable face of mother, the joyless rigidity of the father, the controlling silence of the grandmother, and the cousin's seductive vivacity. The model scenes of the present with Alice and their daughter and the analyst provide an alternative challenge for the integrating self to work with.

Mr. R. did not end his analysis as one might hope. He had not self-righted or reorganized his representations, motivations, and expectancies to have become a man fully prepared to live a life of vigorous emotional fullness. He ended feeling and recognizing a *lot* more than when he started. He knew a great, great deal more about who *he* was. He knew he was a person who could feel. He also knew how he got to be him. His memory and "narrative history" had largely been restored. My understanding of early development helped me sustain the draining effect of the slow, slow progress and to make sense of it, bit by bit, as we went along. With my help, he understood what he had to do if he chose to do it. He was, I think, ready to begin.[1]

---

[1]I was certainly encouraged about his progress when eight months after ending we had a chance encounter in a public place. Mr. R. took the initiative to speak to me and to introduce his wife, all in a friendly, forthright manner.

Chapter 8

The Relevance of Infant Observational Research for the Analytic Understanding of Adult Patients' Nonverbal Behaviors

James T. McLaughlin, M.D.

There are three overlapping sectors of analytic functioning wherein knowledge of the contributions on infancy and early childhood have been particularly influential for me and, I think, for other analysts who work with adults.

First, there is our observational set in perceiving and finding meaning in what we encounter in the patient and in ourselves as we do our work. (This is a fundamental and yet elusive component, and I will need to return to it later.) It interflows with and shapes the second sector. This is our theoretical base. By this I mean our assortment of generalizing expectations, by which we organize what we continue to learn about the psychological development and functioning of the human adult in our culture.

The third and most important sector of analytic functioning involves our interventive capacities, our ability to attain fit and relevance with the analytic needs of the patient.

I want to emphasize the idea of our operational set in

perceiving meaning in order to acknowledge and demonstrate the inevitability of selective bias in our perceiving or knowing anything. It is an analytic truism that we deal with others, and indeed with the larger reality around us, by perceiving via an established set of expectancies or ways of organizing based upon previous experience (McLaughlin, 1981). This, of course, is at the heart of what we have in mind in analysis when we speak broadly of transference, the power of prior experience in shaping current fears and expectancies. For example, *my* expectation of the ubiquity of the phenomenon of transference, and confidence in its explanatory power as a theoretical organizer, have made the concept of transference both benchmark and bias for my analytic perspective.

It is thus delightfully affirmative to read Stern's assertion, based on his studies (Stern, 1977), that the infant's cognitive development, powered by an instinctual hunger for cognitive stimulation, is founded upon an inherent penchant for comparing any new stimulus with a previous and sufficiently similar one (p. 53) or, as Bruner (1975) put it, a central tendency of the infant's mental life is the "active process of hypothesis formation and hypothesis testing."

The infant's inherent penchant to compare the new with the previous lives on forever in each of us, patient and analyst alike, driving us to seek new ways of seeing while limiting what we are able to see as new. We know this as analysts throughout our working lives as we try to peer beyond ourselves and our theory to see the uniqueness of the patient. We spend a lifetime struggling to expand and organize our experiential knowledge gleaned from observing self and other in analytic work, plus extending our cognitive mapping through the observations and theory we pool with others. Then we try just as hard not to let all this interfere with seeing the patient.

Psychoanalytic training thirty years ago educated us to expect to find evidence of the transferential past of our patients in their behaviors in the present analytic relationship, and to organize our understanding of these in terms of the staging and sequence of psychosexual themes clustered around oedipal phase development; yet so much went on between us and our patients that puzzled or eluded us. Some of our patients all of the time, all of our patients some of the time, show a huge sensitivity to and monitoring of all aspects of the analyst's behavior, along with urgent needs for the analyst to stay away, get close, chase, abandon, attack, or rescue. While intuition tells us that these behaviors are reminiscent of early childhood behaviors, I began to find reason and perspective in what Spitz, Mahler, Winnicott, and others had to say about infant–mother behaviors, about separation and individuation, the richness of transitional objects and transitional phenomena and play as transitional behavior, and the skewing power of disturbances in the early mother–infant relationship.

It is not that I could make straight-line extrapolations from these data about the first years of life onto what is there to be observed in the adult. Their value has lain in the greater scope and richness of detail that they provided about what it might be like for the child of the past to be somehow resonant in the person of the present, and thus help me to be more open to such meaning in shaping my understanding of the particular patient.

The closest I come in the analytic relationship to glimpsing the infant and young child in adult behavior has to do with the nonverbal components of that behavior. I shall only sample the richness of what the patient does while on the couch, ranging as it does from primitive kinaesthetic–proprioceptive–visceral experiences (like the Isakower phenomenon) through postural–gestural kinesics to the quirks of verbalization adding meaning to the spoken communication central to our talking cure.

I will consider here chiefly the postural and gestural kinesics of the patient when he speaks or is silent. In general, these behaviors are of the sort he and we have learned to use habitually, from the earliest days of life, in communicating with others, to inform and persuade, to understand and respond.

There has accumulated a formidable mass of data about the development of the human capacity to communicate. Much derives from child observational studies and psychoanalytic exploration of both children and adults, yet remains largely unassimilated into the larger field of linguistics and behavioral psychology. Some consensus seems, however, to have emerged across the disciplines about the sequence of development: the nonverbal gestural, postural, and mimetic components comprise the first communications between infant and caregiver, building out of the bodily and visual involvements between the pair and providing the necessary substrate for the more slowly organizing verbal capacities. The earliest memories of each of us are richly registered in these nonverbal modes, which continue throughout life to extend their own range and refinement even as they are eventually overridden by the emergingly dominant verbal mode that they support.

My point of view about the relevance of infantile experience and behaviors for the kinesic–postural components of adult behavior takes its base in this concept of the primacy and durability of this early mode of psychomotor thought.

Before there were words for the saying, and during the developmental times of separation–individuation, we recorded our experiences of merging and distancing, of clinging and pushing away, of rebellion and submission, by means of the sights and sounds of body movement and gesture, of kinetic mimicry and play.

These gestural modes have undergone their own developmental growth, intertwined with those of spoken thought, and are included in the conscious repertoire of signals used by the verbal adult. But much of what they were, and still resonate about, lies outside conscious awareness, largely suppressed or repressed because of dynamic conflict, or simply because they have been overtaken by more effective communicative modes acquired later. Despite this they persist in alluding to past history and conflict as an incessant accompaniment of the verbally communicated content.

The analytic situation is particularly well suited for bringing into view this nonverbal counterpoint where it can be seen in simultaneity with the spoken thought. Here the concept of intrapsychic conflict finds constant and dramatic actualization: the nonverbal busily reinforcing or negating, affirming and contradicting the spoken words, both subject to the same vicissitudes of regression to unmastered trauma and unresolved psychic conflict.

It is from such observations as these, made in the analytic

situation over extended time (McLaughlin, 1987), that I draw a modest level of confidence that the kinesic activities bear witness to very early levels of childhood experience and thought, never to be clearly articulated, yet directing attention to the existence of the child in the adult.

I wish to point to two general categories of nonverbal behavior, overlapping to be sure, that provide allusion and enactment for two different aspects of the childhood past. The first lies in the conspicuous and idiosyncratic gesture or mannerism that a particular patient may repeat habitually, and which often proves to be a cogent allusion to a specific and unmastered early experience.

The second is of a more general array of inconspicuous kinesics (chiefly hand–arm movements in relation to each other or to the face and other significant body areas) that seem at first glance to be random and meaningless. Only when closely observed over time, in the context of the verbal component, are they gradually seen as rich in metaphor and object-related meaning.

The clinical material I wish to present here will focus upon these kinesic phenomena as seen in one rather average case in which certain rather striking gestural mannerisms as well as an array of inconspicuous kinesics provided rich content and cogent metaphor for furthering the analytic quest.

The patient is one of a small group that I watched over several years of analysis, using a notational system that captured as best I could the gist of ongoing verbal content and simultaneous gestural activity during portions of analytic hours (McLaughlin, 1987).

This crude study gave me much data about both categories of kinesic display that I wish to dwell upon in this paper, both the conspicuous–idiosyncratic and the quiet background activities. Aligning both with their verbal context brought into the foreground patterns of meaning I might otherwise not so explicitly have recognized. I phrase it thus because I am sure that each of us automatically registers, consciously and subliminally, this multimodal range of communication. We do so in ways built into us as part of our earliest acquired capacities to communicate. The data of Stern (1985), Snow (1979), and others give abundant evidence of how facile the preverbal infant is in acquiring and using these nonverbal levels of sending and receiving affectively powerful messages.

CLINICAL MATERIAL

Mrs. M. was in her early forties when she entered analysis. A successful executive and mother of three latency children, she wanted help in becoming more comfortable with people and with herself. This quiet quest masked a tortured self-consciousness and fear of being found flawed that had permeated every aspect of her existence.

For over a year she entered each analytic hour with set face and brisk stride, smoothing her skirt behind her as she passed me, spending several minutes settling onto the couch in a flurry of arranging and smoothing every fold and turn of skirt, blouse, and jacket. Only then could she settle herself to lie stiffly immobile for the entire hour except for her busy hands which went on moving in incessant monitoring and tidying.

Her words poured out in smokescreen fashion, and she fussed over these as she did her clothes, straightening and rearranging her words and syntax, keeping her intonation smoothed and flat.

Mrs. M. was equally vigilant of all that I said or did, looking for any hint of censure or disapproval, and invariably finding what she sought. I quickly felt under surveillance, spotlighted by her unremitting scan. My words became careful and sparse, and I, too, became a wary watcher.

She had grown up on a near-impoverished farm in upper Appalachia, the second child of a rough-cut farmer father, boisterous in his barnyard humor but also sharply critical and somewhat remote, screened from his daughter by a primly genteel mother chronically unhappy with the uncouth way of life an unfortunate marriage to an inferior man had imposed upon her. When not lost in months of bleak depression and hypochondriacal self-absorption, mother turned her relentless concern upon her daughter, holding her close in a vigilant fussing over and remedying of an interminable checklist of defects that likened her to her father and much older brother. The patient had come to accept the accuracy of her mother's viewpoint and saw herself as forever struggling for mother's acceptance, to cover over through incessant self-improvement and anxious monitoring. Her outwardly successful marriage and motherhood did nothing to alter her pained perceptions. Getting back into the business world when her children were safely launched in school helped for a little while; but soon her urgency to be found likable, admirable, and flawless centered on her status and acceptance in the corporate structure. As she patrolled these areas of her life in hour after hour of tense preoccupation early in her analysis, I could sense easily enough her dread of her warded-off aggression and sexual intensities. But these were far away from her awareness, screened by her obsessional and strongly masochistic ways, and accessible only later on.

She gradually revealed a limited collage of painful childhood memories. Some were old and familiar, others only vaguely recalled before, and gradually spanned an increasing range of developmental time. All had in common her image of herself as the squirming or inert target of her mother's clutching concerns: her eyes too squinty, ears too prominent, legs too short.

Especially shameful and painful to retrieve were memories of being infested with ticks, hogfleas, and body lice, of being tortured by pinworms. Some of these were almost impossible to put words to: a feeling of being between mother's knees, high-pitched sounds coming from one or both mouths, and strong visual recall of mother's face, full of disgust and horror, and mother pulling away. She remembered terror, not being able to understand, and an awful conviction that she had or was something forever loathsome.

As I listened I had ample time to become familiar with Mrs. M.'s busy hands and to note the patterns of background gesturing, as well as certain prominent mannerisms that gradually emerged, in relation to her verbal commentary.

She was one of those people who had a fairly reliable lateralizing of body image in terms of gender and identification of important object representations. When she spoke of her mother, of feminine matters, of self as passive object or victim, she gestured chiefly with, or pointed to, her left hand and arm in movements related to her other hand, her face, and body. When she spoke of her self as active agent, of her father or brother, of me or other males, she gestured mainly with her right hand and arm. Mrs. M. was highly consistent in this assignment of gender and object to her right and left, in keeping with the findings of anthropological and psychological observations on this consistent, cross-cultural tendency (Blau, 1946; Domhoff, 1969).

In the context of this paper, however, the relevance of these behaviors lies in the vividness of dramatic enactment her quiet gesturing came to signify for me as I observed her hands moving in synchrony with her words. One hand would fondle or pick at the other, a particular hand would come to rest on lips, cheek, or chest, whether gently or roughly, all this provided a powerful reinforcement of the significance of her words, as well as of my understanding of her inner preoccupation with her object world, and in the process made her communications more richly meaningful.

I do not wish to suggest that this attention to the nonverbal should, or could, take precedence over the usual analytic devotion to the verbal content, nor that the kinesic play provides an alternative royal road to psychic depth. As I noted elsewhere (McLaughlin, 1987) I could not carry out my notational project consistently without jeopardizing my preferred listening modes. However, what came from the effort was a heightened appreciation of how much for me, as an analyst who needs to look while listening, the nonverbal accompaniment added to the amount of information being communicated, infusing the verbal content with significant allusions to past history and lively intrapsychic conflict now being dramatized in the transference.

Also more in awareness was an appreciation of how much I tend to draw upon this level of communication, without deliberate intent, to inform the metaphor and content of how I understand my patients and what I shape to say to them.

So it was in the ongoing work with Mrs. M. For example, there was a moment when Mrs. M. detailed how she had become anxiously aware that she had forgotten to have certain documents with her at the previous day's board meeting. She paused, then spoke of her own anxious heaviness as being like her mother's depressed scanning of her bleak world and her concerns over her daughter's limitations. As she spoke, Mrs. M.'s hands pushed, picked, plucked, flicked at her clothing, hair, and eye glasses. I commented: "Perhaps you felt picked on and ashamed when your mother focused on you?" She responded with quick denial and spoke in vigorous defense of her mother's loving concern that she improve her ways. Then she stopped and ruminated, as she so often did in a defensive response to my interventions, this time in a pained, inconclusive examination of what she had expressed poorly that would lead me to believe she felt picked upon. While she spoke her right hand fingered and pressed upon her left. I said: "Are you saying instead that your way of keeping steady check on you, on how you're doing, became your necessary way of keeping a closeness with your mother?" To this she glumly assented, gave a detailed elaboration of how this was so, particularly since her mother had died three years previously and the patient missed her a great deal. While it was obvious that her content and behaviors carried a level of concern over the fact that she felt under critical attack by me, our prior experience in exploring this sector had made it clear that she was as yet too anxious to be able to address the transference directly.

In a kinesically different example sometime later, the patient's hands, particularly her right, moved about in their straightening and smoothing in slow, soft touchings and pattings as she detailed to me with quiet intensity how hard she was working to maintain her bosses' view of her as able and amiable. It made sense to me to say: "Could it be that you are saying you have indeed learned well how to be pleasing, and that taking such pains assures and comforts you, allows you to go on—and it *is* hard work?"

Hardly a spectacular intervention; certainly she made no spectacular response. What did happen was a silence between us for several moments, not her usual defensive pickup on my words or intonation, just a silence that felt to me to be an easier one as her hands lay quiet, gently clasped on her chest, right hand held in left. She broke the silence to tell me she had been thinking of a close and relaxed time spent with her youngest daughter the previous day.

There were many such commonplace exchanges between us, although some of my interventions were jarring and troublesome when they went too far in touching on utterly unacceptable aggression and hints of conflicted sexuality. Yet these interventions were sometimes retrievable and usable, due in considerable measure to the vivid portrayal of intrapsychic conflict in the patient which the combined messages of kinesics and verbal content allowed me to experience.

Thus, in her harsh picking at herself the patient could be seen as reenacting her mother's incessant attacks upon her, as well as her own attacks upon herself as an attempted defense against her deeper wishes to attack her mother for attacking her. All the while her spoken words conveyed only depressed concern about mother and self.

To the extent that these modes and levels of intervention may have been helpful to the patient's analytic progress, and I think they were, I believe my comfort in keeping on this tack was enhanced by a background awareness, never articulated consciously to either myself or to my patient, of rapprochement phenomena, and knowledge of the hazards for a child moving toward autonomy, in having to deal with maternal depression and self-absorption (Stern, 1985, pp. 115–116). In groping for a good fit between my comprehension of the patient and her state, and the stage we had reached in our work, I had to live, as she did, through the tensions of mismatch and alienation, seeking somewhat different slants and metaphors by which to reapproach and make contact. Attention to her quiet, nonverbal kinesics as she spoke or fell silent afforded me a fuller view into her inner experiences of attachment and conflict, particularly in the maternal transference. The experiencing by both of us of my efforts, which were matched by the patient's efforts and offerings to join again in the endeavor after our lapses—these I see as the bread and butter, the basic nutriment, that sustained the shared struggle of analytic work.

Here I have found it heartening to learn from Stern and others how inevitable it is that mother and infant will "mess up" in their communications (Stern, 1985, p. 75); how necessary it is that the pair must continually make adjustments and corrections to and for each other. Without, I hope, trying to make a virtue out of error, I do delight in those observations that suggest a parallel between this shared groping and measuring and the change-promoting potential of a mother's prevailing tendency to over-shoot, by just a little, her infant's tolerance boundaries, and by so doing induce–invite the infant to stretch and grow.

To return to Mrs. M.: it was not until later in the work that she could endure our looking together at her associative sequences in order to follow their thrust and defensiveness, and look at some of her more obvious kinesics.

One conspicuous mannerism she repeatedly enacted over much of the analysis had to do with her fingering the whorl and parting of her hair. She could be gentle in stroking, patting, and rubbing it with her left fingers as she talked, her left arm and hand hovering above her head, with the elbow on the couch back. Or she could scratch, pick, and tear at it with her fingernails. Most conspicuous was the way her left hand could come down in a whole-handed audible slap on the crown of her head.

The soft touching and fingering tended to accompany verbal fantasy themes of finding herself the center of mother's admiring attention, of Cinderella-like encounters with rescuers of both sexes. At times she would begin this gentle gesturing during some intervention of mine that she found nonthreatening and then carry it on into a relaxed silence.

The combination of repetitive soft stroking and fingering her hair with her left hand while she was raptly absorbed in a soothing verbal fantasy of closeness and love with mother or idyllic other, struck me as authentically transitional and akin to the clinical phenomena Winnicott has described. That such behavior could later be experienced by the patient as a recapturing of old masturbatory acts is not incompatible with the invoking of an earlier pregenital state.

Her harsh rubbing and scratching were far more frequent and had to do with themes of resignation to ugliness, stupidity, and coarseness. Such negative, harsh gesturing with the left hand, in conjunction with a verbal context of self-repudiation and repugnance, seemed to capture both the mother's rejection of the patient's flaws, as well as the patient's loss of contact with the transitional modes of self-soothing. Often, in concurrence with such self-depreciating ideas, she would lapse from her careful enunciation and meticulous syntax into a near-parody of Appalachian vernacular. Early on she had done so when she was at some pitch of self-loathing, or making reference to father, brother, or self as falling below mother's patrician expectations. Later this coarseness resonated as she voiced in growing openness her rebellion and breakaway against being monitored and controlled by mother, and now by me in the analysis. It was at such emerging moments that her loud head slapping became prominent, clearly as a way to stop herself from going farther.

It was this last and loud combination of verbal content and gross kinesics that struck me as an opening—and maybe even an invitation or pleading—to address the matter: an enactment I perceived as reaching out to me as father for help in her release from maternal attachment.

I asked if she were aware of her gesture—what did it feel like? It was clear it had to be explored much as one would explore a slip of the tongue. Her reluctance to engage was intense, as it had been in my few earlier and quite unsuccessful efforts to focus on these behaviors. She insisted that the gesture meant nothing and it disappeared for weeks at a time as she felt herself in a struggle between us over revealing more or covering over. But she came back to it, and gradually she dealt with the gesture as she had grown accustomed to work on dreams, gingerly, but with some safety in viewing dream and gesture as being a happening slightly removed from her. Mrs. M. connected the head slap with memories of literally being batted on the head or slapped in the face by her mother for her bad wishes to go to the barn with father, gallivant with brother and friends, use bad words, show any sign of anger and rebellion. Feeling herself slapping herself gave her a graphic and vivid sense of mother's punishing her: "I'm stuck to her/with her." Our shared focus upon her hand gesture became for her a kind of permission to look. She fitfully became quite absorbed in her hands and what they were doing. She even caught herself in some of her quieter stroking or scratching and made connection with her conflicted needs to soothe or attack herself— and to be succored or punished, first by her mother, now by me. Deeper meanings of masturbatory conflict, or self-stimulation and soothing were hinted at, but not addressed until later on.

One vivid instance of many small increments of analytic work in these areas occurred when the patient opened an hour by bitterly complaining of how she "felt under the big thumb of those guys at work. Always I'm afraid of their anger, afraid to speak out to defend myself or show up their stupidity—that thumb's here in this room over me right now! Yours!" (Her left hand slapped down to clasp her head in familiar fashion.) She was silent a moment (as her left hand moved all the way over to clasp her right temple and partially cover her right eye). "I'm having a headache right this minute—and I don't get headaches! . . . feels like the migraines I had in high school when I was so tied in knots with my religious stuff . . . I want to be so angry and I can't. Instead I'm held down and hurt" (glaring back at me on the oblique past her clutching hand). [long pause]

Mrs. M.: You bastard. It's you! You *want* me to hurt!

Analyst: To be hurting and under my thumb?

Mrs. M.: [long pause—voice changes to coarse drawl] Yo' pore jackass, you *know* that's exactly what I said yesterday about how my mother wanted me . . . (reflective) . . . but I *did* say that about my mother . . . (laughs). Mister, *yo'* thumb ain't so big . . . it's my *mother's* thumb . . . I had to be unhappy because *she* was unhappy. . . . I couldn't go off and be with ma Daddy . . . feel right . . . I have to stay close to mother the only way I knew how . . . (wraps both arms around chest and upper arms in tight hug) . . . *not* go and be with Daddy . . . she'd sneer and get pains when she'd find me in the barn with him or in his lap . . . I just hung in there with her.

Analyst: You holding mother holding you in stuck misery?

Mrs. M.: Yeah . . . and I needed it so much I could kill, 'cause I hated it. . . . It felt safe/feels safe! . . . but it wasn't *safe* . . . it was stuck . . . I don't feel stuck this minute (half-crying, half-laughing) . . . I feels floating and free . . . want to fly like a bird, swoop and soar (arms now outstretched and hands in miming swirl with her words). I could not be happy because she was not happy, nor be free of her because she was so stuck . . . but that was *then*."

It was in the context of such hours as these that the patient began to show, for the first time, flashes of playful humor and pointed wit, increasingly targeted on me. She could become blissfully absorbed in watching her hands swaying and dancing, her comments reflecting her pleased assurance that I, too, was watching and pleased. While this strong conviction about my rapt attention reflected her narcissistic intensities, its qualities of merger, of mutual resonance around playing and showing struck me as congruent with the behaviors of the child in the practicing subphase of rapprochement pleasure between mother and child.

To step back once more, and in closing, I have no doubt that my focusing upon her prominent mannerisms as I did offered her a meeting place and eventual safe playground in which to speak of and often enact the rich complexities of her childhood struggles. With an increasing sense of freedom and space she could move into an action mode with herself and with me that allowed her to live out her memories and fantasies—literally in play, by herself, and by engaging with me. She did so in ways she had only sparsely, and in a conflicted way, sampled in her developmental years as a solitary and often lonely little one in a bleak farm setting. That she was also a responsible and committed woman neither escaped nor constricted her, nor us, as she enacted this play in the safety of the consulting room and within the framework of the analytic situation. I have a strong sense of conviction, without, of course, having any objective way to prove it, that I was seeing in Mrs. M.'s ways of hair rubbing and hand interactions traces of a transitional mannerism linking her to mother as both touched and touching, and as cherished or discarded (Winnicott, 1953). I felt that her conspicuous gestures replayed old traumatic experiences between her and her mother—that they shaped an authentic reconstruction of her childhood past. And in her blissful hand play while feeling benignly watched by me I felt that we were in resonance with the child's need to play and be affirmed in the presence of the watching mother.

To think of these small gestures only as autistic or narcissistic may be conceptually correct, yet robs these proclivities of the rich context of old relatings, a context that comes to life when the action, words, and music are brought into unison in the analytic work.

Chapter 9

Infant Observation and the Reconstruction of Early Experience

Martin A. Silverman, M.D.

Psychoanalytic contributions to the understanding of human development have come in three stages. At first, the only source of information was reconstruction backward from the productions of adult patients, with the emphasis centered mainly on the discovery of the Oedipus complex. Freud did not work analytically with children, and in the one child case in which he participated, by offering suggestions to the child's father, who carried out the therapy, he was guided largely by conclusions he had drawn from his adult analytic work. In this famous case of Little Hans, Freud addressed himself almost exclusively to the little boy's oedipal conflicts, although there also was an opportunity to investigate some of the preoedipal determinants of the form and shape of Little Hans' Oedipus complex and of additional nonoedipal components of his conflicts and anxieties (Silverman, 1980).

A new era began with the advent of child analysis. Now it became possible to learn directly about the psychological struggles of young children. Child analytic investigation not only confirmed what had been learned from adults about the Oedipus complex, but it also contributed greatly to our understanding of preoedipal conflicts. This is exemplified in the almost apologetic tone in which Geleerd comments on the extent to which the contributors to the volume *The Child Analyst at Work* (1967) describe preoedipal issues in the course of their essays.

We are now in the third stage, in which some of the most exciting advances derive from direct child observation. This investigative modality affords an opportunity to extend our inquiries back into the early, preverbal period that cannot be addressed directly in therapeutic encounters. But how are we to interpret the observational data which have been made available to us? It is far too easy to make point-to-point extrapolations back from later psychopathology to very early observations from which they are greatly removed. It is too easy to build early observational data into theoretical constructions which then are utilized to explain problems occurring so far down the developmental road that a panoply of additions and transformations have made it unreasonable to make such simple jumps. It is necessary to be very cautious in our use of early observational data, but it would be equally erroneous to set them aside. They offer us much to think about as we wrestle with the complexities of the clinical situation, and at times there are such strong indications of a correlation between observational research and clinical constellations with which we have to deal that they cannot be ignored.

Although my charge has been that of commenting upon the connection between early observations and clinical work with adults, I find myself unable to set aside my clinical experience with children for two reasons. One is that I have been increasingly convinced, as my experience with the two age groups has grown, that the distinctions drawn between child and adult analysis are misleading and artificial. Although developmental considerations impose technical and procedural differences between the two, the analytic process and even the goals are essentially the same in each. The other reason is that so much takes place in the transition from childhood to adulthood to add to the complexity of the clinical picture and to the possibilities for reworking and obfuscating transformation that the order of inference in adult work tends to be much greater than it is in work with children. Since a psychoanalyst has an opportunity to gather only a limited number of analytic experiences in the course of a lifetime, it would be unfortunate to pass over particularly convincing clinical experiences because they happen to have involved patients of one age group rather than the other.

Let me begin, therefore, by presenting two vignettes drawn from the sphere of child analysis.

The first involves a five-year-old girl, whom I shall call Anna, who had been adopted at the age of two-and-one-half months. No information was available about her innate temperament or about her very early (foster home) experiences except that at the time of her adoption her mother had perceived her as fretful, restless, easily distressed, and difficult to soothe and comfort. Her adoptive mother had had no prior experience with young children and felt insecure and unsure of herself. She had no one to whom she could turn for guidance and assistance and felt overwhelmed by the problems presented by this "difficult" child. It was my impression from what she said and the way she said it that from the first she had felt disappointed and angry at the way things had turned out and that she was still feeling quite ambivalent toward Anna. Not only had she found it extremely frustrating to be unable to consistently relieve the baby's tense irritability, but she also had been afraid that something might interfere with finalization of the adoption (a year after Anna had joined the family). The insecurity that the latter situation engendered, in combination with her ambivalence toward the child, seemed to me to have blocked her from embracing Anna wholeheartedly, empathically, and confidently as *her* child. She had felt particularly perplexed by the alternate clinging and defiant oppositionalism that had begun to appear during Anna's toddlerhood.

By the time I saw Anna, she and her mother were continually at odds with one another. Anna had difficulty parting from her mother, but when she was with her she was defiant and provocative. At nursery school she was so possessive, bossy, and intense that she alienated her teachers and her classmates. She slept poorly and complained of bad dreams. She loved her father intensely and was sad that his work kept him away from the house so much. She was protective of her younger sister, a very easy and easy-going child who was adopted when Anna was four years old, but she was painfully envious of the mother's attentions to her and of her sister's ability to be so much more pleasing to her parents.

During the opening weeks of the analysis, Anna played out an emotional version of the story of Peter Pan, assigning me various parts and instructing me in my lines. The emphasis was upon Captain Hook's agonizing, unbearable, but inescapable envy of Peter for being loved and looked after by Wendy, Nanna, and Tinkerbell. He was distraught at finding himself repeatedly unable either to woo or to steal them away from Peter. What made him most miserable, however, was finding himself intent, without any ability to stop himself, upon pursuing and destroying them so that if he could not have them neither would Peter.

Anna grew more and more anxious as the Peter Pan play progressed. We devoted ourselves for a long time to analyzing her reaction, aided in part by a series of dreams which she recalled. We came to understand her reactions as multidetermined in origin. First to emerge clearly was her competition with her little sister and the guilt and anguish she felt for wanting to get rid of her. We were led from this to her intense distress over her compulsive provocativeness with her mother. We came to understand this in terms of her being so terrified of being abandoned or sent away that she had to test her mother continually to make sure that it would not happen. This led in turn to the emergence, through her play themes, of the enormous guilt, sadness, and rage she felt over having been sent away by her birth parents. We found that she was convinced that it had been her badness that had been responsible and that she was in danger of it happening again; she even entertained the idea that she had been placed for adoption because she had been responsible for her birth mother's death. Strong positive feelings developed toward me as she found herself feeling better and more capable of self-control as a result of our work together. This, in turn, led us to the intense oedipal anxiety and guilt that contributed to her compulsive bad behavior and to her fear of losing her mother.

Her positive feelings for me dissolved, however, whenever I thwarted her by denying a request, failed to adequately provide what she felt she needed from me, or "sent her away" at the end of a session although she did not feel ready to go. She would hurtle, pell mell, into a vengeful, vindictive, enraged state in which she would glare at me, stamp her feet, grit her teeth, hurl vituperations at me, and tear up whatever drawings she had made. She even tore up elaborate Valentine's Day cards she had just lovingly made (including one for me). Within a few hours after such an outburst, I would invariably receive a telephone call from Anna; she needed to ascertain that her angry outburst had neither alienated me nor otherwise driven me off, and she needed to know that I still wanted to see her and work with her. She seemed relieved when, in discussing these calls, we reflected together on her fear of her ambivalence toward her mother and sister.

Somewhere in the middle of one of these telephone calls, Anna would ask me to give a detailed description of the room I was in, my place in it, the weather outside, and what I was wearing. Inquiry revealed that when she was very angry at me, she found herself unable to summon up a clear mental image of me. At such times, I indicated to her, she needed me not only to provide details as to what I looked like but, by providing them in a warm, friendly voice, to demonstrate to her that I still liked her and would stand by her no matter what. I shared with her my impression that over the years she had been exquisitely sensitive to the sound of her mother's voice, feeling safe and secure when her mother was calm and relatively untroubled by her behavior, but so frightened when her mother's voice grew impatient, angry, harsh, and strident that she not only feared losing her, but even felt that she *had* lost her.

As a family trip that would prevent Anna from seeing me for ten days grew closer and closer, she became obsessed with the idea of our exchanging Christmas presents. She gave me a gift of a penny, which she insisted I keep in her drawer, and brought in a Polaroid camera with which she took a picture of me to take along with her on the trip. In addition to the picture, she needed me to *give* her something, a gift that was *from* me. She found it very helpful when I interpreted her exquisite sensitivity to the positive or negative responses she received from me as well as from her mother, but she desperately implored me, at least this one time, to give her something concrete which she could take with her. She was moved, grateful, and relieved when I gave her a gift of a battery-powered memory game.

We have learned a great deal from infant observation about the role of choreographed, to-and-fro interactions between an infant, eager to experience, comprehend, and master the world about it, and a mothering person, responsively tuned in to the child's sensibilities, rhythms, and proclivities. In particular, we have learned that these interactions are necessary to establish a reasonably secure, stable, positively toned, and relatively unambivalent awareness on the infant's part of its own self and of the animate and inanimate world around it (Spitz, 1950, 1957, 1959; Spitz and Cobliner, 1965; Winnicott, 1958, 1965, 1971; Sander, 1962, 1964, 1980; Mahler, 1963, 1967, 1972a, b; Wolff, 1966, 1971; Mahler and Furer, 1968; Stern, 1971, 1977, 1985; Mahler, Pine, and Bergman, 1975; Emde, Gaensbauer and Harmon, 1976; Fraiberg, 1980; Brazelton, 1980; Call, 1980; Lichtenberg, 1981, 1983; Call, Galenson, and Tyson, 1983). Although Anna actually was in greater need of sensitive handling than most children, her adoptive mother was hampered by her own insecurity and ambivalence in her efforts to establish a committed, sensitively attuned, facilitating relationship with Anna as an infant. The kind of data emerging from infant studies have been extremely helpful to me in formulating and responding analytically to the particular aspect of Anna's problems that was referable to this developmental dimension.

Excessive emotional distance and lack of attunement between mother and child are not the only source, however, of interference with the development of healthy self and object representations and attitudes. *Insufficient* distance and use of maternal sensitivity to foster *excessive* dependence on the mother can lead to similar problems. This is illustrated in the case of nine-year-old Ben, who entered analysis because of multiple anxieties and learning problems related to enormous difficulty separating from his mother. His mother had set out from the time he was born to train him to rely closely upon her in satisfying his needs. She had observed him very closely and had become adept at reading his physiological rhythms so well that she could step in and provide for his needs without his having to develop techniques of signaling them to her. When be began to crawl and then to walk, she anticipated his need for assistance as occasions arose, helping him, for example, to avoid danger or catching him as he was just beginning to lose his balance. She encouraged him to learn to speak, but trained him to think *with her* rather than for himself. She taught him to read and write and did his homework with him after he started school.

Unlike his more active, vigorous siblings, who struggled against her imposition of such intrusive involvement in their functioning, Ben acceded, with little protest, to his mother's desire to be indispensable to him. His closeness to her during the oedipal period and early latency was intensified by his excited interest in her repeated, seductive nudity with him. This took place openly at first, only to be replaced, after the psychoanalyst working with one of her other children questioned its propriety, by a surreptitious offering of glimpses of her naked body in mirror reflections which both of them pretended he had not seen.

By the time I met Ben, he was a perplexed, confused, anxiety-ridden youngster who could not concentrate, had difficulty thinking on his own, did not look at or listen to what went on around him, and when he did, was not sure what he had seen or heard. This was exemplified by his asking *me* one day if there had been a fire engine in the street on his way over. He acted as though he did not have a mind of his own and could not think without my continual assistance. This was complicated by the use of mental gymnastics to ward off both castration anxiety and preoedipal anxieties by blurring or distorting disturbing perceptions of ideas. For example, he supported his contention that flies have three leglike protuberances, by focusing his attention on a picture in the family dictionary of a *fishing* fly with three legs. His perceptions of himself were similarly weak and unstable, and he depicted people around him as either controlling or engulfing or as unreliable and abandoning. He was so unclear and uncertain of the world about him that he was afraid to travel in the city lest he become helplessly lost.

As Christmas time approached, toward the end of his first year in analysis, he became increasingly irritated with me for neither proscribing his taking a week off to visit his grandmother nor sanctioning his doing so. He wanted to make the trip, but did not want to lose the time from his analysis, and he was irked that I did not rescue him from his dilemma the way his mother always did. When he arrived for his last session before his departure, he was woodenly distant and his voice lacked animation. When I noted this, he replied, "I know I'm with Dr. Silverman, in Dr. Silverman's office, but I don't *see* you. I can't separate you from the curtain behind you." I said, "I think you're so angry at me for not telling you that you can't go away, that your analysis is important to me and I *want* you to stay here so we can meet, that you can't keep the anger you feel inside you from destroying the picture you have of me in your mind—though if I told you you had to miss seeing your grandmother you'd probably be just as angry at me." I connected his dilemma about separating from me or not with his conflict between cherishing the special closeness he enjoyed with his mother and wishing he could break away and stand on his own without her. "You're right," said Ben, "I am angry at you. I've been angry at you all week. Now I *see* you. Now you're not part of the curtain." We spent considerable time thereafter exploring the connection between his anxieties and neurotic ego disturbances and his ambivalence about his hyperdependent closeness with his mother.

It is evident from these two child analytic vignettes that to make simple point-to-point connections between psychopathology in mid- or even early childhood and experiences during infancy is very questionable. When we get to adults, it is even more difficult to trace out the links between what is observable later on and what might be very early antecedents of them.

Mrs. C., for example, entered analysis in her late thirties because of chronic unhappiness, continual marital strife, indecisiveness, and dissatisfaction with many areas of her life. A pattern emerged early in the analysis in which she alternated between controlling, dominating behavior that kept me at a distance, and insistence that I provide a great deal more care and assistance than I was willing to offer. She began to feel depressed on weekends and to telephone for weekend sessions which I did not grant. When we explored this, it emerged that the analytic arrangements left her feeling alone and abandoned and that giving herself over to free association filled her with terror of losing control.

At first it appeared that this was a regressive response to exciting but frightening erotic fantasies involving me that appeared to be connected with unresolved oedipal conflicts. Her father, she recalled, used to excite her with seductive talk and behavior only to repulse her and become extremely critical and disparaging of her when she responded. A series of floridly exciting dreams led to recall of wild, sadomasochistic battles between her parents which, she came to recognize, she unwittingly sought to reenact with me, as she had been doing with her husband and son. She had become aware of a tendency to stir men up seductively, with the wish for them to pursue her, sweep her up, and carry her off to bed. On those occasions when a man did respond to her overtures she would become terrified and flee. She felt, periodically, that she had seduced me into falling in love with her, whereupon she would introduce distancing maneuvers, plan a vacation, or speak about breaking off the analysis. She often would report enticing dream material or bring up seemingly vital issues only to flee after a partial inquiry into humdrum matters or obsessive doubts about the analysis. It became clear that the aim was to have me "run after" her and forcibly bring her back to the more salient issues, which would both frighten and excite her.

She recalled, as we explored this further, that as a tiny child, still in a crib, she would play a cruel game with her grandmother. She would sweetly beckon, "C'mere gramma," and when her beaming grandmother came to her, would say, in an acid tone, "Go *way*, gramma." She recognized that she had been playing this terrible game with all the important people in her life for a long time. This was traced in turn to a core, ambivalent, hostile–dependent relationship with her mother in which she yearned to be cared for and protected by her at the same time that she wished to flee from or destroy her. Her fastidious mother had found it difficult to deal with crying, messy babies and had managed to impose toilet control on her at the age of five months! The mother had been intolerant as well of her child's rising excitement when she played with her, and would get up and leave, stating that Mrs. C.'s father needed her. All of this emerged out of painstaking analysis of transference reactions, dream images, and screen memories. As we went through this, we wandered back and forth between oedipal and preoedipal issues, although the latter preoccupied us for a long time before her oedipal conflicts took the forefront. During this time, we dealt not only with the obvious rapprochement conflicts, but also with the impact of her central belief that she would only be acceptable to her mother if she were the kind of smiling, unexcitable, unaggressive, pleasing little performing doll she could, as a human being, never succeed in becoming. This belief contributed to her poor self-image and self-esteem, and limited her expectations of herself and of others.

Let us turn now to a different kind of early mother–daughter disturbance. Mrs. D. entered analysis in her early thirties because of the acute onset of periodic phobic anxiety when she had to drive more than a short distance from home. It had started with an anxiety attack while she was driving home from a meeting during which she had become very angry at a woman friend for usurping authority that should have been hers. A few days later, as she was approaching one of the tunnels connecting New York and New Jersey, with her mother sitting in the passenger seat beside her, she had the sudden thought that she might crash the car, killing her or her mother. She was so anxious that she had to ask her mother to take over the wheel. Increasingly frequent anxiety attacks in the car led her to seek treatment.

In the course of a far-reaching analysis, we came to understand what had occurred in terms of a host of past and current issues. In her present life she was caught up in conflicts involving intense but inhibited competitiveness with forceful, domineering, and/or more attractive women friends, conflicts with her husband and children, indecisiveness about her career goals, and certain moral dilemmas that troubled her considerably. She also had had a series of past phobias, extending back into her early childhood. Mrs. D.'s relationship with her mother, not surprisingly, proved to be very important. Her mother was a controlling, dominating woman who was intrusive and manipulative, at times with cruel overtones.

It became apparent that both her mother and her father were anxious and phobic. They had established a mutually protective, phobic system in their family in which Mrs. D.'s mother controlled everyone else via a protector–protected mechanism that kept them close to her. The others were too afraid to defy her and too fearful of going out into the world without her to ever leave her. We came to see that Mrs. D.'s parents had not helped her internalize reliable moral principles nor had they helped her develop the psychological means with which to feel confidently able to control herself from acting upon impulses and urges in ways that might get her into trouble. Her mother still encouraged her repeatedly to do things that clearly were wrong or improper; at the same time she was incessantly critical of her. By encouraging misbehavior while frightening her about the consequences, she had trained her to remain dependent upon her rather than becoming independent and self-reliant. Although she was unhappy and wished to extricate herself from enslavement to her mother's views and authority, Mrs. D. unconsciously both welcomed her mother's control over her and was too terrified of her murderous wishes toward her mother to free herself from her close dependence upon her.

We came to understand Mrs. D.'s emotional dilemmas in terms of intense, insoluble, positive oedipal conflicts. A core childhood experience that had played a part began when she was a little under five years of age. After her mother gave birth to Mrs. D.'s only sibling and, ostensibly, because of a housing shortage, Mrs. D.'s mother left home to live with relatives for several months. Mrs. D. stayed at the home of another set of relatives (in a house which reminded her of mine), where she shared a bedroom with her father.

Analysis of these positive oedipal conflicts proved to be insufficient, however, to enable Mrs. D. to resolve her problems and to free herself from her ambivalent, hostile–dependent involvement with her mother. It proved necessary to delve into her negative oedipal conflicts and into the very early roots of their relationship before she could gain the freedom she was seeking. From the analysis of current relationships, analytic transference expressions, observations of her mother's relationship with her children and with her sibling, dreams, and memories, we were able to reconstruct a succession of stages in which the keynotes were dominance and submission, control of closeness and distance, and mutual ambivalence. An important memory, which her mother confirmed as accurate, was of her mother teasingly rejecting her approaches to deliberately make her cry, whereupon she would tell her that she liked to see her cry because it made her "cute." We came to the conclusion that, from infancy onward, her mother, who had had a very difficult childhood of her own, had promoted or accentuated Mrs. D.'s tendencies to feel so much in need of her that she could not afford to separate from her or alienate her. At the same time she felt so guilty about her rage at her mother that she was enslaved and enthralled by it. Each successive phase of development had transformed and added new meaning to this combination of needy closeness and guilty rage, but it had persisted throughout as a thread that bound things together.

It is evident from these examples that the data emerging from observational research into the development of infants can be extremely helpful in clarifying the beginnings of parent–child patterns of interaction, throughout childhood and even adolescence, that play a major role in shaping ego and superego development. They tell us important things about the evolution of ego attitudes and propensities. We need to be wary about making reductionistic conclusions about early experience that promote genetic fallacies, but infant observation can help us to think about certain things in a way that can help us organize our thoughts about a developmental dimension that tends otherwise to be very subtle and difficult to engage.

Let me present an even more dramatic example. A forty-year-old woman came for treatment because of recurrent depressive episodes that had begun while she was in college. She was referred by someone who had to interrupt his treatment of her because he was moving from the area. One aspect of his description of their working relationship turned out to be especially pertinent. He stated that of all his patients she had been one of several about whom he had been particularly concerned. She was a very likable, extremely fine person, admirable for her honesty, decency, courage, and moral fiber, who did not deserve to struggle so hard and suffer so much. He had tried very hard to find ways of helping her, and she had always been very appreciative of the assistance he had offered her. He was particularly eager to turn her over for care to someone who would appreciate and understand her.

When I began to work with Mrs. E. I found her to be just as her previous therapist had described her. She was every bit as likable, decent, and admirable in her personal qualities as I had been told. I observed that I very much wanted to help her become capable of living an easier, more enjoyable life. As she described her problems to me, she mentioned sadly that she would like to turn to her parents for aid and comfort when she felt depressed but that she could not do so. Although she knew her parents loved her, she had found that their pattern of urging her to fight harder to throw off the depression did not help, and perhaps it even made things worse. Unlike her husband and certain close friends, they didn't seem quite able to understand what she went through when she was depressed. She very much appreciated the daily, solicitous telephone calls her mother had made to her during her most serious depressive episode and she wished she could obtain responses like that at less critical times. She did not want, furthermore, to cause her parents trouble or to make them worry about her, especially since they didn't seem to be able to help her anyway.

Mrs. E. worked very hard in her treatment, too hard in fact. This eventually became understandable in terms of certain attitudes that prevailed in her family of origin. Her father, though kind and generous, always had been very work- and goal-oriented. He had placed a strong emphasis on doing things the "right way," which, of course, was *his* way. In contrast to her older, male siblings, who succeeded academically, athletically, and professionally with apparent ease, she had always felt less capable, unsure of herself, and needed to work very hard to achieve acceptable results. Her mother, she recalled, had said of her, "You've always had to work harder."

But as hard as she tried, Mrs. E. never was able to feel good in any kind of lasting way about what she did. If a piece of work she did was well received, her satisfaction was marred by terrible doubts about her ability to do it again. When she performed well for her team in the athletic pursuit that was her main recreational activity, she felt content, but anytime she failed to perform up to standard she was alarmed. And she dreaded the "lulls" between seasons when there would be no team play in which to participate and show what she could do. An important historical detail emerged in connection with this. Her mother had lost her own father very early in her life and, in an apparently creative effort to psychologically find him, she had become an intense fan—a fanatic in the true sense of the word—of a particular male-dominated professional sport. During its season the rest of the family was told that if a game were on they would have to get their own dinner and they had better not disturb her. It was at the beginning of that sport's season that Mrs. E. usually became depressed.

Mrs. E. insisted from the outset that she did not want to be in treatment and was coming under protest. She did not like depending on someone else, she stated, and should not have to do so; she should be able to do it on her own. Nevertheless, she participated actively in the treatment process and made it clear in many, subtle ways that our work together was very important to her and that my caring interest meant a great deal to her. She alternated between gratitude for my assistance and complaints that I was not helping her. Her conflict was epitomized in her periodic cancellation of a session to do something else, only to call a few days later to say that her plans had been changed and she would like to come for her session if it were still available. She protested when these transference manifestations were linked reconstructively with her conflicted childhood wishes to get hold of a mother who withdrew from her repeatedly, requiring that she do without her and provide for herself. When she looked through her elementary school report cards, during a visit to her parents, she saw that several of her teachers had commented that she had difficulty completing her work on her own. This could not help but give her pause.

From time to time, Mrs. E.'s requirements of me went beyond the traditional expectations a patient would have of a doctor, just as had occurred with her previous therapist. She demonstrated an urgent need both to know enough things about me as a person to substantiate an otherwise insufficiently clear and solid image of me as an important other in her life and to elicit statements from me that would tell her what I thought of her and felt about her as a person. I cannot overemphasize the obligatory, urgent quality of these requirements.

At one point, for example, as she was coming out of a depressive episode, she interrupted her narrative description of the signs of improvement she had noted in herself and of some helpful changes she was making in her life to criticize me sharply not only for not commenting on what she had been saying but for not even showing very much in my facial expression. "*You* don't think I'm doing well," she exclaimed; "*You* don't think I'm getting better; *you* don't think much of what I'm doing." When we looked into this together, it became clear that it was not sufficient for *her* to observe indications that she was coming out of her depression. It was not enough that she was taking charge of her life again and assuming the reins as the active, effective agent determining her own destiny. She needed *me* to acknowledge and confirm what she perceived with her own senses, to mirror back to her in a beaming, approving, encouraging way that I shared in, agreed with, was impressed by, and was contributing to her efforts and accomplishments.

From instances such as this we were able to reconstruct her sense of something missing or inadequate in her relationship with her parents, especially her mother, so that she had not gotten all that she had needed from them to build up a secure, solid, firm sense of herself as a capable, successful, good person who was appreciated, admired, and sufficiently pleasing and satisfying to others that they liked her, wanted to be with her, and enjoyed participating in her achievements. Her ability to sustain a positive self-image and to feel good about herself and her place in the hearts and eyes of significant others in the face of intermittent small defeats and failures, or even of temporary lulls in an otherwise unbroken string of victories, was compromised. This appears to have disposed her to periodic depression when her inability to mobilize her aggressive capacities to pursue, catch hold of, and obtain desired responses from her primary libidinal objects or those who later came to stand for them, led instead to turning of her aggressive inclinations back against herself in the form of scathingly self-critical, self-punitive attacks.

Infant observation offers us help in understanding this kind of clinical experience by providing a means of conceptualizing and dealing with the issues involved. Daniel Stern, for example, has organized the data of infant observation he has been gathering in terms of the development in a child of a sense of a core self and then of an intersubjective self (Stern, 1985). One aspect that seems to me to be very helpful is the formulation of this process as a multifaceted one in which the young child comes to view herself or himself as an intact, consistent, strong, capable, good, likable, admirable being, not only via repeated observation of the child's attributes and abilities but also via repeated, more or less reliable and consistent, sensitive, maternal (and paternal) responses that are confirming, rewarding, encouraging, assisting, and subtly shaping and structuring. Perhaps a *shared* or *connected* sense of self would be an even more precise term for what Stern refers to as the intersubjective self.

Stern also emphasizes, and I concur entirely on the basis of my own observational and clinical experience, that the basic patterns of parent–child interaction observable in the course of infant observation are likely to persist or to recur repeatedly over the years thereafter. The problems between Mrs. E. and her mother which we were able to reconstruct were not limited to her infancy, but extended more or less throughout her childhood and, in attenuated form, even into adulthood. The problem is that by the time children get to be just a few years old, let alone become adults, so many psychological issues have emerged and the earliest trends have become so intermingled with later ones and so transformed, that the complexity of the observational field becomes enormous. When some colleagues and I embarked on a long-range, normative longitudinal study at The Child Developmental Center of The Jewish Board of Guardians over twenty years ago, we were dazzled and flabbergasted by the swirling, shifting developmental currents we encountered, with such a profusion of issues and conflicts that were referable to multiple developmental levels, that we had to make serial, detailed assessments over a year to a year and a half before we felt we had an idea of what might have been going on. The advantage afforded by infant observation is that it gives the investigator an opportunity to look into the beginnings of ego maturation and development, drive expression, self-awareness, object relations, and so on, *before* they have progressed so far and have become so complex and so intertwined that they are difficult to identify, let alone to assess.

It would, in my estimation, have been unwarranted and

clinically ineffective to reconstruct experiences Mrs. E. might have had during her first year or two of life. It was extremely helpful to her, however, for me to call repeated attention to the subtle transference enactments with me, and the more blatant ones with family members and friends, of her hypersensitivity to indications of failure by those to whom she turned for consistently affirming, approving, encouraging, appreciative, or even affectionate and delighted responses. We were able to reconstruct together a pattern of parent–child interaction, throughout her formative years but probably beginning very early, in which her parents, because of their own particular problems and needs, the most notable of which probably involved her mother's periodically reduced emotional availability, were unable to respond optimally in response to her particular needs.

We further postulated that, because of her own particular emotional makeup, she had had considerable difficulty tolerating, acclimating, and adapting to the limitations she was discovering in her parents. We hypothesized that she had been hampered in building up a perspective of her parents that would allow her to perceive them in a balanced, multidimensional, integrated way that would permit her to feel reasonably secure about their responsiveness. We postulated that she had had difficulty coming to appreciate that she could become frustrated and angry at them without incurring the danger of driving them away still further. Mrs. E. found this extremely helpful because it catalyzed her making changes to overcome the naive, innocent, "Cinderella" attitude she came to recognize in herself. It helped her reduce her fear of incurring disapproval and permitted her to become more assertive. It helped her replace her dependency on the chief objects in her life with sublimatory activities that afforded her an opportunity to do enjoyable, satisfying things with new people and "opened her eyes" to the world and what she could expect from it. Her depressive diathesis greatly decreased. Clinical experiences like this demonstrate the value of infant observation in enhancing our understanding of human development and in facilitating our ability to be clinically useful to our patients.

SECTION III
THE DISCUSSIONS

Chapter 10

The Challenge Posed by Infant Observational Research to Traditional Psychoanalytic Formulations: A Discussion of the Papers

Morton Shane, M.D.

Phyllis Tyson's extensive, open-minded review of psychoanalytically inspired infant and child research emphasizes the increasing appreciation of the interaction between infant and mother, and the increasing complexity and technological sophistication by means of which this interaction can be studied.

The panorama of divergent views in psychoanalytic theory as applied to developmental study is well portrayed. I hear Tyson as implying that the preponderance of evidence drawn from observational study leads us to question the utility and value of the primacy of a dual drive motivational system, and even to question the usefulness of the drive concept itself. She herself does not, of course, take a position in this area, nor does she take a position regarding which might prove to be useful: organizing psychoanalytic thinking concerning development around the ego, or around the self, or around some amalgam of the two, and if the latter, whether or not one is better off placing them in a hierarchical order. Tyson also does not make value judgments regarding conceptualizing the infant as possessing the capacity to distinguish self from other from very early on. These are certainly pertinent current issues which were addressed, more or less, in many of the papers in this monograph, and in this discussion I am urging further consideration of them.

Novick began his paper by asserting that while, beginning with Freud, observational experience with infants and children has always been integral to psychoanalytic training and practice, something is distinctly different in the field at present. He says that, with the current plethora of activity, the term *infant observational research* must refer specifically to the body of data accumulated exponentially in the last ten years. He then presents us with a most creative assignment: to look at his own psychoanalytic work on a borderline adolescent, Dave, completed fifteen years ago, and ask the question, how would that work be viewed today in the light of current knowledge? Novick himself answers that, for one thing, he would entertain more firmly the conviction that Dave's "addiction to pain" began in infancy and led from that point to persistent delusions of omnipotence and a life-long search for relationships that involved hurtful interchanges. He adds that were Dave in treatment now, he would not have terminated with him until he had made further headway into his patient's need to actualize this dominant fantasy. Novick bases these changes from then to now on both his own and others' researches into the infant–mother dyad, most specifically the microanalysis of interchanges between the infant and mother where there is a failure to repair a mismatch. He postulates that this failure escalates and persists throughout development.

The material Novick presented is rich and potent for speculations about the ways in which newer theory subtly changes the way in which the case is seen. To begin with, in the light of current research, what is the place of the dual drive theory of libido and aggression as it applies to his patient's pathology? Novick speaks of the reconstruction he made that Dave's mother's inattention to him as a child created in him a feeling of not being loved. This reconstruction, he says, broke the increasing spiral of rage, projected rage, panic, and further defensive aggression. Does this mean that Novick conceptualizes, consistent with Parens, destructive aggression as secondary to frustration, and not as an innate drive? He does not answer this specifically in his paper. As drive constructs have not proven useful to many infant researchers as a basic building block of the mind, would Novick now be less likely than he had been then to think in terms of thought and fantasy emerging from drive inhibition? Would he think today in terms of shifts of cathexes? Would impulsive expression be conceived of now as complex wish rather than drive?

Another series of questions, although ostensibly for Novick, is actually for all of us: Would the general agreement among infant researchers that Novick points to, that the Mahlerian scheme of development is "utterly refuted," influence his own readiness to see defensive merging in his patient? Might he now see the same phenomenon as wishes for dyadic attunement without a loss of boundaries? Or, if the merger idea still seems persuasive to him, would he see this, rather than as a regression to an earlier phase of normal development, as a pathological state that borders on loss of reality testing? As a corollary, would Novick still see Dave's nose picking earlier in the treatment as objectless, or would he be persuaded by Stern's assertion that the infant is never without objects, whether he is alone or not, and conclude that autisticlike withdrawal is never a regression to an earlier phase, but rather the most extreme pathology. In other words, would Novick be more likely to posit the nose picking even at the beginning of treatment as a way of relating, the fantasy of a messy, damaged, anal child connected to the preoedipal mother, just as later in the analysis he posits the nose picking as a part of the fantasy of the oral child related to the preoedipal mother?

Eleanor Galenson's paper is based on her own original research. In that research she postulates an early genital phase, identifying it as a psychic organizer wherein the child's psychic system is reconstructed on a higher level of complexity, the child being capable of changing from passively experienced stimulation by mother, to active, self-induced genital stimulation which has the effect of consolidating self–object differentiation; that is, the new capacity for masturbation facilitates repression of regressive fantasies of merging with the mother of earlier infancy. The effective psychotherapy of the three-year-old boy who wished to be a girl demonstrates the clinical usefulness of her formulations, as well as providing a beautiful illustration of how infant and child research can inform clinical practice. Her work not only raises questions for further research but also allows us to contrast her developmental theory with that of others.

Galenson has significantly extended Mahler's work regarding the second year of life in the areas of gender identity and gender confusion. Her research demonstrates a most important finding: the discovery of sexual differences by the child is traumatic in proportion to the quality of object relationship with the mother prior to that discovery. However, her research is based upon Mahler's view of the first year of life, her conceptualizations relatively uninfluenced by what Stern has termed the "revolution in infancy research" which calls into question the developmental task assumed by Mahler of differentiating out of an undifferentiated symbiotic merger. When Galenson writes about a shift in passive–active balance as a significant aspect of the early genital phase as psychic organizer, she conceptualizes this shift from passive to active as consolidating the normal developmental process of self–object differentiation. Also, she speaks of regressive fantasies as merger with the mother of early infancy. I am certain that it comes as no surprise to Galenson that this view is inconsistent with the view of prewired emergent structures of self separate from other almost from birth on. I will raise the same question with Galenson that I raised with Novick: how does she conceptualize aggression? The material might indicate that she sees it as parallel to and comparable with libidinal strivings, namely, inborn and epigenetically unfolding during the course of development, when she speaks of her young patient Jim as having to negotiate sufficient separations of libidinal from aggressive strivings so that he can express phallic strivings toward his mother without fear of destroying her. Jim had more than enough to be angry about. There were the desertions, first by his mother at two months, and then by his mother–surrogate housekeeper at fourteen months, and then by a series of housekeepers after that, until a second long-term person was employed. When she asserts that phallic strivings carry with them destructive aggression, does she mean just in Jim's case, which would be understandable because he is so angry with his mother, or does she mean that destructive aggression is built into phallic strivings in normal development? Galenson seems to emphasize the danger of these phallic strivings over Jim's longing to identify with the lost housekeeper by becoming like her, that is, feminine. In the same way, Jim wished, in sucking his thumb, to become like the daughter of the new housekeeper, and thereby prevent her loss as well. Since these are subtle differences in accent, I wonder, again, how a reactive view of aggression might alter the therapy. For example, I wonder if there then wouldn't be less emphasis on the therapeutic maneuver of having mother encourage phallic aggressiveness, that is, little boy behavior, and more acknowledgment with Jim of his attempting to control his sad longing for his lost housekeeper and his desiring her attention to his needs, by his clinging to femininity and the feminine accoutrements he gathered around him to replace her.

Turning to Mel Scharfman's paper, it is clear that he has been influenced by current infant research; it is also clear that he sees limitations and complications in attempting to apply this research to the clinical situation. Scharfman begins with the challenging statement that, to his mind, the discovery that the infant has the ability to respond much more actively in the environment than had been thought previously, and that, in addition, the infant is capable of fine discriminations between his mother and others very early in life, has little applicability to the clinical situation at this point in time. I say this is a challenging statement because it is just this ability to discriminate early in infancy which leads to the hypothesis of the existence of separate schemas of self and other almost from the beginning of life. What leads from this hypothesis is that there need be no normal developmental task of separating self from object. To the extent that this hypothesis is accepted, significant modification of traditional developmental theory, including Mahler, Hartmann, Jacobson, and many others, would be required. Scharfman does see as extremely useful the newer findings regarding the match and mismatch within the infant–mother dyad. The issues he raises regarding the potential for correcting emotional deficits and skewing through the vehicle of a new object relationship are most intriguing. Child analysts have always wrestled with this issue because, like it or not, we cannot help but provide new object functions for our young patients. But what Scharfman highlights using infant research is our need as clinicians to reassess the quality of the analyst's responsiveness to all patients. For example, research tells us that the infant cannot emotionally survive the effects of a deadpan mother. The infant's average expectable environment should provide an affectively attuned, friendly, and responsive other for adequate social refer- encing, for affect attunement, and for intersubjective health. Scharfman raises the question, how responsive should analysts be to their patients? Should they be their unguarded selves in response to the patient's affects, or should being openly oneself be reserved for selected patients, for example, those who manifest self pathology? With such patients, who may have experienced deficient or defective affect responsiveness with their caretakers, would the analyst treat the patient face to face, avoiding the mutual affect deprivation the couch involves? Scharfman's ques- tions stimulate me to wonder how much affect misattuning we inadvertently subject our patients to by being our muted selves in our attempt to achieve an analytic neutrality? Might we be telling our patients the opposite of what we intend to say: we want them to feel free to be as affectively expressive as possible, while we respond to their affects in a much lower register. Are we in this way tuning them down as mothers are shown to do so effectively and continuously with their infants? A psychoanalytic candidate said to me, after facing a group of analysts reviewing her case presentation, "The trouble with analysts is that they lack the social smile." Finally, I wonder, should we consider a tradition-shattering idea for all of our patients: do the drawbacks of the couch in terms of affect deprivation and physiognomic information blocking outweigh the well-known and well-considered advantages of using the couch? I think it may even be possible, based on what Scharfman is pointing out, to consider redefining analysis, without the couch as an *obligatory* aspect of the analytic situation. Scharf- man demonstrates many of these issues in his clinical example of Donny.

In Jules Glenn's paper on work with prelatency children, he uses the beautifully executed case of Jan, first seen at age three-

and-a-half, to illustrate most clearly and cogently his particular approach to the clinical situation. Glenn, like Galenson, applies Mahler's separation–individuation theory to his understanding of the conflicts and developmental difficulties that unfold in the analysis. I therefore must raise with him the same questions I have already raised with Galenson concerning the challenge made by infant research to the concept of symbiosis. Glenn makes some important generalizations on the role of infant observation in insight-oriented psychotherapy. Among others, he says infant observation helps us to know what infants are like and thereby enables us to get a feel for what developmental level our patients are at. He illustrates this point when, during the case discussion, he tells us that the analyst, looking at the patient, Jan, clinging to her mother, and appearing at one with her, was reminded of the infant-with-mother in the symbiotic stage. Glenn thereby demonstrates the unavoidable tendency of all analysts to read their theoretical formulations into the behavior of their patients. We see a child clinging to her mother and we infer symbiosis. But reading into the appearance of oneness the psychic reality of symbiosis requires a knowledge and an acceptance of that theoretical formulation as opposed to competing formulations, such as the wish to return to the womb, the wish to be eaten, or, now more recently, the wished for experience of security and attachment with a self regulating other. I think this range of choice indicates the necessity for an increasing reliance on infant observation and experimentation in order to gain approximation of the psychic reality of the infant and preverbal child, and thereby provide as solid a basis as possible for our reconstructions. Which brings up another of Glenn's helpful generalizations regarding infant research, his warning that the reconstructions we make on the basis of our knowledge of infants may not benefit the young child who is cognitively incapable of grasping them, and, in any case, is more interested in the here and now. He illustrates with Jan's behaviors which are reminiscent of earlier periods, but are complicated by her current conflicts, in this case, conflicts on an oedipal level. Thus, reconstructions are not made of the original, unmodified patterns, but of current, here-and-now issues.

Arnold Cooper demonstrates the strong influence current

infant observation has had on his reconstructions with adult patients. He makes the point that while our patients are concerned with their genetic past, analysts have never derived their picture of the patient's life solely from what the patient has told them. Rather the portrait described by the patient is elaborated by the analyst's inner vision of development. Cooper finds the depressed visage, the pinched face of a sad infant and child in the facial expression of his thirty-five-year-old woman patient, and later hears in her voice the tremulous fearfulness of a three-year-old left alone, holding back tears. Thus, like Glenn, and like all of us, he draws upon his own particular theory of development to make inferences about the patient's psychic reality. Cooper states further that with certain manifestations in the patient one would anticipate particular features in the past history. For example, his patient suffered from low self-esteem. His theory of development led him to expect to hear about parental failure, in contradistinction to the nice mother and ideal father that the patient actually recalled. In other words, he infers that in some ways we know better, or we know earlier, aspects of the patient's life narrative, a position that can of course lead to disruption in the analytic relationship if it is not tempered by tact and by the capacity in the analyst to be surprised. And, as Cooper points out, there are times when the unique stories our patients tell may generate research questions and disrupt fondly held presuppositions.

In looking at the history of infant research, Cooper notes with characteristic irony that in the past, developmentalists sought to confirm and extend existing psychoanalytic theory, whereas now the goal seems to be to discover what babies are actually like. He himself appears to be attracted to the most recent research work, including that of Emde, Stern, and Greenspan, as well as the work of Bowlby and those inspired by him. He contends that the better the conception we have of actual plots of early interpersonal life, the more likely we are to help our patients relive them within the transference. Thus, his conviction concerning the profound effects of early mothering on the developing self and the defensive attitudes and activities initiated to maintain well-being in individuals whose lives have been lived under less than optimal circumstances informed his contention that his patient must have been traumatized by the inadequate responsiveness of her parents. However, one possible alternative to that view is to see the patient's unhappiness while a child as the result of inadequate solutions to conflicts regarding unsatisfied drives. Perhaps, then, he sees that more accurate plots, or life narratives, can be extrapolated from developmental theories focused on self and affects rather than on the epigenesis of drive.

In this regard, it seems most appropriate to discuss Joe Lichtenberg's presentation next, because he has contributed much to the range of plots, or, as he calls them, model scenes, on which analysts may base their reconstructions of life narratives of their patients. His paper contends that, based upon current infant observation, understanding model scenes from childhood in our adult analytic patients through the concepts of libidinal stage progression or autistic isolation is either inadequate or inaccurate. Rather, the newer research provides a different set of model scenes closer to the lived experience of the child, enabling the analyst to be more empathically perceptive, and presumably more accurate, with his adult patients.

Lichtenberg gives us the benefit of his thinking about the complexities of motivation, substituting a group of five motivational systems for the dual drive theory of classical analysis. The five systems include needs for: physiological regulation; intimacy and affiliation; exploration and assertion; aversive reaction; and sensual and sexual pleasure. One can locate the dual drives of aggression and sexuality among these five types of motivation but the totality obviously includes more, is organized to be consistent with the newer findings of infant observation, and each system is interactive with the environment rather than only fueled from within. In his case discussion, it is clear that Lichtenberg uses not only model scenes from childhood, but, in his responses, he models his own interchanges with the patient after model exchanges between infant and parent. For example, his patient Robert Roseman mentions in one of the excerpts at the end of the analysis that he can now resist the pessimism of his parents, and Lichtenberg responds, "Were you saying to me implicitly, 'why didn't I let you leave the analysis when you were in an optimistic state? Why didn't I match your optimism with mine?,'" and the patient replies, "I hadn't thought of it, but yes." Lichtenberg's statement is reminiscent of infant research related to affect attunement and misattunement. At another point, Mr. Roseman complains about his loss of curiosity to explore. "I need you not only to undo my parents' command, but to reinstate my curiosity," he says. By this time, after seven years, he begins to sound like Lichtenberg, and Lichtenberg replies, "Do you sense yourself waiting now for me to stimulate your interest, reinstate your curiosity?" Again, Lichtenberg probably is seeing the patient as attempting to use him as the interested other who offers the active self opportunities for appropriate interesting stimulation, an affect-intensity-regulating other. One other exchange is reminiscent of affect tuning. When the patient complains that he has never internalized the spark of his cousin's enthusiasm in order to generate enthusiasm by himself, Lichtenberg says, "That's what you have to do now." Mr. Roseman then responds in a way which indicates that he has experienced an affect-attuning other, saying, "It's easier because you have not been as ebullient as my cousin. I *had* to do it more for myself." Here is a model scene of infant–other interaction transposed to the adult level and within the transference, or, more specifically, a new object experience in the analytic relationship. I am left with the impression that Lichtenberg has himself been inspired by the new view of human interaction that modern infant research has brought us. The whole ambience of the analytic situation seems altered in Lichtenberg's hands, characterized by active, to-and-fro exchanges, the kind of intersubjective activity reminiscent of the infant–mother dyad. The classical analytic ambience, perhaps in caricature, is the analyst as a more inert iconic object of desire who need offer little to stimulate the patient. Much more is expected to arise from within the patient, and more is expected of the patient to integrate laconic interpretive remarks. The analyst's affective profile is traditionally lower, and lower keyed. An "other" of this caliber would not be as suitable for the real infant and child, and perhaps Lichtenberg, like Scharfman, is telling us that a patient with this pathology requires an interaction different from patients who suffer difficulties either in other motivational systems, or with a healthier, more stable, integrated self. Or perhaps Lichtenberg is implying that all patients would benefit from more of this activity. I hope he and Scharfman, too, will comment on this.

McLaughlin is particularly interested in the multimodal range of communication as it is registered and dealt with automatically and subliminally by all of us as a part of our earliest acquired capacities to communicate. In addition to paying his long-standing respects to Spitz, Winnicott, and Mahler for their ideas about mother–infant interaction, transitional phenomena, and the separation–individuation process, McLaughlin states that the newer data of Stern and Snow provide evidence for the infant's capacity to acquire and use nonverbal levels of communication to send and receive affectively powerful messages. It is on this issue that McLaughlin concentrates his discussion of his patient, Mrs. M. He describes his observations of her on the couch, and the interchanges between himself and his patient, and then refers to Stern, who, McLaughlin notes, reports the same types of interchange between infant and mother, noting that the pair must continually make adjustments to one another and for one another. I believe here McLaughlin has in mind a model scene of interaction based in what Stern calls the intersubjective realm of relatedness: that is, relatedness between the subjective self and the intersubjective other. As in earlier writings, in his discussion of Mrs. M., McLaughlin uses the focus on her gestures to bring to the reader the analytic experience as lived. The focus on his patient's postural, gestural kinesics, and his interpretation of them, does make her self-conscious. While it leads to productive analytic work, we can see that it is never possible to make interventions without simultaneous iatrogenic ramifications. This aside, McLaughlin's attention to the nonverbal may provide a more direct pathway back to the preverbal period. His uncanny, incredibly acute attention to his patient's body–self and her associated affects, may have enhanced the patient's feelings of psychic human membership. Though his attention to her might have run the risk of making her feel physically transparent, that it, too, intruded upon and laid bare the overall effect of his tactful involvement seems to have created in Mrs. M. a much needed sense that she is not alone, could be understood in her misery, and that her mood could be attuned to by the analyst as an empathic intersubjective other. It is obvious that someone less skilled or less tactful could easily botch it (and I include myself in this group). I wonder what McLaughlin's experiences have been in teaching his approach.

It is appropriate that Marty Silverman's presentation is last because in his use of patients from both child and adult analysis we are given a welcome sense of unity. He demonstrates that infant observation may be useful in a patient of any age, but at the same time, he wisely cautions us against too much enthusiasm, echoing the warnings regarding the complexities and complications in developmental progression advanced by others, and the danger of reductionistic genetic fallacies. Just because something begins early does not mean it has powerful effects continuously throughout life.

Silverman provides vignettes from five patients, two children and three adults. It is interesting to note that the connections drawn between infant observational data and interactions in the analytic situation are not necessarily closer or more convincing with children than with adults, as one might have presumed. In fact, in the second child case he refers to, that of Ben, the nine-year-old child with learning disabilities, multiple anxieties, and great difficulty in separating from his mother, an understanding of the case is not dependent upon data drawn from infancy studies. The mother in the here and now is intrusive and controlling and overstimulating to the point were the pathology can be understood just from Ben's current interactions with her. Of course, we infer that she has been doing this all Ben's life, but, as I say, we don't even need to make such an inference to understand why Ben is unable to think for himself.

The other child case, that of five-year-old Anna, is much enhanced by an understanding of what transpires in the first year of life. But the most convincing demonstration to my mind of the usefulness of infant observation to the organization of subtle developmental material is in fact not with a child case at all, but with the adult patient, Mrs. E., whose mother, a fan of a sport that was linked to her dead father, withdrew periodically from her child when that sport season was in process. Silverman interprets the patient's failure to get what she needed from her mother in order to build up and sustain a secure, solid, firm sense of self, requiring a beaming face and an approving, encouraging manner from her analyst. Silverman states that Stern's experimental data in particular established for him an understanding of the functions required by the individual, these functions beginning in infancy and recurring throughout childhood, and, in attenuated form, into adulthood as well. Also, like others, Silverman notes that it would have been ineffective to reconstruct experiences Mrs. E. might have had during her first year or two of life, but it was helpful to point out to Mrs. E. her hypersensitivity to failure of affirming responses in the present. The pathology of Mrs. E. raises the question that was addressed by Scharfman in relation to the balance between insight and new-object corrective emotional experience. The sense I have when reading the excerpt from Silverman's treatment of Mrs. E. is that interpretation and insight were greater factors than some might anticipate with patients who exhibit such ego and self pathology.

In summary, in reading these excellent papers, I was reminded of something Anna Freud emphasized, the distinction between the reconstructed infant and child, and the actual infant and child. Her implication was that too often analysts are in love with their reconstructed versions and are made uncomfortable in the presence of the actual infant and child. This monograph, it seems to me, is dedicated to the proposition that we ignore the real infant and child only at our peril.

Chapter 11

The Value, Use, and Abuse of Infant Developmental Research

Harold P. Blum, M.D.

This very thoughtful series of papers provides a stimulus and information overload very much like the infant sometimes experiences, related to the exponential explosion of papers in the fields of infant psychiatric and psychoanalytic research. Infant research is identified with what "every mother" does; a mother attempts to make sense out of the communications and behavior of her infant. There is a long history of infant observation and formulations. John Locke, the seventeenth-century philosopher, assumed that the infant was a tabula rasa, born virtually without any individual proclivities or temperament. Kretschmer (1925) proposed the inheritance of psychobehavioral attributes and the determination of mental life by constitutional factors. Alas, the days of simple developmental theory are over and the field has grown ever more complicated and sophisticated.

Psychoanalysts developed their own developmental theory primarily because of their attempts to understand pathogenesis. Our initial framework, by today's standards, was rather simple yet quite elegant, still useful, appropriate, and pertinent. I refer here to psychosexual developmental theory with its progressive, linear, but hierarchical sequence of oral, anal, phallic phases through the

Oedipus complex, latency, adolescence, and to maturity in adult-hood. Pathogenesis was at first thought to be related to regression to simple fixation points. There have been references to psycho-sexual phase regression, and fixation in the preceding papers; for example, the obsessional patient with "anal fixations." Today we have added considerably to the original psychosexual develop-mental lines, but with much greater developmental complexity. The work of A. Freud (1936), Spitz (1965), Mahler (1967), and now of Sander (1980), Emde (1984), Stern (1985), and many others have brought new perspectives to both theory and therapy.

The intention of this series of papers is to assess the clinical application of infant research to work with patients. The assump-tion is implicit that there is clinical application. The title of the volume tends to favor, to accentuate, the positive in terms of applying the current research; it probably also resulted in the choice of authors (discussants included), who have a positive interest and investment in infant and developmental research. Multiple research interests and methodologies have flourished, with infants or infant–caregiver dyads of different age, sex, state, phase, and condition. Infants are in different states when asleep or awake, satiated or hungry, and much of the new research has utilized the state of quiet alertness. The research has been and promises to be of great value, but the serious limitations of method and mode of research, infant phase and state, interdisciplinary discourse, and levels of conjecture have to be kept in mind.

This brings me to one of the first controversies we have to consider, the use and abuse of research data. Several authors have sounded notes of caution, and I agree that we have to be cautious about applying the results of infant research, particularly research on the early preverbal period. Inferences from both direct obser-vation and preverbal reconstruction are at high risk. It is exceed-ingly difficult, even in analytic work, to be sure that we are discerning the persisting influences of earliest life and to feel that we can accurately reconstruct back into the earliest phases of life. The earliest phases invite the greatest speculation. Today, we attempt to reconstruct the onset of structural conflicts but also conjecture concerning the prestructural period, a time when structure is in the very process of formation. Infant research has great promise of shedding light upon the mysteries of structure formation and malformation, on developmental arrest, deviation, and deficit. These issues are of great current relevance to developmental theory and to the understanding of severe psychopathology.

I have singled out six underlying problems which figured in the course of discussion but were not made fully explicit.

1. The first I have already indicated: What is the value of the research itself, its relevance, its correlation, its meaningfulness for clinical work with patients? We can divide that problem into questions raised for theory: ego theory, drive theory, affect theory, object relations theory, and so on. The new knowledge of infancy colors, enriches, and informs our work. Conversely, the findings may be misleading or lead to misinterpretations.

2. Continuity versus discontinuity is a significant issue in clinical and developmental theory. Developmental transformations are actually new formations which were not previously present. We have reason to believe that there really is no direct line between early infancy and adulthood. The adult neurosis is not simply a continuation or replication of the infantile neurosis; we deal not only with continuities but with discontinuities as well. Genetic fallacies and adultomorphic fantasy can lead to misconstruction of the relationship between infantile and adult characteristics.

3. Another problem concerns the translation of biobehavioral studies into the psychological realm. There is an indistinct boundary in infancy between the biological and the psychological, but biological and psychological data and inferences are in different categories. Somatic forces and factors contribute reciprocally to the foundation of psychic structure and to later psychic conflict. Interdisciplinary studies may entail a "mysterious leap" between different domains of discourse in analytic developmental theory and biobehavioral research. We have to be very careful to distinguish different conceptual frameworks. Infants cannot really tell us about their inner life experience. We attempt to establish a balance between our observations of the infant's reactions and our hypotheses, but our knowledge of the primordial psyche is necessarily very limited.

4. Another problem concerns differentiation of the preverbal from the verbal dimension of infancy. Infancy was defined by Dr. Galenson as the first three years of life, but there are, of course, varying definitions. Certainly the first twelve months are quite different from the second year, and the neonatal phase quite different from three to six months. Before the advent of language and symbolic thought, with all its special developmental influence, we are confronted with the prerepresentational psyche. The preverbal sphere has been the locus of important constructs, e.g., basic trust, narcissistic and need-satisfying objects, and so forth. The nonverbal sphere encompasses elements from both preverbal and verbal development. Nevertheless, most forms of psychological treatment, derivative from psychoanalysis as well as psychoanalysis itself, are based primarily upon verbal exchange. We have to be particularly careful about the translation of the preverbal into the verbal. The degree to which the prerepresentational later achieves representation, and what changes it undergoes in the process, remains an open question. The accretions and alterations of later phases may render the earliest phases ever more inaccessible. How reliably can we retranslate into an understandable form what occurred in such an early phase of life? Earlier organizations may not be reinstated during periods of regression, and the alterations that occur with regression may not reflect normal earlier development. Yet traces and acquisitions may persist in various forms, such as confidence or optimism.

5. What is the relationship of normal development to deviant or pathological development? Is normal development continuous or discontinuous with developmental deviation or developmental arrest? Developmental potential and plasticity, the drive to complete development (A. Freud, 1965), and self-righting tendencies, are important for understanding later change, compensation, and correction. There has always been an important and valuable tension between attempts to formulate normal development and inferences drawn from psychopathology. From the treatment of patients we have often generalized to normal development, and that again may involve assumptions, such as those relating to analogy and continuity. There is no reason, ipso facto, to assume that the normal and the pathological are always continuous, or

closely related, as in such classic formulations as perversion being the negative of neurosis. There is no clear boundary between the so-called normal and the neurotic—everyone is neurotic. But this does not mean that all forms of psychopathology have no clear boundary from the normal. Assumptions have proven to be generally correct that certain forms of psychopathological difficulties are universal; everyone has symptoms; conflicts can be found in everyone's dreams and daydreams; and we always see the precipitates of such conflicts in character formation. Nevertheless, we have to be very careful about inferences derived from severe pathology. Such psychopathology does not simply represent fixation to, arrest at, or a particular version of an early developmental phase. Our reconstructions should be consistent and convergent with developmental knowledge and, at the same time, used as a test of each other. A major value of infant research is that it adds to, it amplifies, it supplements, and complements our reconstructions and our developmental hypotheses based upon clinical experience. Reconstruction and developmental knowledge are synergistic and interdependent (Mahler, 1971; Blum, 1977a).

Contemporary developmental knowledge helps to clarify Freud's pioneer reconstructions. The Wolf-Man witnessed the primal scene at eighteen months of age, and reported he had seen his parents having intercourse from the rear three times. It is extremely unlikely that a child of eighteen months, with a life-threatening illness like malaria, could see anything that discretely or in the correct sequence. Cohesive and convergent evidence for the Wolf-Man's primal scene preoccupation is apparent, suggesting overdetermination and the multiple perspectives that characterize contemporary reconstruction (Blum, 1980). Reconstruction can be more accurate, expanded, and deepened.

6. Finally, nature–nurture controversial issues reappear on new levels of complex interrelationship in object relations theory. The research we have been looking at has a number of special emphasis. The emphasis today, as compared to the pioneer days, is on object relations, on the interaction between the caregiver and the infant. In the early days, the infant's psychosexual development was assumed to be largely generated from within along a maturational–developmental timetable. New questions have arisen

about the significance of object relations for drive and affect differentiation and regulation.

The actual characteristics of the caregiver—attunement, empathy, consistency, and organizing influence—were hardly discussed in the past. Most of the difficulties that arose were seen in terms of trauma, with either overindulgence or deprivation. Analysts spoke of harsh weaning, harsh toilet training, and castration threats when the child was masturbating during the phallic phase. More subtle relationships came much later. Freud (1909, 1920a) reported pioneering studies of Little Hans and of his grandson's play. But there was no systematic research of early development until after World War II, and by today's standards, it was rather crude. René Spitz (1946b) observed hospitalized children suffering from maternal deprivation and discovered "anaclitic depression." Margaret Ribble (1943) and others were already implying that the child needed more than food—children don't live by bread alone—the child needed love, warmth, care, protection, comfort.

Spitz (1965) offered a brilliant formulation which stimulated analytic interest in the primary object relationship. Referring to Harlow's monkeys, he said what was missing was not simply warmth or the opportunity to cling to either the wire or the terrycloth mother. What was missing was reciprocity; a reciprocal reaction was needed. It was no longer an object relationship based upon the infant's gratification of sucking *and* of hunger and nutritional needs, the oral drive having an anaclitic relationship to the physiological need for nutrition. Now the psychological input from and to the caregiver was also important. This reciprocity was what was most human and humanizing. Current research on the human infant, summarized by Phyllis Tyson in the present monograph, indicates that the neonate is cognitively competent, stimulus seeking, and socially interactive—capable of reciprocal interaction with a great deal of subtle communication.

Spitz's initial formulation of reciprocity was crude by today's standards. It is true that it introduced the notion not only of feeding but of feedback; and of a constant feedback between mother and child, necessary for the child's further development on higher levels of organization. But the components of the

interaction—the components of the reciprocal process—were really not then recognized. Only hinted at in the concept of
"dialogue" were the mutual shaping, the reciprocal regulation, the
fact that the infant could not only initiate but also terminate some
of the exchanges: that the starts and stops represented a type of
precursor conversation between mother and child; that the very
foundations of verbal language could be seen in the early reciprocal communications. Today we have an idea of a much more
sophisticated, very complex type of interaction in which both
infant and mother regulate each other from day one. What
Mahler and Furer (1968) called "mutual cueing" refers to a
selective, organizing form of affectomotor communication. Infant
and caregiver have a capacity to read each other's signals. This can
eventuate in an early communications gap if there are special
problems of miscueing and mismatch. When there are multiple
caregivers, as is the case, for example, with day care, where the
child has to read signals from more than one caregiver, the infant
may be more or less ready to cue anew. The mother's tendency is
never to simply engage in mirroring her infant's cues. The match
of mother and infant varies over time with implications for
developmental process and, clinically, for therapist–patient match.
    What is mirroring, a concept suggestive of congruent reci-
procity? It is a term that is frequently used, but it is imprecise and
ill-defined. It is not simply imitation or empathic echoing by the
caregiver of the infant's behavior, though imitation is very important on the part of both dyadic partners. The infant has an inborn
phylogenetic capacity to imitate, hence the name "to ape" for
imitation. Imitation also reciprocally occurs on the part of the
mother. As the child opens his mouth, the mother will often open
her mouth. In the very process of feeding the child, there is an
ongoing reciprocal, primitive identification process. But "mirroring" involves something that transcends imitation or echo or
mirror imagery. When the child, who has an innate capacity for
intermodal transfer, signals the mother with activity, or with
speech, or with crying or fussing, the mother responds to the
child's communications in a way which not only "overshoots" but
which *usually* translates the response into a different modality.
This has been designated as attunement (Stern, 1985). The child

may talk; the mother may move. The mother may talk; the infant may move in synchrony with the mother's speech. I would propose that the crossover and linkage of different perceptual and cognitive modalities has something to do with the *tremendous* importance of integration in the human organism. The mother joins and invites integration from different points of view, and with different components of the apparatuses and of the responses which are organized by her. The mother's reciprocal advancing reorganization of her infant's cues and communications suggests formulations similar to those of Loewald (1960), Spitz (1965), Mahler (1967), Mahler, Pine, and Bergman (1975), and to the therapeutic reorganization of primary process to secondary process. In infancy there is an ongoing developmental process in which bilateral communications advance to higher levels of integration and organization. Analogous processes may promote developmental thrust in psychotherapy, and may be a silent influence in analytic structural change.

There is another important mirroring concept. An important dimension of mirroring concerns the mother's affirmation, her positive pleasure in what the child is doing and in the child's functioning. This has been discussed as the "gleam in the mother's eye," and Kohut (1977) has particularly emphasized it. The term and metaphor were used earlier in a related developmental context by Winnicott (1967), indicating the child's self-discovery in the mother's facial response to her infant. And we know today that development is indeed very much influenced by the mother's approval or disapproval of various developmental lines and tendencies. What the mother wants she will, to some degree, be able to facilitate, and what she doesn't want she may be able to inhibit. Her baby, with his own influence upon the object world, will be the child of that particular caregiver, or caregivers, the father also exerting influence.

What have we learned from this? We know the tremendous importance of the mother's fantasies, the mother's feelings. The caregiver has extraordinary potency to power development in various directions. But we know something else now as well; in the early literature, what was called "function lust," the child's pleasure in his own functioning, was really partly also the mother's pleasure in the child's functioning. There is a kind of synchrony between the pleasure of the caregivers in the child's functioning and the child's own, biologically predisposed pleasure in functioning—a genetic contribution. I would presume that this reciprocal pleasure in functioning is a major dimension of pleasure in mastery and motivation toward mastery. Without the mother's so-called "mirroring," or let us say without the mother's positive affirmation and pleasure in her child's functioning, impairment of function ensues, with a tendency toward developmental inhibition or deviation and, in extreme forms, developmental arrest.

I now return to reciprocity and its relation to object relations, affects, and drive theory. In a much more complex understanding of development, other forces and motivational systems than drives alone have come into focus. Affects and affective ties to objects coexist alongside and are very much interrelated to, and sometimes psychologically and even biologically inseparable from, the drives. The infant–caregiver relationship is an affective reciprocity, and without affects we do not have object relations or ego development. Affects have been subsumed under both drive development and ego development. Later, affects were assumed to also represent signals; for example, signal anxiety. Affects have importance to both internal and external object related communication. We do not yet have a comprehensive, consensual view of affects, particularly as a communicative–motivational–activating system. Anxiety, the affect so central to psychoanalytic theory and study, has a complex development with innate somatic, signal, and experiential referents (Emde, 1984; Rangell, 1984).

So long as affects were regarded as drive derivatives, particularly with a discharge function, their motivational goal-directedness tended to be somewhat overlooked. However, even in the early formulation, the pleasure principle was implicit. There was a tendency to repeat what was pleasurable and to avoid what was unpleasurable. Today we think of affects in a more complicated way. Following Darwin's (1872) lead, Tompkins (1962) and Izard (1971) have demonstrated that affects are linked to phylogenetic species-specific facial expressions which are cross-culturally understood. Mother–infant and doctor–patient pairs communicate affective exchanges all the time with circular translation and response. Affective ties–exchanges are extremely important in the "bonding" of mother–infant. The "match" of doctor and patient may be significant in certain cases as a factor in the therapeutic relationship. The primary object tie is not established purely on the basis of drives. Some affects are clearly drive-related, for example, the affect of anger and the drive of aggression. In the case of other affects such as shame or disgust, the drive connection is by no means so clear. There are at least eight or nine distinct, inherited affective facial expressions. Darwin became interested in the "evolution" of the infant, and kept a log of the development of his own infant, watching his son's personality evolve. Darwin drew attention to the fact that the facial expressions of animals—the growl, the scowl, the frown, and so forth—could be related to facial expression in human beings in a homologous series. The fundamental roles of affect and of human identity are intrinsic to the preference of human beings to be face-to-face in their social and sexual relationship. Early reconstructions of optimism, pessimism, poise, serenity, smugness, and other complex affect states and attitudes can now be integrated with direct infant research.

A whole series of questions has arisen in the preceding papers relating to these issues and to the tilt toward discussion of the mother–child relationship. There was very little discussion of constitutional factors; for example, the biological disposition of the child born with very low thresholds to anxiety or distress, the child who is not easily consoled or comforted, the hyperactive or the hypoactive child, and so forth. There was more stress in the discussion on the mother's capacity to respond to a particular type of child, and in the mix and match of mother and child. The discussion more often was on the mother's own particular way of relating, the impact of her fantasies and feelings on the child, and her pathogenic influence, for example, when she is not emotionally available, as in Dr. Lichtenberg's case, for the child's optimal development.

I have a series of questions for each of the authors. These questions will give us an opportunity to test the clinical application of what we have been hearing. I would like to go on with the discussion of theory, but at this point I am going to turn to clinical correlation.

First, let me start with Dr. Glenn's stimulating paper which brought up the application of Margaret Mahler's work and the great importance of the rapprochement phase for an understanding of the infantile neurosis. "Infantile neurosis" might even be a misnomer in terms of our definition of infancy because it mainly refers to a period after three years of age. How do we translate the rapprochement struggles that Dr. Glenn observed into their antecedents and into their influence and effect upon the Oedipus complex? An issue which was only implicitly stated was how do we understand the preoedipal in terms of the oedipal? There is an old struggle between those who favor a primary oedipal view and oedipal core of all neurosis, and those who view this formulation as correct but not sufficient. The latter group point out that there are antecedent preoedipal influences on the formation and resolution of the Oedipus complex. In sicker patients, the problems seem to be more rooted in the preoedipal period and pathogenically more closely related to the very beginnings of the personality.

Dr. Scharfman's paper raised a fascinating question of treatment variations, particularly with patients who have affect disorders. Dr. Scharfman's case sounded almost like it might be close to the category of "alexithymia" as described in the American and the French psychiatric literature. The patient could not recognize and express affects, perhaps had not differentiated his own affects very well. One could not tell if it was a developmental inhibition and arrest, or if the affects remained, to a degree, repressed. The technical question in such patients is whether face-to-face treatment is to be preferred to analytic treatment, where the patient does not see the therapist. This is not an issue in child analysis or child therapy which is face-to-face anyway, but I think it does raise a very important question about certain categories of adult patients. These patients might benefit from face-to-face therapy because of the presumed enriching effect of the affective exchange and the opportunity to identify with the therapist's normal affective responses. This issue is apart from the question of interpretation and insight. Could this "affect repair" become a therapy in itself, or would such treatment be extremely limited? Should such affect enrichment only be viewed as a preparation, a kind of preparatory psychotherapy for later, more insight-oriented therapy, if that were possible? Are there not patients for whom the relationship experience is the paramount instrument of therapeutic benefit?

Dr. Silverman gave us a repast—a banquet—of clinical vignettes, and I want only to refer here to a particular aspect which I would like to enlarge upon. That is the impact of the mother's fantasy system upon the adopted child. Dr. Silverman mentioned that the child had fantasies about the other parental set, the invisible double, the biological parents. We know that the images, the fantasies about the biological parents are mediated through the adoptive parents. If the child has never seen and knows nothing about the biological parents, the fantasies about them are a function of the child's own fantasy system; but they are also what is conveyed and communicated by the adoptive parents' knowledge of and fantasies about the biological set of parents. Some adoptees have the fantasy that the adoptive parent has stolen the baby from the biological set of parents. The child's fantasy of having been kidnapped sometimes turns out to be a fantasy shared with the adoptive parents. We need to consider the impact here of the joint set of fantasies that are seen in such situations where there is the sharing of the fantasy system between the mother and the infant. The same shared fantasy system is true when the child becomes frightened of separating from the adoptive mother, becomes threatened all over again with loss, having lost the biological parents; the adoptive mother assumes that the child will prefer the biological parents and will want to return to them. The adoptive mother becomes threatened by the child "deserting" her, especially if she feels guilty. She may unconsciously fantasize that she stole the child, and not truly regard herself as the parent.

This is an example of how infant research impacts upon our work with patients. We become much more aware of the importance of the mother's fantasies—not only from birth, but even from pregnancy and from her own childhood, including her expectations of some day becoming a mother. It reminds me of a situation where a mother was presented with her newborn daughter right after delivery and said, "She's ugly." That one comment was so portentous because, as you can imagine, it was rich in underlying meaning, in this case, unfortunately, a good deal of negative meaning, which impacted throughout all subsequent phases of development.

Another aspect of the fantasy system that has to be teased out at this point is the following: mothers are more or less adequate, as are children, in terms of a mix and match, at different phases of development. For example, a mother may be more adequate with a very active child during the first year or two of life and less adequate during the phallic–oedipal phase. Or a mother may be nurturant and better able to respond to an infant during the oral phase in the first year of life, and may be more strained and less responsive and attuned during the second year. When we talk about the impact of earliest life, we have to raise the following question: Do certain issues between caregivers and child express themselves continually throughout all of development? If a mother is coercive, feeding her child very rigidly by the clock, and requiring the child to sit on the toilet for hours until he defecates, does the coercive behavior continue in later phases? The same mother makes castration threats in the phallic phase and pulls the child's hands away coercively when he masturbates. A controlling, coercive, intrusive quality runs right through the developmental phases. Another mother may be far more responsive, empathic, and able to attune to the child's needs and is only out of sync, so to speak, during a particular period. We have to differentiate those two situations of strain: one continues throughout development while the other remains a phase-limited, specific strain. It is important to look at the match from the child's side as well, to recognize that a child may adapt much more readily during one particular phase than another.

Dr. McLaughlin's and some of Dr. Silverman's cases raise questions not only of conflicts, but of deficit. How much can conflict and deficit influence each other? Can early deficits be resolved or compensated for in later development, or in later childhood or adult therapy?

Conflict versus deficit is an issue that should be absolutely explicit because most of our clinical work, and certainly work in analysis, has been work with intrapsychic conflict, not with deficit. We do not know, as Dr. Scharfman was very careful to state, to what degree analysis can reverse early deficits, early developmental deviations, and arrests. Analytic work is primarily geared toward the resolution, at least the attenuation, of unconscious infantile conflict. Some deficits are related to conflict; for example, the impairment of reality testing because of the defenses of denial and projection. We can expect that such impaired reality testing may be reversible, at least in some cases, by the work on defenses and the attenuation of the conflicts connected with those defenses. On the other hand, certain children with impaired reality testing may have this difficulty on a constitutional basis. They are not prepared to invest in reality in the same way as other children, or they lack some of the underlying integrative mechanisms, and so on. The deficits may not be reversible. This is a whole area for further research.

One of the advantages of Dr. Novick's presentation is that it is graphically linked to current research. This research uses instrumentation not available to the early pioneers. Classic pioneer movies have been superseded by the simultaneous split video screen, by audio–video microanalysis. What is actually occurring is too fast for conscious perception but can now be observed, and not only in the infant. The researcher can screen and study the infant and the mother side-by-side at a moment which would be missed by the naked eye. We can see the child's smile being wiped off his face as the mother scrapes the child with the spoon. Similar electronic movies of abused children may have profound implications. For example, one can see the converse, a child in distress and discomfort, with psychic pain and also see a flicker of a smile on the mother's face. For just a moment, the mother is enjoying the child's discomfort. And one must also look for the opposite— the flicker of displeasure, the momentary irritation on the part of the caregiver when the child is enjoying himself or herself. The distress on the part of the caregiver when the child is having some fun is the mirror image of the pleasure on the part of the caregiver when the child is in distress or pain. These reciprocally paired responses alter the pleasure–pain balance, and they give us new food for thought about the role of these early influences in later development. Dr. Novick's case lends itself very readily to the examination of such questions because the patient, after a very primitive beginning but with the marvelous help he received, developed an organized beating fantasy out of the chaos. Based upon Valenstein (1973), Blum (1980), and Novick (chapter 2), I would say that the beating fantasy already represented a higher level of organization of his sadomasochism. The fantasied pain and suffering probably represented not only biological factors, not only an ego signal of distress, but also a dimension of the object relationship itself. Did the earliest sadomasochistic struggles, in the second or third year of life, and before the oedipal phase, contribute to the oedipal beating fantasy rather than representing oedipal regression? This case was a negative oedipal beating fantasy—the father was beating the boy over the buttocks; there was no question that the fantasy, by adolescence, represented a homosexual oedipal submission to the father. But what did the fantasy mean in terms of earliest life, and the reconstructions that Dr. Novick made concerning that particular child's development? Did that child's mother show, from day one, some degree of sadomasochistic involvement, perhaps too subtle for us to have surmised in the later clinical situation? There was some association of her pleasure in the child's pain in earliest life. The preoedipal mother disappears into the depths of later fantasy because it is the father–son relationship that underlies the final manifest content of the adolescent beating fantasy. Could we reconstruct the roots of that beating fantasy in the caregiver exchanges during the first years of life? We also want to be sure that we don't overinterpret and misinterpret the significance of the preoedipal period compared to the oedipal and later phases. If sadomasochistic infantile interaction between mother and child had not been continuous in later developmental phases, would it have been developmentally transformed and lost to any possibility of reconstruction in analytic work after childhood?

Dr. Lichtenberg's paper convincingly demonstrated the emotional deadness that can occur when there is a lack of reciprocity between mother and child. But, because he used an unfamiliar theoretical framework, I do want to ask if he would discuss his different viewpoint. He described pathogenic development in terms of the aversive responses of mother and child rather than in terms of traditional views of conflict. This was an overfed child, an obese child, with a "fed-up" mother who was probably offering the child inappropriate supplies. The mother may literally have shoved a bottle into the baby's mouth, feeding him in order to "shut the child up." His other needs were not attended to or recognized. One then deals with underlying rage and inappropriate need satisfaction, as well as wishes and defenses and potential traumatic fixation or developmental disorder. Unconscious infantile conflict and danger situations would be intensified under these circumstances. We did not hear about oral fixation, or narcissistic injury and demands, about defensive withdrawal, or pathogenic object relations and identifications. The analytic work did not seem to progress through traditional conflict interpretations. I wonder to what degree Dr. Lichtenberg thought that some of the early difficulties between that particular mother and child were based upon the child's constitutional tendencies to overeat, with a greater degree of oral need and greed based on physiological factors. To what degree did an early derailment of dialogue contribute to later intrapsychic conflicts?

Dr. Lichtenberg's reasons for his mode of understanding and his nonutilization of many psychoanalytic concepts should facilitate our comparison of different ideas about the influence of early development upon conflict and character.

Dr. McLaughlin's paper was a fascinating return to considerations of the relationship of psyche and soma, and the development of the body image and symbols. Dr. McLaughlin pointed out the role of kinesics, the use of posture and gesture, and how this can be viewed carefully, artfully, and also with a degree of appropriate caution so as not to overread these nonverbal communications. He felt that he could see derivatives of the earliest mother–child affective transactions in the posture and the kinesics, in the movements of this patient, in the way she separated right and left. I believe that right was masculine, left was feminine. We also know how often one represents good and one represents evil; one the superego and one the id, and so forth. That type of split also suggests a high degree of isolation, or dissociation, which may come from a later phase of development. When do right and left differentiations occur, and when do they acquire psychological meaning? When does the infant express such body representation in symbol and metaphor? I would like to know more about how the early tendencies coalesced with later developmental transformations and alterations. Can we be further educated about the process of decoding and inferring the earlier phases, given the overlay and reorganization of the later transformations? Right and left differentiation, and more complex splitting of the body image to represent opposites or paired conflict, is not within a one-year-old's conceptual capacity.

Dr. Galenson's paper is in an area of shared interest, and one of great importance for our understanding of pathogenesis, particularly of gender disorder. Homosexuality does not have a uniform structure, and there are different "homosexualities" which do not necessarily involve gender disorder. We learn in Dr. Galenson's case that separation traumata during the first year of life were of great importance. In this case a male child dealt with the separations by identifying with the lost object—a classical formulation. This was a kind of global identification with the missing mother, an attempted merger instead of separation and separateness. The separation traumata also contributed to the heightened aggression, the rage of the child, as well as the child's profound feminine identification. This child also experienced the problems of inconsistent parenting because there were a series of housekeepers and multiple objects with whom he had to cope. This case is probably quite different from the type of gender disorder in which we see the pathogenic influence of shared fantasies (Blum, 1988). In a subgroup of gender disorders, the mother with a rather exclusive, intense, and highly invested relationship with her infant conveys a feminine developmental orientation to the child. She conveys or indicates her reward, her appreciation, her pleasure in the child's interest in and identification with her feminine attributes. Such children, by the time they are two years of age, are walking in high heels and have a preference for mother's clothes. A preference has been transmitted by the mother to a child who is constitutionally compliant and passive. The mother rewards feminine interests and indicates her disapproval and devaluation of the masculine line of development. Her feminine cues and directives are internalized without her child being initially or necessarily traumatized. In Galenson's case, separation traumata led to massive maternal identification. There are different pathways to perversion, different homosexualities, and different routes and types of feminine identification in the male.

Galenson's work on prophylaxis extends from the work of Selma Fraiberg (1980). Early intervention is an area of great significance for primary prevention. Can we facilitate healthy development and constructive internalization by treating infant–parent pairs? Current infant research has sharpened and deepened our diagnostic and therapeutic skills. At the same time, early intervention with a case of intractable crying, feeding, or sleeping disorder, and so on, becomes infant psychiatric research with implications for adult disorder. The human infant is born with a brain which continues to grow and differentiate during early childhood. Human infants are particularly endowed to learn from experience; we, in turn, have much to learn from them.

Chapter 12

The Viewpoint of a Devil's Advocate

W. W. Meissner, S.J., M.D.

We have been privileged in studying these papers to read the thoughtful reflections of skilled clinicians regarding the impact of child observational research on clinical practice. The material has been clinically astute and sensitive, displaying, in a variety of forms, the ways in which knowledge of developmental vicissitudes plays a significant role in ongoing clinical work with patients.

It is generally agreed by analysts that the information gained from the study of infant behavior plays a significant role in the work of the clinical analyst. There is an unspoken presupposition that we have some notion of the way in which early infantile developmental vicissitudes play a role in later, clinically relevant, forms of psychopathology, including those of adults. The lines of connection between early developmental vicissitudes and later expressions of pathology and personality functioning are easier to establish when the time lapse is shorter. The developmental connections between infant and toddler are more immediate and closely interwoven than the linkage between infant and adult. As the time span lengthens, the connection between developmental features of different levels becomes increasingly obscure and difficult to define.

Psychoanalysis is essentially a developmental psychology; its

175

most powerful tools are its understanding of psychopathology and personality functioning at all levels of development. Even in the treatment of adult patients, psychoanalysts have never abandoned or retreated from their insistence on the necessity for exploring and understanding developmental factors and on gaining insight into the manner in which developmental factors have come to influence the patient's current life. To a large extent, psychoanalysis depends on the connections of predictability, transformation, and continuity between various phases of the developmental progression for the continuing vitality of that developmental perspective. In my role as devil's advocate, I will argue that all of these elements are uncertain and open to question. Predictions from infant or child observation to adult psychopathology or behavior have proven abortive. The hypothesis of continuity in development runs into rough waters and troublesome obstacles in confronting the obvious discontinuities between developmental phases. Also, it is not always clear how the various forms of psychological transformation, which are so central to the psychoanalytic perspective, can be justified on any more than heuristic grounds.

In carrying out my self-appointed role as devil's advocate I will pursue my agenda in three steps. First, I will address the issue of predictability, second, I will address the issue of developmental reasoning within psychoanalysis and discuss some of its conceptual difficulties, and, finally, I will offer some assessment of the approaches to the use of infant observation in psychoanalytic practice that have been offered during the course of the preceding discussions.

First, the issue of predictability. I can do no better in focusing this question than to cite Freud's observations on the issue. In 1920, he wrote:

> But at this point we become aware of a state of things which also confronts us in many other instances in which light has been thrown by psychoanalysis on a mental process. So long as we trace the development from its final outcome backwards, the chain of events appears continuous, and we feel we have gained an insight which is completely satisfactory or even

exhaustive. But if we proceed the reverse way, if we start from the premises inferred from the analysis and try to follow these up to the final result, then we no longer get the impression of an inevitable sequence of events which could not have been otherwise determined. We notice at once that there might have been another result, and that we might have been just as well able to understand and explain the latter. The synthesis is thus not so satisfactory as the analysis; in other words, from a knowledge of the premises we could not have foretold the nature of the result. . . . Hence the chain of causation can always be recognized with certainty if we follow the line of analysis, whereas to predict it along the line of synthesis is impossible [1920b, pp. 167–168].

Thus, Freud seemed to recognize the precariousness of prediction and seemed to rest the psychoanalytic case more on retrospection and a possible connection of continuity than on the capacity to predict from childhood to adult behaviors.

Freud's assessment has been reinforced, and to some extent qualified, by the results of a recent review by a Harvard group of researchers on the role of childhood development as predictive of adult adaptation (Kohlberg, Ricks, and Snarey, 1984). The report comes to conclusions which are not very encouraging regarding the issue of continuity or predictability. They conclude that available research does not support the continuity assumption, namely, the assumption that emotionally disturbed children are necessarily prone to become mentally disturbed adults. Psychoanalysts generally accept the theory that if nonorganic, conflict–defense types of psychopathology are formed in childhood, they become crystallized and result in a warping and malformation of personality which endures into adulthood as adult psychopathology. This theory is soundly refuted by this research. They observe further that the critical period model, in which forms of pathological deviation tend to become more rigid with time so that, by implication, they are more amenable to effective therapeutic intervention at earlier rather than later stages of their evolution, is also open to severe questioning. They claim, to the contrary, that genuine longitudinal studies tend to reverse the impression of earlier restrospective studies and seem to indicate that early childhood is not an important period for social and emotional development; rather, emotional deprivation, trauma, or conflict in this early period need not lead to irreversible damage to socio-emotional development or functioning.

Distinctions can be drawn regarding the bases for prediction. Predictions based on cognitive assessments are different from evaluations of emotional development. Predictability was maximal for measures of development that had a heavy cognitive ability base, as, for example, measures of I.Q. or moral judgment maturity, which tended to yield ten-year correlations in the 0.70 to 0.80 range. This may be due to the fact that cognitive traits are largely cumulative, sequential, and irreversible, as contrasted with affective traits and experiences which do not share these charac-teristics. Thus, the trauma theory of neurosis is in jeopardy from the lack of any solid evidence for irreversible effects of early childhood trauma. When emotional experience has enduring effects, it may be due to the fact that these sequences of emotional development involve cognitive–structural components, as would be stipulated, for example, in the cognitive–developmental theo-ries of Piaget, Werner, and others.

The case is much different for emotional disturbances than for cognitive deficits or behavioral deviations. Predictions fared considerably better in dealing with psychosis, where there is an associated cognitive deficit, or with forms of character pathology and sociopathy, where criminal, antisocial, or unethical behaviors are present, than it does in the area of symptomatic or character neurosis, where the disturbance is more restrictively emotional.

Assessment of these factors is severely limited by the lack of adequate data, particularly by the paucity of effective and well-conducted follow-up studies of child clinical populations and the lack of well-designed follow-up studies concerned with adult neurosis in contrast to adult psychosis or criminality. Within the limits of available data, the findings are not encouraging. First, they conclude that we have little practical ability to predict which children will turn out to be adult neurotics rather than well-adjusted adults. The behavior of children who turn out to be adult neurotics can be distinguished from the behavior of children who become psychotic or sociopathic, but cannot be distinguished from children who become normal adults. Second, children referred to guidance clinics for emotional problems without accompanying cognitive or antisocial problems are as likely to become well-adjusted adults as a random sample of the population. Third, cognitive defects and antisocial behavior in children can be accompanied by emotional symptoms, but inclusion of the emotional symptoms, in addition to the cognitive or antisocial deficits, adds little predictive power. Similar conclusions are reached about sexual problems in childhood. Kohlberg et al. (1984) write:

In summary, there are few basic data on the role of childhood sexual attitudes and symptoms as prognostic of later sexual pathology. The limited evidence suggests that insofar as deviant childhood sexual behavior is predictive, it predicts in the same way as nonsexual deviant behavior to deviant or irresponsible social behavior in adulthood [p. 131].

Along with cognitive factors, antisocial behavior is a singularly powerful predictor of later adjustment problems. Juvenile antisocial behavior is associated with psychiatric diagnoses of sociopathic personality, alcoholism, hysteria, and schizophrenia. Nearly all antisocial adults, along with other maladjusted adults, have a record of antisocial behavior as children, but many well adults also have engaged in antisocial behavior during childhood. In other words, almost no children who are free of antisocial behavior will become antisocial adults, but only a moderate proportion of children who engage in antisocial behavior can be predicted to become antisocial as adults.

Prediction based on the opposite behavioral syndromes of withdrawal and dependency behavior is by no means as clear-cut or decisive. Such children may be described as withdrawn, introverted, seclusive, or shy, but this behavior does not predict later adult maladjustment. There is no connection, for example, between patterns of withdrawal and later psychosis. Such children are unlikely to follow criminal or psychopathic paths and are no more likely to become neurotic than controls. Some studies suggest that children showing predominantly shy, withdrawn, anxious, or fearful behavior tend to find sheltered life-styles which emphasize stability and security, but, in general, their adjustment is as good as that of children in a random sample of the general population. Kohlberg et al.'s report concludes:

> In summary, the contrast between the predictiveness of anti-social behavior and that of behaviors on the withdrawal–over-dependent dimension is marked. Antisocial behavior predicts well and predicts on the level of "like is to like." In contrast, withdrawal and overdependency predict poorly, and their possible predictive value is not based on a prediction of like to like [1984, p. 143].

The conclusion of the review is sobering; the continuity hypo-thesis which states that emotionally disturbed children tend to be-come mentally ill adults, has received minimal or, at best mild research support. The report thus casts doubts on the prognostic or predictive merit of most clinical, psychiatric, or educational diagnoses of young children. Research *does* demonstrate that there is more change than constancy between childhood and adoles-cence or adulthood, as well as suggesting that there is greater constancy than change on the adult level. Recent evidence is also supportive of the notion of continuity between adolescence, early adulthood, and later adulthood.

There are two major exceptions to these conclusions regard-ing predictability and continuity from childhood to adulthood. The first is that some forms of schizophrenia in adulthood can be predicted on the basis of a biological disposition that can be discerned in childhood. The second exception is that tendencies to criminality and sociopathy are predictable from a combination of factors, including genetic endowment, familial environment, and the occurrence of antisocial behavior in childhood. The presence of intrapsychic emotional disturbance does not make any useful additional contribution to predictability in these cases. In view of this report, the question remains open whether additional refine-ment and extension of research methodology can gather better long-term data that will allow for better levels of prediction in these questionable areas.

The foundations of psychoanalysis rest on the retrospective dimension in Freud's view of the developmental process. The theory presumes that the roots of psychopathology are formed in the childhood years and the resulting defensive and conflictual warping of the personality is assumed to endure into adulthood in various transformations including adult symptomatology. The psychoanalytic approach regards the present as a direct derivative of the past. The infantile past is repeated in the psychic reality of the present. Beneath the facade of maturity and reason and adaptation, there is a hidden stratum of infantile motives and dispositions. The residues of various developmental states from earliest infancy through young adulthood persist and coexist within the mature man.

We have to face the fact that there are conceptual difficulties with this form of developmental reasoning. One reason, possibly, why Freud's observation about the ease of reconstruction and the impossibility of prediction rings so true is that there is in fact no chain of causation. Or, more conservatively, one might argue that the data do not support a causal connection or conclusion. Later forms of maladaptive personality functioning may not be the outcome of earlier deprivation, trauma, and conflict, but rather may simply be reactions to the current stresses of adult living and defensive conflicts. In this view prediction suffers because there is no cause-and-effect connection, and reconstruction becomes possible since one can always find earlier versions of later patterns and can retrospectively attribute causal significance to them. Genetic reconstruction is both seductive and dangerous, because it is so easy to attribute causal significance to what on a phenomenological level amounts to no more than structural parallels. A similar conceptual difficulty underlies the distinction in psychology more generally between correlation and causation. In psychoanalysis it is this difficulty that is often treated under the rubric of the genetic fallacy.

A second conceptual difficulty is the risk of overemphasis on phase-specific deficits and their connection with specific forms of psychopathology. By and large, the deficits and failures in the developmental process do not take place exclusively at any given developmental stage, but are distributed throughout the full range of developmental experience. The failures of parental empathy or traumatic deprivation are usually not phase-specific. While care-taking adults may have particular difficulties at different develop-mental stages, there is also a strong likelihood that difficulties of some sort or other will be encountered at various stages of the child's development. The mother who tends to be unresponsive to her infant's needs and affects and is unable to engage her child in playful interactions may also have difficulty in guiding her latency-age child or, further, in setting limits for her acting-up adolescent. We can all think of countless clinical examples of parents who have recurrent and repeated difficulties in dealing with the develop-mental crises of their children.

Developmental reasoning, however, searches for the earliest prototypes of any developmental difficulty. While this sort of ana-lysis can alert us to the earliest expression of particular difficulties, it also runs the risk of assigning disproportionate weight to early developmental levels, assuming a kind of fixation of the develop-mental process at these early points. Subsequent developmental difficulties are often referred back to the earlier prototypical stages. Early difficulties are assigned a causal weight, which in fact outstrips their actual impact on the course of development.

This difficulty arose particularly in the effort to connect borderline psychopathology with particular phases of the separation–individuation process, most particularly the rap-prochement phase. This early suggestion from Mahler (1971) became a fundamental aspect of the thinking of a number of theorists about borderline pathology, particularly Kernberg (1975, 1976) and Masterson (1976). It did not take Mahler long to revise her opinion and to retract her hypothesis. In 1971 she wrote:

> My intention, at first, was to establish . . . a linking up, in neat detail, of the described substantive issues with specific aspects of borderline phenomena shown by the child and adult patients in the psychoanalytic situation. But I have come to be more and more convinced that there is no "direct line" from the deductive use of borderline phenomena to one or another substantive finding of observational research [p. 415].

And again in 1977, she commented:

> In our assessments of the personality organization of narcissistic and borderline child and adult patients, the overriding dominance of one subphase distortion or fixation must not obscure the fact that there are always corrective or pathogenic influences from the other subphases to be considered. [Mahler and Kaplan, p. 84].

From this perspective, then, it has been questioned whether the severity of any given form of psychopathology reflects the impact of earlier developmental deficits so much as the depth and pervasiveness of the pathogenic disturbances. More important than parental failures to provide early nurturance and an adequately facilitating environment is a failure to provide the appropriate space and stimulus for psychological growth throughout the entire cycle of development from earliest infancy into adulthood.

A third conceptual difficulty has to do with the distinction between analogy and homology as heuristic components of scientific investigation. The distinction can be drawn in relation to biological processes. If we are trying to seek out a common denominator for diverse conditions as, for example, among various forms of addiction, such as addiction to cocaine, alcohol, or heroin, we can assume that knowledge of one addiction may provide a basis for insight into the others; and this would have heuristic advantages. But such an assumption may not be valid. Throughout the biological world, there are examples of species with widely separated genetic origins that have evolved similar behaviors and even similar organ systems. Such behaviors or organ systems are described as analogous. Though similar in appearance or function, they derive from separate genetic origins. Successful prediction from one such species to the other is based upon a similarity of environmental pressures rather than a common genetic origin.

Such analogies do not necessarily extend beyond the phenomenological similarities. The jealousy of the goose and the jealousy of humans are analogous behaviors; the analogous details are quite striking, but there is no common origin and consequently no necessarily common mechanism. In contrast, different organs or behaviors can derive from common genetic sources and develop out of common embryonic tissues. Such organs and behaviors are described as homologous, implying that they result from a common genetic origin in contrast to analogous organs or behaviors that do not. Since the embryonic origins of homologous organs are the same, knowledge of one of a set of homologous organs or behaviors almost necessarily has an important heuristic value for the study of others, even if they happen to be superficially dissimilar. The wings of bats, the flippers of whales, and the limbs of dogs and humans are all superficially quite dissimilar, but they are nonetheless homologous organs.

Applying this to the study of human psychological development, the question is whether later forms of behavioral or functional deviation in the adult are to be regarded as analogous to earlier forms of developmental or functional deficits in the infant or child, or whether they are in fact homologous. Can any conclusions be drawn beyond the simple observation of phenomenological similarity? Homology, it would seem to me, cannot be assumed, but must be demonstrated.

The last conceptual difficulty is the role of the baby as a "blank screen." The complexity, inconsistency, and obscurity, I might even say density, of the behavior of babies makes them quite suitable receptacles for the projected fantasies of observers and infant researchers. We are all familiar with the phenomenon of observer bias and experimenter expectancies in scientific work, the degree to which prior theoretical commitments can influence the process of observation. We are also all well aware of the fact that what we observe in babies is not only theoretically biased; it is also influenced by the cultural and social milieu that can change significantly with the passage of time.

The last difficulty we have to take into consideration is whose baby are we talking about? Psychoanalysis has been blessed with quite an elaborate array of offspring on which to base its efforts. When it comes to psychoanalytic babies, we have an embarrassment of riches. Freud's baby originates wrapped in a narcissistic cocoon out of which he only gradually emerges into the world of objects. In classical drive theory, he is driven by powerful instinctual forces, fantasies, and fears. He is torn between the powerful pulls of pleasure and pain, and his sensuality is dominated by the polymorphously perverse chaos of poorly organized sexual drives and impulses. The Kleinian baby is the victim of powerful destructive forces in the form of the death instinct, which must be countered, split off, and projected in a basically paranoid resolution. The Kleinian infant's world is divided into good and bad breasts, poisonous milk, good and bad internal objects, persecuting objects, destructful envy, and the constant threat of destruction of the inner world by bad internal objects. Kernberg's baby does not follow the Kleinian developmental time table, nor is it cursed by the Kleinian death instinct, but it too struggles painfully with early elements of oral envy and powerful aggressive drives which must be modulated, modified, and defended against if the child is to live. Kernberg's baby is forced into Kleinian-like struggles and defenses, primarily that of splitting, in which the infant's experiences are organized into all-good or all-bad images. The success of subsequent development depends on the difficult task of modulating the excess of unpleasurable and painful experience that is connected with this primary and primitive aggressive force.

Mahler's baby, much like Freud's, begins life wrapped in an autistic cocoon, out of which it only gradually emerges into states of infantile symbiotic dependence followed by gradually increasing degrees of separation and individuation. The Kohutian baby provides a striking contrast to these somewhat negative and aggressively tainted portraits of the infantile state. Kohut's baby is joyous, smiling, lovingly and happily interactive with the maternal caregiver, joyously caught up in the fascinating interaction of eye contact and mutual exchange with the empathic and responsive mother. Such a baby is a joy to behold, and his progression into the joys of development is impeded or corrupted only by the failures of his caretakers when they deny him the empathic nutriment that is required for his continued unimpeded development. The infant of modern observational research is likewise a *Wunderkind,* not seeming to be far removed from the Kohutian baby. He requires the same sort of basic environmental conditions and empathic parental responsiveness for his growth and development. It is only when these conditions are not adequately provided that tensions and difficulties arise and growth is impaired. While the Freudian or Kleinian babies are essentially troublemakers, driven by irresistible aggressive and destructive drives that clash with the external world, the modern baby resorts to aggressive alternatives only in the face of deprivation and frustration. When conditions are right, however, he responds positively and comfortably to the growth-enhancing inputs from his responsive environment. Rather than running into conflict with the demands of reality, this infant is preadapted and has the inherent capacity to elicit the appropriate responses from the caretaking environment. He is more competent, more active, more engaging than previously imagined. He is busy, almost from the beginning, in the process of building a core sense of self and engaging in the intersubjective realm of object relatedness.

Certainly, the array of psychoanalytic infants is stunning in its variance and in its contradictory emphases. It is not difficult to recognize the degree to which these varying portraits of the baby are saturated with theoretical suppositions, so that we can at least question the extent to which they involve a concretization of preexisting theoretical commitments. The issue is not so much a conflict of observations between various approaches, as it is an issue of what these observations mean and within what theoretical contexts they are to be interpreted.

In spite of all these problems and cautions the model of the baby can become an organizing metaphor for integrating our clinical experience and for devising a therapeutic approach. In particular, regressed and primitive material can be integrated into more coherent and intelligible patterns through the perspective of our understanding of infantile experience. Viewing the adult analysand in terms of the implicit child within often provides a perspective that allows us to make sense out of the analytic material. The image of Freud's baby, for example, allows us to understand the way in which the basic psychic life is torn in different directions by powerful conflicts, by wishful desires, and forbidding and threatening prohibitions, by situations of anxious danger and threat that arise in the inevitable clash between inner drives and outer realities. The modern baby, however, is seen more as the victim of developmental deprivation or lack. He requires the correct nutriments for growth to be regained and continued. Rather than the renunciation of infantile desires that is required of the Freudian baby, this baby requires nurturance, understanding, and the provision of previously lacking parental functions within the analytic matrix.

How does the developmental perspective enter into and influence clinical work? Not too many years ago (1974), the COPER Committee on Child Analysis addressed this question. It will be helpful to review their contribution which I will now summarize. The first emphasis is that the developmental viewpoint sees the disturbance in the patient not in terms of the medical model of a diseased entity, but as a functional disturbance which not only impairs current functioning but presents an obstacle to the further development of psychic structure and function in one or another developmental line. Treatment aims, therefore, at facilitating development and enabling it to proceed along all of its various dimensions. The purpose of psychoanalysis in this context is the ultimate enhancement and furthering of psychological development that has been impaired by deficits or traumata in the course of previous development.

The developmental perspective emphasizes the ongoing formation of psychic structure. Psychopathology is viewed as a form of psychogenetic or psychodynamic deviation from normal development, and this deviation is viewed as reversible, at least in part. Psychoanalysis does not treat syndromes so much as developmentally arrested human beings who have in some degree participated in the formation of their own pathology and, correspondingly, have the capacity to participate in its undoing.

Despite obvious differences in capacity and function at various developmental stages, development itself is a continuous process. This implies that even the earliest experiences, including those of the preverbal period, antedating the advent of conscious memory, enter into the determination of evolving psychic structure and function. The study of early development helps us to understand how such experiences and their derivatives can be represented in adult personality structure and functioning, as well as in the analytic situation and analytic material. While such early experiences do not achieve direct symbolic representation and may be concealed or reorganized in later developmental stages, our greater understanding of early developmental vicissitudes assists our understanding of their expression in psychoanalytic work.

The traditional psychoanalytic method is limited in its capacity to deal therapeutically with such preverbal issues, but this should not prevent us from deepening our understanding of these issues and from making the effort to develop meaningful psychoanalytic techniques for addressing them. The developmental orientation has already had noteworthy success in its application to the analysis of neurotic children. The diagnostic assessment includes an evaluation of the degree of development of ego capacities that are necessary for analytic work. Where such capacities are underdeveloped, the analyst can serve as an auxilliary ego in supporting the child's engagement in the analytic effort. Learning and identification with the analyst, together with ongoing development, allow many young children to then acquire these ego capacities and thus to fully participate in the analytic work. By the same token, the developmental approach has proven particularly valuable in the treatment of adult patients whose ego capacities are similarly lacking as a result of developmental arrests or severe and primitive defensive pathology (COPER, 1974).

A further point that has been urged by some of the authors of this monograph is the contribution that our increasing knowledge of infantile behavior makes to our capacity to respond empathically to our patients. Lichtenberg, for example, argues that, as we make progress in the refinement of what he calls "model scenes," and as they become increasingly congruent with actual infantile experience, we acquire a basis for a more sensitive empathic involvement in the intersubjective experience with the patient as it occurs in the unfolding of transferences and in the therapeutic relationship. Similarly, Lichtenberg argues that if empathic failures in caretaking have created a background of distrust or of traumatically determined pathological fantasy systems, can we then argue that empathy in the psychoanalytic situation is the means to repair this damage? He argues that empathy is the means to the means for repairing the damage. It allows the analyst to fully comprehend the analysand's meaning and thus provides the basis for meaningful interpretation. Empathic attunement between analyst and analysand not only echoes the earlier empathic attunements between infant and mother in the first year, but also makes an essential contribution to the matrix of relationship within which it becomes possible for interpretations to be given and received. We can question, of course, whether research into infant behavior is necessary for the attainment and implementation of such empathic responsiveness. Perhaps not. Perhaps analysts have always intuitively and instinctively responded in terms of such empathic responsiveness, but certainly the contributions of developmental research have made the bases and the understanding of the role of such empathy in the psychoanalytic situation much more decisive and precise.

There is little doubt in my mind that developmental research has had a significant impact on psychoanalytic theorizing and on the modification of technical emphases within the psychoanalytic process. The shift from Freud's baby, caught up in the vicissitudes of drive, defense, and conflict, to the modern baby, involves a decisive shift in both theoretical formulation and technical implementation toward an object relations model. The impact of the more modern view of the baby has brought with it a considerably greater emphasis on relational aspects of the psychoanalytic situation and on a more explicit and purposeful elaboration of object relations thinking in its application to psychoanalytic work. Scharfman, for example, emphasizes issues of the therapist's emotional availability and the role that the therapist's range of emotions might play. If developmental disturbances in the self-system are a problem, are such patients better treated face to face? To what extent should the therapist allow himself to express a range of emotional responses? What are the implications to be drawn from developmental knowledge with regard to issues of match or fit? The latter point was also focused on by McLaughlin. A parallel issue is the question of the balance between interpretation as opposed to relational factors as the vehicle for therapeutic action. The shift in emphasis points toward earlier levels of disturbance in significant object relationships that may otherwise elude interpretation. Certain more global patterns of individual responsiveness, where the means of relating and coping may not be accessible to change by interpretation, may be influenced by the relational transactions that take place within the therapeutic matrix. Even timely and apt interpretations may have their major burden of impact not from the content of the interpretation but from the relational context within which it functions. Lichtenberg, for example, cites Stone's opinion as follows:

> The interpretive function, I believe . . . has a tremendous primary transference valence, but only when linked by compelling unconscious associations, via a recognition of the impulse to help, to relieve suffering, with primary caretaking attitudes which give all early teaching its affirmative infantile significance [Stone, 1961, p. 63].

The emphasis shifts from what is interpreted to an understanding of how and why the interpretation works, and this involves greater emphasis on the qualities of the dyadic relationship discovered originally between mother and child.

An additional shift is from the oedipal to the preoedipal level, or at times more specifically, to the preverbal level of development. The preoedipal baby can be taken to antedate Freud's baby, or in terms of the psychoanalytic situation to underlie the oedipal dynamics of Freud's baby. But there is also an important theoretical shift involved, which has to do with the kind of past that is seen as relevant to the analysand's current experience within the analytic process. The most heated arguments in current psychoanalytic theorizing have to do precisely with the discontinuity of interpretation between these two divergent development levels. Particularly in the discussions regarding the treatment of narcissistic and borderline disorders, the issue of the relative impact of preoedipal as opposed to oedipal dynamics and the implications for the treatment process are hotly debated, controversial, and have by no means reached any secure degree of closure.

Several authors in this volume, perhaps most notably McLaughlin, have emphasized the link between early child and adult behaviors with regard to nonverbal components of the analytic situation. McLaughlin refers specifically to the Isakower phenomenon and various forms of postural and gestural kinesics. Such a view may have retrospective validity, but it is not at all clear on what theoretical terms it can be based. We also run afoul of issues of analogy versus homology as I have previously suggested. McLaughlin gives the interesting example of his patient's picking, plucking, and flicking at her clothing, hair, and eye glasses. He relates this to earlier childhood experiences she had previously discussed and comments that the patient must have felt picked on when her mother focused her critical attention on her. The problem with such an example is that there may indeed have been the implicit developmental connection, but we would be hard pressed to prove it. There would seem to be no reason, for example, that the patient could not be expressing a feeling of being picked on, derived from experiences in her current life situation, or even in her relationship with the analyst—even if one were to assume that the picking, plucking gestures were in fact expressing that mental content. We would have to forge a good many and somewhat stronger links between the earlier infantile fear of the mother's scrutiny and the picking behavior, or even some elements of the patient's self-critical grooming involved in the picking and flicking operation.

A further question that strikes me as particularly important has to do with the extent to which patients may or may not use the analytic situation and the relationship to the analyst to further the developmental process. This concern focuses particularly around the issues of internalization derived from the experience with the parent–analyst. We can ask whether such developmentally relevant internalizations do in fact take place, and, if so, in what manner, and how do they influence the developmental potential within the patient. What aspects of the analytic relationship become available for such internalization, and on what terms? What is it in the analytic situation that we might control that would facilitate such developmentally constructive internalization?

The authors of the COPER report (1974) addressed this question in rather unequivocal terms. The object of such developmentally attuned internalization is the analyst in his role and function as analyst. They comment:

The question does not refer to the idiosyncratic, personal qualities of the analyst which may be revealed despite the principle of anonymity, but to those qualities, attitudes, and values which are universal to all analysts as a part of the analytic method: empathy; understanding; belief in cause and effect, logic and reason; viewing behavior as determined significantly by past experience; belief in the dynamic unconscious; a non-judgmental attitude; non-reactivity; acceptance of drive representations and affects as needing to be tamed, not proscribed; and respect for individuality and autonomy with recognition of the fact of normal dependency. All of these are, of course, essential to the capacity for self-analysis which ideally continues after termination in all patients, and is of crucial importance in the analyst-to-be [p. 18].

They go even further, however, to focus the core developmental internalizations in the therapeutic alliance. They write as follows:

There is another facet to structure building through internalization and identification with the analyst. The child patient often makes developmental use of his analyst. The new (real) object relationship that the analyst provides not only mediates the therapeutic alliance but furthers structure-building experiences and ego and superego alterations. This same function is provided, though in a less easily discernible fashion, in adult analysis as well. This is particularly so in the case of the training analyst. His qualities, such as intellectual curiosity, capacity for empathic relationship, integrity, and a level of self-esteem are all evident to the candidate for evaluation and identification. The analyst serves as a model for structure of both superego and ego, and for attitudes toward instinctual drives. The candidate learns how to be an analyst in part through being an analysand himself and by identification with the analyzing function and professional commitment of his analyst. When the usual therapeutic understanding is complemented by a developmental orientation, the training analyst, and his candidate patient as well, may be better able to maintain the integrity of the analytic process and keep the therapeutic alliance consonant with working through, while the developmental process is also furthered [pp. 35–36].

The same viewpoint has been echoed in the present volume by Glenn, when he refers to the child's use of the therapist as a real object, and in Silverman's discussion of the reverberations of parent–child patterns of interaction as they occur throughout childhood and even adolescence, and the manner in which they play a significant role in the shaping of ego and superego development. He argues that the reconstruction of these interactive patterns in their expression throughout the formative years and their emerging evolution as the developmental process moves forward provide an effective basis for therapeutic insight and change. At the same time, he notes that efforts to reconstruct experiences in the first two years of life are more likely to be both unwarranted and clinically ineffective. By implication one might argue that a substantial burden of the potential for therapeutic change may in fact rest on the experience that the patient has with the analyst in his reconstructive effort, which not only does not repeat the pattern of interaction experienced with parental figures, but actually exposes the patient to a much more mature, mutually respectful, and growth-enhancing interaction.

I would conclude from this line of argument and from the uncertainties in the causal and predictive links between childhood and adulthood that the data from infant observation provides us with little more than organizing metaphors which both profess and explicate theoretical orientations and convictions more securely than they reflect any identifiably real and specific vicissitudes in a given patient's childhood history. At times our knowledge of infant development can help us in the task of reconstruction, which only exceptionally attains the status of verifiable veridicality, but which almost always serves as a basis for plausible integration that is sufficient to serve the purpose of therapeutic modification. Thus, I would argue that while the data of infant observation has a role and function in the channel of interpretation, it may simultaneously have a more powerful and persuasive impact along the channel of the analytic relationship and its vicissitudes. To my mind, the data of infant observation bring into focus aspects of the interaction between child and caretaker at many levels of the developmental experience which serve as hints toward a more precise understanding of what is involved in the psychoanalytic relationship. Infant observation provides an avenue of understanding of those interactions between analyst and analysand that can elicit and facilitate developmental potentials in the toddler, in the latency-age child, in the turbulent adolescent, and in the continuing developmental struggles of adulthood. Our increasingly refined understanding of these aspects of the therapeutic relationship increase the effectiveness of our therapeutic efforts and maximize the potential of the analytic situation to support meaningful therapeutic change.

Chapter 13

The Significance of Infant Observations for Psychoanalysis in Later Stages of Life: A Discussion

Leo Rangell, M.D.

From the beginning, psychoanalysis has aimed its method toward uncovering the past to explain the present. It has never sought, nor even permitted, direct methods to ascertain previous history, since past events as filtered through the mental apparatus of the particular patient were the subject matter under exploration. Analysts do not welcome diaries, or other "proof," nor invite parents or siblings into the treatment room to provide the "real" evidence. Some analysts even eschew the taking of an anamnesis, which they feel might start both the patient and analyst in a wrong direction, or at least a restricting one, by allowing actual events and history too important a role.

These aims and concerns are in line with Cooper's opening statement that analysts are interested in psychic, not material, reality. It was Freud's discovery of the overriding importance of psychic reality, a milestone comparable to his discovery of resistance or transference, that led to the shift of etiological interest from seduction to fantasy. It was trauma "felt" (i.e., affectively experienced), with its cognitive ideational accompaniments, that was pathogenic, whether or not an event actually occurred. Fantasy was as often pathogenic as external occurrences.

Freud did not abandon his original insight into the frequent pathogenic significance of seduction when he became aware of the more common dynamic of inner fantasy. He saw that internal and external are aspects of one continuous interaction. Each can both reflect and be initiated by the other. Material and psychic stimuli have equivalent and predominantly combined operational and causal effects.

All of this is by way of introduction or background to the question posed by this monograph: What, if anything, is the relevance of the new infant observations to the theory and practice of psychoanalysis? We have been treated to an array of new, directly observed data, original "facts," we do not see or come to in the retrospective views of psychoanalysis. Some analysts consider this the tapping of a valuable resource. Curiously, these often include the same analysts whose theoretical convictions preclude being influenced by facts or historical reality. What are the relationships of these new facts of observation to the psychoanalytic pursuit?

How much and in what ways does knowledge of the facts, of the earliest observable origins of behavior, help in reconstructive psychoanalysis, at any later age? The answer is the same as the response to the question posed about the relative roles of fantasy and external trauma in neurosogenesis. In both instances, the background "facts" do and do not influence the process and the outcome. The events, the origins, the sources, the "real," are simultaneously both relevant and irrelevant. Is this solution to a dilemma or conflict a surprise to any analyst?

How do these seeming opposites both apply? The "no" has been stated: psychoanalysis centers only on psychic reality, not external reality. Some analysts insist on this. The "yes," however, is the opinion gradually registered in the unconscious of the analyst, as in the patient, of the actuality of events or conditions. McLaughlin states that his knowledge of rapprochement phenomena improves the precision of what he observes and understands. Every patient presents to every analyst information about his specific separation–individuation experiences, his oedipal life, anal conflicts, and earlier oral phase. The analyst builds up a memory bank for each patient's life which comes to include the analyst's version of the ratio of seduction versus fantasy and inner versus outer, during all stages of the developmental process. He utilizes and calls upon these unconscious cognitive constellations as they are built up and modified by continuous analytic experience with the patient. Through his analytic instrument, which includes conscious and unconscious strata, he fashions and formulates the patient's life history, communicating and sharing this process with the patient.

All of the contributors to this book, each in his own way, has answered the major question of the symposium in the same overall manner. Knowledge of infant observations is undeniably useful. Its application to the immediate analytic process, however, needs to be treated with caution. The patient has a right to, in fact a requirement for, individuality. What is known in general cannot be imposed specifically, automatically, and routinely to the individual patient. While the knowledge gained is universally applicable, it must be administered in accordance with analytic principles.

For some this means it can be transmitted only indirectly, for example, through the transference, in the here and now. The age of the patient has little to do with the principle being discussed as in the case of Dr. Glenn's young patient. The strength of primary repression and the closeness to oedipal and infantile anxieties can keep the connecting paths as closed in a child as in an adult patient. Analysts of children, adolescents, and adults agree on the undesirability of confronting the patient, at any age, with what the analyst knows, without the analytic ego of the patient having initiated the links to the material, or being accessible and in readiness for it.

This applies to the new data being discussed in this book, however stimulating it is to the practicing analyst, and however it seems to have been confirmed and convincingly added to the analyst's intellectual armamentarium. The child of three to five (Scharfman's, Glenn's, Galenson's) does not have easier access to infantile experiences, which have undergone primary or secondary repression, than does the older person, adolescent, or adult. A qualitative barrier exists and seems to be the same throughout life.

The young child in fact has less equipment to understand, absorb, or utilize such connections. To bridge from the present to the buried past requires special development of analytic ability and motivation. Not just a special age but a special patient is required.

For the patient, the goal is to connect the present to the past via insights won, and with connections available for the patient's ego to affectively absorb. It is well to remember that no analyst has been without knowledge of the infantile past since the advent of psychoanalysis. The connections have always been made by tunneling from one to the other, from the current analytic age to the past etiologic years. The principles and problems which underlie the process of making connections to any etiologic period in the past are the same. What is now added about the neonatal past confronts the same problems, though to a quantitatively higher degree, than do any other stages.

From the point of view of advances of theory, the path from observation to theoretical understanding does not follow automatically, or with methodological certainty. There is nothing in current findings at this earliest period which qualitatively alters the status of general psychoanalytic theory in one direction or another; they neither confirm nor disprove previous theory. If Stern (quoted by Tyson) feels he makes his observations "unencumbered" by theory, by the same reasoning he can feel equally unencumbered in observing the analytic patient. Or he can be guided by theory, of his own choosing and preference, in both sets of observations.

Theory does not follow automatically from observations. It needs to be constructed and tailored to best fit the observed data at any age or level. The new observations do not confirm nor do they invalidate structural theory, or self psychological or object relations theory. One could equally say that Stern is observing "the dawning ego," as Greenacre (1941) postulated about the same period, and that his observations confirm her theorizing. Or with Kohut (1971, 1977), that he is observing evidence of an early developing self, or with Winnicott (1953), and Fairbairn (1954), that the infant is relating at this early stage to an apperceived object. Stern (1984, 1985) bringing our attention to an early active agency is consonant with my (Rangell, 1955, 1963a,b, 1969, 1971,

1986, 1988) having uncovered the fact of unconscious ego choice, of active secondary process ego operations in the unconscious, which is as new, theoretically, in the adult as the current findings of the infancy observers. In fact, these adult observations have been viewed with as much resistance and surprise as Stern's novel, yet convincing, neonatal observations.

Changes in theory do not come automatically. Scharfman discusses the erroneous theory that consideration of preoedipal factors not only leads to object relations theory but also convincingly demonstrates the need for specifically responsive corrective emotional experience in analysis. Scharfman correctly anticipates the objections elicited by the analytic technique of supplying the "missing ingredient" of empathy and emotional feedback. This theory and technique was strongly suggested and equally questioned prior to the new infant observations. These observations do not automatically make a case for the correctness of the view, long held by some, that the analyst should supply what might have been missing from a parent. If empathy is indicated, it is not because of these observations.

While I have stressed the centrality of psychic reality and agree with the universal role of narrative truth (Spence, 1982a,b) I am one who still believes that "what happened on the staircase" (Kris, 1956) has relevance in reconstructing a life history. It is hardly possible to diagnose a delusion, or distortion, or a borderline state without some assessment and appreciation of the actuality. Only when superimposed upon a reality platform can one assess a patient's reaction to events as well as his input in eliciting them. Anna Freud (1976) said that the ego can only do something about what it did, not what was done to it.

The comprehensive summary presented by Dr. Tyson serves as background for the psychoanalytic experience against which the subject of these discussions can be tested.

Tyson's paper shows the difficulty of creating revisions of basic theory from infant observations alone. The substitution of affects for drives as primary motivational forces, as suggested by Stern, Emde, Bowlby, and supported by Cooper, has also been postulated by Kernberg (1975, 1976) from adult analyses rather than child observations. The same alternative theories, stemming from data of earlier or later stages, will be tested by the validity of their total explanatory scope and accuracy.

Another major revision of theory, noted by Tyson, is based upon a broad organizational model as an alternative to the classical model rooted in drive theory. "System" is favored over "structure," and is considered more of an ongoing process than the latter. Such a model, Tyson states, would be characterized by change and plasticity rather than stability, and is consonant with the emphasis of current research on the activity of the infant as compared with a previous view of the infant as "a passive recipient of maturational determinants and environmental forces." I am perplexed by what I consider misinterpretations of classic explanatory psychoanalytic theory in which neither stability nor passivity are emphasized. Freud's instinctual drives were always striving, active, and object-seeking. Tyson's description of the complexity and instability of system theory is no more complex or in keeping with the diversity and unpredictability of life than the classic psychoanalytic intra-psychic sequence I have described. It is the opposite of static; it is in a constant state of flux, instability, and change. The new model she describes is our old one, complex, multiple, kaleidoscopic.

The "electronic revolution" referred to by Tyson, which has resulted in more detailed direct observations of the most minute somatic changes and processes, cannot detect the contents of psychological impulses or motivations, nor prospectively the effects these will have in the future. It still requires a leap over uncharted ground—the somatopsychic synapse—to interpret from somatic event to the mind, or, for that matter, from the mind of the infant to that of the adult. I am reminded of Freud's statement that a man standing on the shoulders of a giant can see further, unless he is blind or has defective vision!

Galenson's interesting and convincing theoretical–clinical paper responds to the repeated assertions, both by direct observers and analysts, that theory stifles. She demonstrates the advantage of "knowing and understanding"; that is, of having in one's possession a theoretical framework relevant to the clinical phenomena. The framework is the result of her own and Roiphe's (Galenson and Roiphe, 1974; Roiphe and Galenson, 1981) hard-won experimental and observational efforts. The clinical handling demonstrated here is a microcosm of the macrocosm of a more complete analysis at any later age, and of more complex clinical phenomenology. The distance between the data and the explanatory formulations are close and, most important, are within the grasp of the patient's ego. Felicitously, despite the anxiety and the resistance, they also happen to be syntonic to the supporting milieu.

Jules Glenn also deals with a three-and-one-half-year-old child. The treatment of such young prelatency patients demonstrates what is applicable, in principle, at any age, but in a more complex and more sophisticated way at later periods in life. Glenn points out the advantage of having as much data as can be made available. He benefits from and freely uses Mahler's observations on separation–individuation in the second year as well as on symbiosis from five to twelve months. He grants that the earlier infancy observations of Stern are equally valid as a theoretical framework and cognitive guide for the analyst. However, Stern's work does not invalidate Mahler's, and each can only be used when the data observed and the readiness of the child patient make such knowledge, and interpretations based on them, applicable.

In this case, the Mahler material became actually utilizable and ego syntonic. This occurs, Glenn feels, not by reconstructions, which, especially in this analytically oriented psychotherapy, would have been inaccessible, but by the transference interaction providing understanding and necessary support. He provides many cogent examples of current dynamic moments when this was possible. On the other hand, Glenn feels, correctly, that to have utilized Stern's observations of the earliest postnatal period for cognitive communications with this patient would not only have been useless but also antitherapeutic. This last point can be kept in mind as a principle in analytic as well as psychotherapeutic procedures at any age.

Scharfman also discusses a child between the preoedipal and the oedipal phase. While stating that knowledge of infancy helps, Scharfman also cautions against automatically applying direct observational knowledge of infancy to later analytic situations, even in child analysis. Not only is interpretation itself sometimes ineffective compared to a transference experience with a traumatized or deprived child, but interpretation without proper linkages or ego readiness is all the more inappropriate and antithetical to the analysis.

As Scharfman points out, many analysts feel that when infant observations are applied to the conduct of an analysis, they favor a self or object relations theory and a type of corrective emotional experience. In these cases, a "new relationship," often debated among analysts, is felt to be necessary and desirable. Scharfman then cautions against this recommendation. An analyst must be what he is; a warm analyst cannot act (i.e., role-play) as constricted, and a cold or controlled one cannot put on a warm look or attitude which is not his own.

Again we must question whether the new empirical infant data alters the analytic prescription in the conduct of adult analyses. Many previous authors (Escalona, 1953; Brody, 1956; Spitz, 1959; Benjamin, 1959; Mahler, Pine, and Bergman, 1975; Brody and Axelrad, 1978; Fraiberg, 1980) have described how, from its earliest origins, progressive ego development takes place, in conjunction with the developing self and early object relations. We have always thought that later pathology runs genetically back to the earliest stages. Within the framework of this general, theoretical, working guide, our theory of therapy espouses an analytic attitude which has always been complex, as well as easily misunderstood and misapplied. Our theory of therapy is always what Scharfman describes in his case; the therapist cannot change to become more affective or warm or giving in certain cases. The effective analyst is always analytic, i.e., objective, *and* warm, giving, appropriately affective and natural. To be seemingly distant most of the time, and then add warmth or an affect appropriate to the moment, usually indicates the kind of difficulty Scharfman describes in his teaching experiences with young residents or therapists.

Scharfman brings up several interesting and stimulating points which relate to an area of my own analytic research. He quotes Emde's (1984) discussion of the affective core, and cites the importance of his patient watching the analyst's face. He suggests the reverse as well, perhaps analysts should see their patients' faces. My own work (Rangell, 1954) on the face, the snout, and the perioral area as "the window to the emotions" and to the somatic and psychological "human core" (Rangell, 1967) is consonant with the findings of Brazelton, Koslowski, and Main (1974), Sander (1978), Stern (1984, 1985), and Anders and Zeanah (1984). Further, that the infant from birth on is not a passive but an active agent, appropriate to the developmental stage, is confirmatory and synchronous with my work on the active ego and its directing functions. These active ego functions have been as much submerged in theoretical discourse about adult life as they seem to be novel at the very earliest stages. Emde, in his studies, describes active ego affective functions akin to drives. This too is reminiscent of the previous works of adult analysts, such as Hartmann (1939, 1950) on "ego drives," Hendrick (1942) on the impulse to mastery, and Karl Buhler (1951) and Charlotte Buhler (1954) on function pleasure or pleasure in function.

Novick, moving the discussion to the treatment of the adolescent years, asks himself an interesting question: What did he do analytically before knowing about the current wave of infancy research? He reports a clinical case, then asks what he would do differently now. The patient was a severely disturbed pubertal boy, analyzed from ages eleven-and-one-half to eighteen, with classical and florid symptoms of obsessive–compulsive disorder. Because of "atypical ego development," the diagnosis was changed from neurosis to borderline. I have always wondered what "typical" ego development would be in this or even milder cases? The fact that there was drive discharge as well as defense was not atypical but is characteristic of the ambivalent two-pronged symptomatology of this syndrome.

More important, what effect did the more severe diagnosis, which carried with it the implication of a very impaired mother–child relationship in earliest life, have upon the course of the treatment? Did Dr. Novick become more open in his affects? Did he gratify more, reveal more affects, become supportive, less objective, less analytic? I feel that none of these took place, but that an analytic stance, with the required humanism and affective support, was evident at every point of the analysis, both before and after the change of diagnosis. Novick withstood the severe aggression, trying to maintain necessary limits, permitting revealing material to emerge which could then be treated by interpretation. The transference was the vehicle for this approach. The content of the past became evident to the analyst through his subjective transference experience of the patient's psychopathology.

What would he do differently now, Dr. Novick asks. He would not terminate the patient when he did or as forcefully as he did but, instead, would analyze the patient's "addiction to pain" more thoroughly. However, one might ask whether the analyst's timing of the termination was due to a lack of knowledge of infancy, or to a miscalculation and misdiagnosis of the patient's dynamic issues at the time of termination. I think the latter is more likely. (The treatment issues are reminiscent of those of Kohut's Mr. Z. [1979].)

However, just as a patient can improve with inexact interpretations (Glover, 1931), so did the analytic work already achieved allow the patient to overlook this lapse at the time of termination, and to consolidate the gains he had made sufficiently to compensate by unconscious analytic work of his own. His prognosis was good. The outcome also seems to confirm the fact that the original diagnosis of neurosis was more suitable than that of borderline or possible psychosis. In this respect one would wonder about the "delusion of omnipotence." Magical thinking, yes, as in any typical obsessive, but delusional thinking is doubtful.

This well-conducted clinical case demonstrates a point I have always stressed. It is preferable to err in the direction of applying the straight analytic technique to severely neurotic and borderline patients than to use parameters of technique with benign or more severely afflicted neurotics. I once stated (Rangell, 1956), at a time when borderline meant borderline, not just any demanding case, that the analytic attitude is more of a safeguard in a borderline patient, whose hold on reality is wavering, than it is in a structured neurotic condition where the hold on reality is more secure. The analysis and the analyst provide a line back to reality for the severe obsessive neurotic, with one face of his ego looking outward, and the other toward further regression.

Novick quotes a number of authors to the effect that the "revolution in infancy research . . . utterly refutes" Mahler, Kernberg, Klein, as well as Freud's "image of the infant as a passive receiver of oral supplies." I find such claims to be a straw man with clay feet; they are hardly credible as well as regrettable. More important, such opinions percolate down to "the average analyst," who will eagerly follow his leaders. How many times and how regularly will a good piece of work discredit itself by having to discard equally good work which preceded it? It does not do credit to current research to tolerate such views.

As I pointed out in my discussion of Tyson's presentation, Freud never thought the infant was "a passive receiver of oral supplies." The outward thrust of drives exists from the beginning. I have previously noted the many significant contributions to our understanding of the earliest active ego. Among these, to reemphasize their centrality, Hartmann wrote decades ago about constitutional ego apparatuses, ready to exert their active effects, and of "ego drives," present from infancy and before (innate, even evolutionary). Ives Hendrick wrote of the instinct for mastery, the Buhlers of pleasure in function, existing from infancy onwards. Spitz and Cobliner (1965) in their careful descriptions of the early organizers of behavior spoke to the same effect. I have elaborated in many writings upon the active functions of the ego in directing and influencing human life. An awareness of these functions as existing in adults is as frequently repressed as the complexity and competence of infants is obscured or camouflaged. It needs the lifting of repression among analysts themselves to admit the active role of the unconscious ego, a finding which is complemented, not counteracted, by the demonstration, in this new research, of these effects from earliest life onward.

The findings of Stern in the 1970s and 1980s enhance and are synchronous with the observations of Mahler in the 1960s and 1970s, on primary autonomy and hatching. The observations of Mahler, and of Mahler and McDevitt (1982), on early biological and psychological sequences, enhance and expand the observations of Spitz, and of Benjamin, in the 1940s and 1950s, of Erikson (1950), of Winnicott (1953) on mutuality and reciprocity, and of Piaget's (1924) cognitive–intellectual studies as well. More currently, such works as those of Herzog (1984) on the infant's need for the father, of Anthony (1984) on the active role of the infant in influencing his surround, of Lebovici (1983) and his group in France, and of Perez-Sanchez (1987, personal communication) in

Spain, confirm and expand the works of Stern, Mahler, and their predecessors who opened the path before them.

Silverman shows, in his analyses of both children and adults, how knowledge of all developmental levels routinely and reciprocally interacts with data gained during the course of an analysis. The problem is the same in the analysis of children, adolescents, and adults, to connect the present with the etiologic past in a manner which facilitates insight into both past and present and into the connections between them; further, to make the patient's own analytic ego able to absorb the insights, and from them to gain the ability for self-improvement and continuing self-analysis. The knowledge which Silverman uses routinely, built into his analytic instrument, comes from his analytic knowledge of the oedipal period, of the entire preoedipal period back to infancy, as well as the postoedipal periods of latency, adolescence, and beyond. From all of these phases, united into one ongoing continuity, Silverman surmised mother–child interactions in infancy, convincingly documented and described in his patients from childhood to adults in their forties.

Yet Dr. Silverman properly pointed out in all instances how inappropriate and ineffectual it would have been to make connections beyond the capacity of the ego to acknowledge and affectively absorb them. Reductionism and the genetic fallacy were to be routinely avoided, at the peril of rendering the analysis academic and easily defended against. This applies especially to material concerning the first and second years of life. Infant observations are valuable; of this there is no doubt. They should be used appropriately; this should be routine. As has been true since the beginnings of psychoanalysis, the inappropriate use of analytic knowledge produces a caricature of the analytic position.

In Silverman's recapitulation of the use of observational and clinical data, one sees his understanding of infancy in terms of the beginnings of drives, ego maturation, awareness of self, and object relations, that is, in terms of the total existing psychoanalytic theory. New theory does not emerge automatically or in a proven way from the new early observational data.

Lichtenberg presents a clear and convincing report of how he, as an analyst, works and thinks. His paper demonstrates that early infant observation cannot be separated from consideration of comparative analytic theories. As the background orientation through which he filters his clinical data from the analysis of children and adults, Lichtenberg presents the complex theoretical system he has personally evolved. It is not the purpose of this discussion to analyze and compare psychoanalytic theories; a proper integration of Lichtenberg's intricate theory with the material of this monograph would need special attention to do this justice. To briefly seek common ground, his five motivational–functional systems include all that I require to explain observational data. These factors were present in my own total evolved psychoanalytic theory prior to Lichtenberg's version of self psychology.

Thus, Lichtenberg's sensual–sexual pleasure system is our id, his exploratory–assertive functions, our ego psychology, his aversive motivational system, our anxiety mechanism, and his declared need for intimacy, our object relations. (In a previous work, [Rangell, 1985], I made a similar comparison between Fairbairn's new theoretical system and cumulative, evolved psychoanalytic theory.) All the necessary and sufficient divisions are there, under different labels and formulations. Lichtenberg sees the ability to enter and confront and negotiate controversy as a maturational gain when positive feedback enables the personality to achieve a position of security and satisfaction. Perhaps what I have just said about our comparative views will enable us to both embark upon and discover resolutions in the play of controversy.

In his analytic case report, Lichtenberg presents his interesting dynamic and productive analytic experience in terms of the theory which he has sketched in for us as the background. This can no doubt be done equally as well with the interstructural conflicts recognized by Freudian psychoanalysis and exposed in the analytic process by the equidistant stance recommended by Anna Freud (1936). Lichtenberg's explanation replaces these concepts and techniques with his five motivational systems.

I found of particular interest his description of the fate of altruism, its inhibition or its joyful development, either upon liberation by analysis, or better still from optimum initial growth and development. These thoughts apply not only to the so-called structured neuroses but to all psychopathology which, in every instance, consists of a combination of deficits (as well as special talents) and intrapsychic conflicts which have overtaken them.

Cooper describes his appreciation and improved functioning as an analyst as a result of knowledge derived from direct observations of infantile development. Cooper adds this to the body of knowledge analysts have acquired from the experiments and observations of Harlow, Bowlby, Robinson, and Engel. I would add Spitz, Benjamin, and others who predated the modern observers. The former have not come upon the field de novo. As Novick indicates, the tradition of such interest and observations has existed from the onset of psychoanalysis, and with increased vigor from the 1930s and 1940s on.

Although Cooper points out that the analyst's primary interest is in psychic reality, he adds the thought that knowledge of material reality is the bedrock of the analyst's armamentarium, and plays a significant and realistic part in the composition of his analytic instrument. This is no different from stating that biology is the bedrock underlying psychological reality. Both pairs also share the quality of reciprocity in that the biological and the psychological are reciprocally interactive as are infantile experiences and the exigencies of further development.

I do not feel, as Cooper does, that object relations theory opened up the possibility of preoedipal analysis. The latter was present in general analytic theory from the beginning, as was the active, universal, expectable interaction between self and object. Nor do infant observations require or validate object relations theory as contrasted with drive theory. They do not validate self theory, or any variation of interpersonal theory, or of any derivative extension of these such as a stated requirement for corrective emotional experience in the therapeutic process.

Observations, whether of infant or adult, are best explained by a theory which both encompasses them, and, as much as possible, achieves parsimony with completeness. Direct infant observation, like treatment of children, adolescents, and adults, neither confirms nor invalidates drive and structural theory. Self and object relations theories do not depend on infant observations for proof or acceptance. Each version of theory is held and maintained by its adherents because they believe that it best explains facts throughout the life cycle.

I agree with Cooper when he states that the Oedipus narrative is not supplanted by knowledge of preoedipal experience but is enriched by it. I would, however, apply the same principle to arguments concerning conflict versus regulation of affect or tension, or the experience of safety; all have a place in each individual's intrapsychic sequence, his intrapsychic process. Drives, tension, anxiety, safety, conflicts, and affects are all links in the intrapsychic chain.

The interest of the analyst does not stop at the patient's narrative. As Cooper agrees with Sandler about the layering of the unconscious, so does the narrative historically supersede the actual seduction, or frustration or state of satisfaction. It helps the analysis of lack of empathy to know whether the bedrock reality was a fantasy or an actuality (Erikson, 1962). Infant observation, Cooper points out, can guide an analyst to entertain the thought that a patient's narrative consists mainly of screens and defenses. This is as true for positive as it is for negative actualities.

McLaughlin, like the other contributors, appreciates the increased knowledge coming from the studies of infants and children throughout the forty years of his career as an analyst. Again, his knowledge guides his observations and understanding although, as with others, the danger of having prior knowledge influence the data is recognized and guarded against. The infant's tendency to rediscover underscores for him the ubiquity and centrality of the transference. McLaughlin is pleased with Stern's finding that the infant, from the beginning, has "an inherent penchant" for comparing any new stimulus with previous, sufficiently similar, ones, finding here the biological and early psychological origin of transference. One must of course leave room for the inroads and effects of new experiences, from infancy into later life; psychoanalysis is a prime example of such a change-inducing experience.

McLaughlin, adding his experience to this monograph, glimpses the earliest years through "transitional behaviors" (this is not literally Winnicottian), especially as seen in the transference. These transitional behaviors are mostly in the form of nonverbal,

sometimes inconspicuous phenomena: sounds, accents, expressions, attitudes and mannerisms, Isakower phenomena, and the
like. The patient he cities as clinical material is one of a small
group of patients upon whom he used a notational system in an
ongoing experimental observation over several years of analysis.
Both conspicuous foreground idiosyncratic material and more
quiet ongoing background activities were observed. Psychoanalytically valid observational data are not limited to the observation of
newborn infants—nor even nursery school situations; they can
also be obtained from carefully observed analytic phenomena, as I
did for a period of time in my study of snout phenomena.
Through his observations, McLaughlin gleaned linkages to infantile struggles around relationships to primary objects and to
transitional modes of relating: clinging and parting, dominance
and submission, merger and separation.

Besides an affectively convincing and revealing historical life
account which the analyst reconstructed from his patients' words,
an affective agenda, expressed in a quite different mode, was
observed, pursued, and organized through the filter of analytic
understanding. This was the expression of affect through the
patient's movements, mannerisms, and habits on the way to the
couch (such as smoothing her skirt behind her as she walked past
him), and while lying on the couch (her busy hands picking,
plucking, pushing, flicking at her hair, face, glasses, and the like).
McLaughlin gives credit to his close knowledge of rapprochement
phenomena and early infancy for his sensitive understanding of
good fits and mis-fits between infant and caregiver, and in
communicating the relationship of the movements he was observing to infantile affects with mother and other primary objects.
Much was learned and passed back and forth between patient and
analyst; for example, there were both subtle hints and broad
avenues of insight from the patient's changes of accent, similar to
reported reversions to long-forgotten mother tongues. McLaughlin has demonstrated elsewhere that a laterality of actions and
body musculature may result from memories and reenactments of
father or mother. Here different accents represented each parent.
The end result of the analysis of this patient's movements was
increased playfulness and relaxation with wider and more soaring
movements instead of small, careful picky ones.

A parallel case came to mind as I read McLaughlin's clinical account. This patient's presenting symptom was trichotillomania (hair-pulling); he performed an intricate ritual with his hair such as the one McLaughlin describes. Equally symptomatic, but at the other end, he patted, rubbed, and played with his thighs, legs, and sometimes toes. I would emphasize my restraint in moving from such observed phenomena to interpretation. Even these observations, without verbal associations, present problems similar to those connected with infant observations. They are always good and valuable to know, but sometimes challenge one's capacity for control. McLaughlin's understanding of such symbolic and indirect communications, and the analytic interventions he described to us, are affectively satisfying and cognitively impressive.

Chapter 14

Epilogue

Scott Dowling, M.D.

Curiosity about the psychological development of infants and children began, historically speaking, only yesterday. Though folk wisdom had long proclaimed that "as the twig is bent, so grows the child" it was not until the nineteenth century that science hesitantly joined art and literature in recognizing that infants and children are neither miniature adults nor mindless, soulless receptacles awaiting infusion with human characteristics at baptism, by way of the rod, or at puberty (Aries, 1962). During times when far more infants died than lived, and unbaptized infants could be disposed of like trash, the personhood of infants was inconceivable, much less the notion that infancy contained the fragile makings of the adult personality. To this day, sentimentality about children alternates with indifference, and in the process the world of childhood is denied equal significance with that of adults, and isolated from it. We need no reminders of how pervasive and destructive such attitudes are in the educational and political arenas, but we do need reminding that even today there are prominent voices in child development that minimize the impact of childhood experience on adult life (Kagan, 1984). Analysts are not free of such attitudes; as Anna Freud (1970) pointed out, psychoanalysts sometimes prefer the child created by interpretation in adult analysis to the actual child of direct or analytic observation.

Darwin's observations of his infant child, the true beginning of scientifically inspired infant observation, were made near the time of Freud's birth. Less than fifty years later Freud not only recognized the complex sexuality of childhood but established forever the formative link between the psychology of the child and that of the adult.

Freud's initial attention to children (I like to think it was inspired by the observations *he* made of his own six children and by his work with neurologically damaged children) was taken up by others, first in response to his request for relevant observations from friends and followers and, later, as a more organized psychoanalytic commitment to the observational study of children. Anna Freud's work, both in Vienna and at Hampstead, is a model of these highly productive studies. Hartmann's theoretical support, Kris's enthusiastic involvement both in his writing and in support of the Yale Child Study Center, and the pioneering work of Mahler and her colleagues added significantly to our knowledge of early development and to the respectability of observational studies. Most of this work was with the toddler and preschool child.

Fifty years after Freud presented his findings in *The Three Essays* (1905) and *Analysis of a Phobia in a Five-Year-Old Boy* (1909), a psychoanalyst galvanized the world of observational infant research. In 1958 Peter Wolff (Wolff, 1959) published his paper describing the objectively definable states of infants. Previous behavioral research efforts on neonates and young infants had been poorly controlled and therefore unverifiable because of the difficulty in establishing a baseline condition for making comparable observations. With Wolff's success in identifying universal, definable states, the psychophysiological condition of study infants could be objectively determined. This elimination of otherwise uncontrollable variables came just as the technical aspects of observation and analysis of audio and visual data underwent a revolution of their own. Behavior of mother and infant could now be studied in ways never before dreamed possible. Among the esoteric techniques developed were simultaneous, split-screen images of mother and child; films taken in the dark with infrared illumination; films of images reflected in an infant's eyes indicating visual fixation; and slow-motion films, permitting examination of second-by-second details of behavior and correlations of behavior and vocalizations. Measurements were made and the inner life of the child tapped by new techniques; for example, a pacifier attached to a transducer was utilized as a device through which an infant expressed preferences and controlled his visual or auditory environment by the rate or intensity of sucking.

What followed was a deluge of research on the infant. During the first decade or more, research focused on the competencies of infants, the amazing abilities of the human infant, never previously appreciated. It was a time of astonishment, of "Look what infants can do!" research. It was also a time of new research strategies. One such technique, exploited by John Bowlby, Mary Ainsworth, and their followers, has been to isolate and study definable components of infant behavior such as "attachment" or "feeding" or "sexuality" without regard for confounding aspects of mentation and behavior in other aspects of the child's life. The yield from this approach has been impressive, with the limitation, recently addressed by Ainsworth (1982) and others, that it does not permit an integrated understanding about the actual life of children.

In recent years the emphasis of the questions asked by infant researchers has shifted toward the complex interactions of mother and infant. Researchers are not only asking, "What can an infant do?" but "What and how does this behavior contribute to the formation of human attachments, to the development of skills such as speech and motor competence, to the formation of psychological structures and to other aspects of human adaptation?"

The new research is powerful; many of the techniques and results are innovative and original and some of the findings have shattered long held theories. Infant investigators are increasingly emboldened to also claim a general validity and priority for their theoretical results. It is these studies, and these theoretical claims, that have become most challenging to psychoanalytic theory. Lost in the excitement of the new research, the earlier, less technically spectacular but equally important and ground-breaking studies of older toddlers and preschoolers has been eclipsed.

As Dr. Tyson has described, the infant is now recognized as an active, more organized and organizing, more perceptually acute and discriminating, and more motorically complex creature than neurologists or child development specialists, including psychoanalysts, had previously believed. It has been firmly established that the infant is equipped with complex, adaptive, perceptual and behavioral capabilities which help to assure the interest and involvement of caretakers. These capabilities can be understood as enhancing the infant's likelihood of survival, especially through abilities that elicit and support caretaker actions that improve survival, and through techniques which facilitate his utilization of necessary inanimate aspects of his environment.

Granted the unforeseen skills of the newborn, we do not know enough about the organization of these capacities. There appears to be a transient, primitive, "hard wired," psychological organization, an *instinctual* (in the original, biological sense of the term) organization prior to intentionality and psychological representation as we know it in older infants, and therefore prior to *ego organization* as we usually use that term. We do not know enough about the kind or degree of psychological representation that accompanies these early activities; to what extent are they "experienced" in some unclear sense. Are these abilities innate, reflexive, and automatic, with as little psychological representation as occurs, for example, with the rooting reflex? At an opposite extreme, are they interpersonal activities with psychological representation comparable to that of adults? Or is there a midpoint, a poorly understood level of awareness that accompanies these activities? Our better understanding of the psychology of the infant awaits further clarification of this issue, among others.

Several speakers have discussed the "psychoanalytic baby" and his evolution. Although it is difficult to speak for others, the "model baby" who most influenced my thinking as a physician— and left me with an inaccurate view of the newborn—was not a "psychoanalytic baby" but a "neurological baby" as presented in neurology textbooks and in my pediatric training. This was the baby on whom we did circumcisions and vein cut downs without anesthesia and without concern for causing pain. This brain stem baby, who saw, heard, and felt nothing but a blur and who had stimulus–response reflexes but no effective perceptual capacity or complex interactive skills at its command, has been declared nonexistent by infant research. However, the baby of Freud, pressed to action by innate forces, capable of experiencing pleasure and pain, and soon engaged in the differentiation of inner need and outer reality, showed glimmers of becoming an effective agent, the "competent infant" revealed by modern research. As elaborated by many other analysts of the "pre-infancy research era" (Middlemore, 1941; Levy, 1928; Ribble, 1943; Fraiberg, 1959) this Freudian baby was respected as a feeling, responding, sociable creature, albeit a thoroughly immature one. The birth of psychological structures and functions, as they are known in the older infant and child, were viewed as hard won accomplishments, not innate endowments. Of the early Freudians, Melanie Klein was almost unique in her direct application of a portion of psychoanalytic theory (the death instinct) to the infant without regard or attention to direct experience. She ascribed destructive thought processes to the infant which have few, if any, specific expressions in infant behavior. Similarly, it has been a source of much confusion that Margaret Mahler, influenced by her medical, neurological background, forged inaccurate metaphorical links between early infancy and psychosis through her use of the terms *autism* and *symbiosis* to designate and describe both psychological phases of infancy and types of psychosis. In contrast, Mahler's observational studies of older infants and toddlers make use of metaphors drawn from nonpathological terminology.

The authors of this volume distinguish three overlapping categories of influence by infant research on psychoanalysis. First are specific challenges to psychoanalytic theory due to newly discovered facts about infants; second are new or revised "model scenes" of infancy based on the observation of babies; and third are approaches and attitudes toward infants and infantile experiences which have been inspired by this research.

Several contributors to this volume, most notably Drs. Lichtenberg and Cooper, are convinced that specific changes in psychoanalytic theory are required by the findings of infant research that Dr. Tyson and others have enumerated. Other contributors range from those who recognize an intense challenge to psychoanalytic theory (e.g., dual drive theory and psychosexual stage theory—Drs. Tyson and Novick), to those who are unconvinced of a valid challenge by infant research to any important aspects of psychoanalytic theory (Drs. Galenson and Glenn). Many of the authors warned of the dangers of the "genetic fallacy," an attribution of continuity or etiology from an early form of response or behavior to a later, seemingly similar, form of behavior. Others, especially Dr. Lichtenberg, see this concern as exaggerated, shielding psychoanalysts from necessary consideration of changes in theory. Whatever the degree of conviction about the need for changes in theory and practice, there are two topical areas in psychoanalysis which are most challenged by infant research. They are: (1) the dual drive theory and its associated theory of motivation, and (2) theories connected with the emergence of self/other differentiation.

Although differing in the details (and these are important), all the authors of these papers were agreed that the *model scenes* of infancy, to use Dr. Lichtenberg's well-chosen term, have been deeply affected by the new infant research. There is much less consensus about the clinical relevance of these new model scenes; for example, their usefulness in reconstruction or in formulating interpretations within the transference. Drs. Cooper, Lichtenberg, and McLaughlin seemed to find the new model scenes particularly helpful. Dr. Scharfman pointed out that it is quite possible to recognize the enormously different view of the infant that has emerged from research on the neonatorum and first year of life without that new knowledge necessarily having a place in the reconstructive and interpretive aspects of clinical work. For example, it is apparent that the model of the infant as autistically isolated from the environment or as fending off all stimuli behind a stimulus barrier is no longer tenable. But does this change of model scene perceptibly alter the clinician's response to child or adult patients?

Without attempting to be exhaustive, we can say that most of the new model scenes derive from an understanding of the infant as more active and autonomous than previously appreciated, from altered views of aggression and motivation, and from a change of emphasis concerning the issues which hold a central position in human development. "Aggression," as it was previously described psychoanalytically, by Hartmann, Kris, and Lowenstein (1949), has been fragmented into separate pieces, particularly in the work of Stechler and Halton (1987). Motivation, principally viewed within psychoanalysis as variously transformed manifestations of the sexual and aggressive drives, has been assigned by different investigators: (1) to separate and distinct affects; (2) to interpersonal relationships and interactions; or (3) to motivationally distinct and separate aspects of the drives. The new infant research has totally set aside the central developmental issues of traditional psychoanalysis, the link of ego and drives to the body and its physiological processes, and the interaction of the developing ego with the various manifestations of the drives. This emphasis has been replaced by a central concern with the formation and quality of interpersonal bonds and with the development of a sense of self.

Thus, for example, many of the new model scenes concern activity and efforts toward autonomy by the infant on the one hand, and frustration and experiences of failed empathy or other forms of inadequate environmental (caretaker) response on the other (as described by Lichtenberg). In others, there is an emphasis on assertion (Stechler and Halton, 1987) with active rejection of the possibility that assertion may include transformed destructive impulses or wishes. Interpersonal events take precedence over intrapsychic events (Stern, 1985). Separate and behaviorally distinct affective states (Tomkins, 1962; Emde, Gaensbauer, and Harmon, 1976) take precedence over underlying, drive-related impulses.

It is evident that these model scenes follow from the emphasis and interpretation given by the researchers to their empirical findings. It is a process familiar to psychoanalysts. After all, this is precisely what Freud did in discovering the Oedipus complex and the stages of psychosexual development; each finding triggered the formation of a wealth of "model scenes" which have been used by psychoanalysts ever since. Similarly, the results of earlier infant and toddler observational studies, such as those of Anna Freud, Margaret Mahler, and Donald Winnicott, have been the source of such "model scenes" as the anal stage child giving or withholding the gift of feces, the separated toddler "keying in" and "refueling" with its mother, the rapprochement toddler, torn asunder by the recognition of his separateness and ambivalence, and the child or adult seeking a transitional object–activity when lonely.

Unlike Freud, the "new" infant researchers and some analysts are assigning special clinical relevance to scenes based on the first year of life. A problem which they encounter, a problem which is encountered by all who attempt to utilize "model scenes" from the first year in work with older children and adults, is uncertainty about the psychological status of the young child as compared with older children. Let me illustrate with an example from cognitive psychology. Jonas Langer wrote a book some years ago which attempted to delineate precursors of later logical skills such as division, coseriation, symbolization, and reciprocal operations in six- to twelve-month-old infants (Langer, 1980). The book provides a wealth of data, drawn from many hundreds of experiments. To stay with the example of symbolization, he shows that the six-month-old tends to carry out certain actions (e.g., such actions as "drop," "push," or "hold") with a given object more often than another action; he suggests that these preferred actions are "protosymbols" of a group of objects that the infant identifies as "dropables," "pushables," or "holdables" (p. 32). The problem is that there is no assurance that this behavioral preference, related in a logical sense to a variety of later skills, is not simply the way in which a young infant is either preadapted or guided to respond to such objects. It in no way confirms that this grouping is represented within the child's awareness or that the action is used as a symbol to indicate a particular group of objects. Within the researcher's awareness, these actions connect, logically and behaviorally, with later symbolization, but that has no necessary relevance to the psychology of the child. In a similar vein, when Daniel Stern sees the beginning of self and object differentiation in the differential response of the infant to his mother's voice, he is undoubtedly right from his vantage point as an external adult observer. It is less likely that he is right from the vantage point of the infant. There may be no awareness or continuity of meaning for the infant from the earlier to the later behavior. The genetic fallacy is a very real concern in drawing conclusions from early infant behavior to later infant behavior, let alone to adult psychology. The issues of psychological organization, of the birth of meaning and concept formation, are central to the assignment of psychological equivalence of infant awareness with the awareness of older children or adults.

In his concept of levels of psychosexual organization—oral, anal, phallic, and genital—Freud introduced the notion of a complex of motivations, actions, attitudes, interests, and capabilities under the organizing influence of a developmentally ascendant group of drive derivatives. The corresponding periods of childhood have certainly engendered "model scenes" which most analysts utilize—the nursing infant, the gift-giving or withholding toddler, the charming, exhibitionistic four-year-old, and the tender, possessive oedipal lover—these are model scenes familiar to us all. Issues of loss and attachment, of progressive differentiation of self from other, of physical gratification and of interactions of the infant with the world around him, and between aspects of his personality, are attached to each of these levels and form part of the vision of early life that is deeply woven into the fabric of psychoanalysis.

Some infancy researchers have taken exception to these "Freudian" scenes, in particular decrying the "oral" emphasis (Bowlby, 1960). Several of the authors represented in this book suggest that when the researchers turn their attention from the "alert inactive" satisfied infant to the hungry, crying, active infant, it is likely that orality and "drive pressure" (however it may be termed) will again gain prominence.

The final category of influence of infant research on psychoanalysis is in the analyst's attitude toward his analytic patient. Dr. McLaughlin is very explicit about this influence and gives clear illustrations of it as do Drs. Cooper and Lichtenberg. These analysts find themselves more sensitive to the frequency and specificity of nonverbal sensorimotor communication than they were prior to infant research. Verbal and nonverbal expression, they find, are intricately interwoven to an extent not previously appreciated. They point to an increased awareness of the complex sensorimotor forms of knowing and interpersonal interaction in later life, an awareness that had its origin in the research of Jean Piaget.

The infant's influence on his caretakers and environment and his penchant for activity are attitudes which have been strikingly demonstrated by infant research. There is an interesting and controversial change in analytic attitude which is a result of this emphasis on the interactive component of infant behavior. It is exemplified in Dr. Lichtenberg's paper; his more conversational and interactive mode of analytic technique reflects the interpersonal emphasis of infant research.

I would like to mention a number of other, indirect influences of infant research on psychoanalysts and psychoanalysis which were not mentioned in the papers presented here. Psychoanalytically oriented infant researchers have influenced society's provisions for infants, educating analysts as well as the general public about the issues involved; for example, Robertson (1958) (hospital care of young children), René Spitz (1945b) (institutional care of infants), Joseph Goldstein, Anna Freud, and Albert Solnit (1973) (legal rights of infants and children), Marshall Klaus and John Kennell (1976) (hospital care of newborn infants and their mothers), Sally Provence (1962, 1977) (institutional care of infants and day care standards), Stanley Greenspan (1988) (care of developmentally disabled infants and physically and psychologically abused infants).

The surge of research and of corresponding social concern for infants has stimulated a growth of academic programs dedicated to the study of infants and young children. Organizations such as the Society for Research in Child Development and the National Center for Clinical Infant Research have flourished and are influential in the development of standards and priorities of care for infants and children.

Many of the questions raised by the authors of this book concern investigative methods and methods of interpretation of data. Infant research has confronted psychoanalysts with many questions about how we regard clinical evidence and about the ways in which we view our theoretical formulations. The most direct question is simply this: if infant research, a "harder science" than psychoanalysis, derives useful and successful theoretical formulations to explain its findings and to guide further research, are analysts obliged to alter their theories to conform with those of the new research? Or is psychoanalysis justified in maintaining skepticism about the usefulness and fit of the new theories to its field of study based on the integrity of its own findings and on the usefulness of its own theories? My wording makes it clear where I stand on the issue. Psychoanalysis is a broader and less empirical science than infant research. Its emphasis is on the intrapsychic life of man. It deals with aspects of human psychology throughout the life span, not just infancy or adolescence or adult life. Its data are derived from the psychoanalytic situation. Psychoanalysts have an obligation to be aware of and attentive to findings from research other than their own, whether that research concerns infancy, old age, or some other discrete period of life or concerns other fields of study, such as cognition, neuroendocrinology, or human genetics. But each field is separate one from the other, each has its own methods, and each makes its own claims. Psychoanalytic theory derives strength from its broad applicability in understanding development and psychopathology throughout the life span and from its unique and powerful investigative technique; it is not a detailed guide for research on a particular period of life or a particular ego function.

There is value in recognizing that valuable observations may coexist with doubtful theory in our own and other sciences. Many, including myself, view Stern's observations and theories concerning interpersonal behavior in early infancy in that light (Solnit, 1987). Although this essay is not the place to attempt to resolve the many conceptual problems involved in the interpretive aspects of infant observation, I will list some relevant considerations. Most important, adherents and critics alike seem to lose track of the fact that infant observational research is an independent area of study—free to develop its own methods and theories. It is properly unrestrained by conclusions drawn from other fields. The neurologists who could see only confusion and immaturity in the neonatal cortex and owed a frozen allegiance to the concept of "no function without myelinization" were wearing conceptual blindfolds against the possibility of motoric and perceptual discrimination and complexity. But much like Newtonian mechanics confronted by Einstein's relativity, the utility of theoretical ideas fitted for a limited psychological area under study must, at some point, come into contact with human psychology as a whole, including the findings of psychoanalysis. Prior to the day when the constraints on theory established by each area of study can be evaluated and brought into harmony, one point of view cannot dictate what will or will not prove useful to the practitioners of another field of investigation. It has been experimentally useful for attachment theory investigators to isolate an area of human activity without troubling themselves with the variables introduced by other areas of human activity, an approach, which, within the limits of those studies, has been very successful. But, when such findings are transformed into recommendations for public policy or infant care, a line must be drawn and the limitations recognized. Similarly, infant researchers are unduly constrained by drive theory, preferring the greater discreteness and operational directness offered by a separation of drive from affect and of affects from each other. There has been a return to faculty psychology and a "useful" retreat from the transformational psychology of psychoanalysis. Assertion can be studied apart from aggression if we can be untroubled by any link between them; individual aspects of experience can be more neatly studied if the unification of separate libidinal trends and of separate aggressive trends implied by the dual drive theory can be set aside. That position has been useful to the immediate progress of infant study. Accepting that position means acknowledging that everything emerging from infant research applies, with assurance, only to the limited area being studied, namely, to infants. A larger unity of understanding, an encompassing unity that includes toddler, child, and adult psychology, must address the powerful evidence from psychoanalysis for a transformational, conflict-oriented, drive psychology. That eventual unity will be one in which psychoanalysis, itself a limited method of study, will also gain new perspectives.

In summary, there was a wide range of opinion among the authors of this volume about the impact of infant research on interpretive and reconstructive processes and on the degree to which psychoanalytic theory has been changed in response to infant research. Several contributors saw broad applications of the findings of infant research, from important revisions of psychoanalytic motivational theory to changed forms of interaction and interpretation within the psychoanalytic paradigm. This group of psychoanalysts, representing a wide range of opinion concerning the influence of infant observation on analysis, were agreed in seeing its greatest influence as a source of new "model scenes" and in a greater appreciation of nonverbal communication.

References

Abelin, E. (1971), The role of the father in the separation–individuation process. In: *Separation–Individuation: Essays in Honor of Margaret S. Mahler*, eds. J. McDevitt & C. Settlage. New York: International Universities Press, pp. 229–252.

———(1975), Some further observations and comments on the earliest role of the father. *Internat. J. Psychoanal.*, 56:293–332.

———(1977), The role of the father in core gender identity and in psychosexual differentiation. Paper presented at American Psychoanalytic Association Meeting, April 1977.

Ainsworth, M. (1982), Attachment: Retrospect and prospect. In: *The Place of Attachment in Human Behavior*, eds. C. Parkes & J. Stevenson-Hinde. New York: Basic Books.

———Blehar, M., Waters, E., & Wall, S. (1978), *Patterns of Attachment*. Hillsdale, NJ: Lawrence Erlbaum Associates.

Alexander, F., & French, T. (1946), *Psychoanalytic Therapy: Principles and Application*. New York: Ronald Press.

Als, H. (1984), Discussion. In: *Frontiers of Infant Psychiatry*, Vol. 2, eds. J. Call, E. Galenson, & R. Tyson. New York: Basic Books, pp. 211–223.

Anders, T. F., & Zeanah, C. H. (1984), Early infant development from a biological point of view. In: *Frontiers of Infant Psychiatry*, Vol. 2, eds. J. Call, E. Galenson, & R. Tyson. New York: Basic Books pp. 55–69.

Anthony, F. J. (1984), The influence babies bring to bear on their upbringing. In: *Fontiers of Infant Psychiatry*, Vol. 2, eds. J. Call, E. Galenson, & R. Tyson. New York: Basic Books, pp. 259–266.

———(1986), The contributions of child psycho-analysis to psychoanalysis. *The Psychoanalytic Study of the Child*, 41:61–87. New Haven, CT: Yale University Press.

Aries, P. (1962), *Centuries of Childhood*. New York: Vintage.

Barrie, J. (1910), *Peter Pan in Kensington Gardens*. New York: Charles Scribner's Sons.

Beebe, B., & Sloate, P. (1982), Assessment and treatment of difficulties in mother–infant attunement in the first 3 years of life: A case history. *Psychoanal. Inq.*, 1:602–623.

Benjamin, J. D. (1959), Prediction and psychopathological theory. In: *Dynamics of Psychopathology in Childhood*, eds. L. Jessner & E. Pavenstedt. New York: Grune & Stratton, pp. 6–77.

———(1961), The innate and the experiential in child development. In: *Lectures on Experimental Psychiatry*, ed. J. W. Brosin. Pittsburgh: University of Pittsburgh Press, pp. 19–42.

Bergman, A. (1987), Comments made during the 18th Annual Symposium on Child Development, Margaret S. Mahler Symposium Series, Philadelphia, May.

Bertalanffy, von L. (1968), *General System Theory: Foundations, Development, Applications*. New York: George Braziller.

Blau, A. (1946), The Master Hand. *Research Monograph 5*. New York: American Orthopsychiatric Association.

Blos, P., Jr. (1985), Intergenerational separation–individuation. *The Psychoanalytic Study of the Child*, 40:41–56. New Haven, CT: Yale University Press.

Blum, H. (1977a), The prototype of preoedipal reconstruction. *J. Amer. Psychoanal. Assn.*, 25:757–785.

——— (1977b), Comments made at the American Psychoanalytic Association Meeting, Panel on the Role of the Father in Preoedipal Years, Quebec, April.

———(1980), Paraonia and beating fantasy. *J. Amer. Psychoanal. Assn.*, 28:331–361.

———(1988), Shared fantasy and reciprocal identification, and their role in garden disorders. In: *Fantasy, Myth, and Reality: Essays in Honor of Jacob Arlow*, eds. H. Blum, Y. Kramer, A. & R. Richards. Madison, CT: International Universities Press, pp. 323–338.

Bowlby, J. (1958), The nature of the child's tie to his mother. *Internat. J. Psycho-Anal.*, 39:350–373.

———(1960), Grief and mourning in infancy and early childhood. *The Psychoanalytic Study of the Child*, 15:9–52. New York: International Universities Press.

———(1969), *Attachment and Loss*, Vol. 1. New York: Basic Books.

———(1973), *Attachment and Loss*, Vol. 2. New York: Basic Books.

———(1980), *Attachment and Loss*, Vol. 3. New York: Basic Books.

———(1988), Developmental psychiatry comes of age. *Amer. J. Psychiat.*, 145:1–10.

Brazelton, T. (1973), *Neonatal Behavioral Assessment Scale*. Philadelphia: J. B. Lippincott.

———(1980), New knowledge about the infant from current research: Implications for psychoanalysis. Paper presented to the American Psychoanalytic Association, spring meeting, San Francisco, May 1980.

————(1984), Why early intervention? In: *Frontiers of Infant Psychiatry*, Vol. 2, eds. J. Call, E. Galenson, & R. Tyson. New York: Basic Books, pp. 267–275.

————Als, H. (1979), Four early stages in the development of mother–infant interaction. *The Psychoanalytic Study of the Child*, 34:349–369.

————Koslowski, B., & Main, M. (1974), The origins of reciprocity. The early mother–infant interaction. In: *The Effect of the Infant on its Caregiver*, eds. M. Lewis & L. Rosenblum. New York: John Wiley, pp. 49–77.

————Tronick, E., Adamson, L., Als, H., & Wise, S. (1975), Early mother–infant reciprocity. In: *Parent–Infant Interaction*. Ciba Foundation Symposium 33. Amsterdam: Elsevier, pp. 137–154.

Bridger, W. H. (1962), Sensory discrimination and autonomic function. *J. Amer. Acad. Child Psychiat.*, 1:67–82.

Brody, S. (1956), *Patterns of Mothering: Maternal Influence During Infancy*. New York: International Universities Press.

————Axelrad, S. (1970), *Anxiety and Ego Formation in Infancy*. New York: International Universities Press.

———— ————(1978), *Mothers, Fathers, and Children. Explorations in the Formation of Character in the First Seven Years*. New York: International Universities Press.

Broussard, E. (1984), The Pittsburgh first-borns at age nineteen years. In: *Frontiers of Infant Psychiatry*, Vol. 2, eds. J. Call, E. Galenson, & R. Tyson. New York: Basic Books, pp. 522–530.

————Hartner, M. (1970), Maternal perception of the neonate as related to development. *Child Psychiat. & Hum. Develop.*, 1:16–25.

Bruner, J. (1975), The ontogenesis of speech acts. *J. Child Lang.*, 2:1–19.

Brunswick, R. M. (1940), The preoedipal phase of the libido development. *Psychoanal. Quart.*, 9:293.

Buckley, P., ed. (1986), *Essential Papers on Object Relations*. New York & London: New York University Press.

Buhler, C. (1954), The reality principle: Discussion of theories and observational data. *Amer. J. Psychother.*, 8:626–647.

Buhler, K. (1951), On thought connections. In: *Organization and Pathology of Thought*, trans. & comment. D. Rapaport. New York: Columbia University Press, pp. 39–57.

Call, J. (1980), Some prelinguistic aspects of language development. *J. Amer. Psychoanal. Assn.*, 28:259–289.

————(1984), From early patterns of communication to the grammar of experience and syntax in infancy. In: *Frontiers of Infant Psychiatry*, Vol. 2, eds. J. Call, E. Galenson, & R. Tyson. New York: Basic Books, pp. 15–29.

————Galenson, E., & Tyson, R., ed. (1983), *Frontiers of Infant Psychiatry*, Vol. 1. New York: Basic Books.

Casuso, G. (1965), The relationship between child analysis and the theory and practice of adult psychoanalysis. *J. Amer. Psychoanal. Assn.*, 13:159–171.

Cath, S., Gurwitt, A., & Ross, J., eds. (1982), *Father and Child: Developmental and Clinical Perspectives*. Boston: Little, Brown.

Condon, W., & Sandler, J. (1974), Neonate movement is synchronized with adult speech: Interactional participation and language acquisition. *Sci.*, 183:99–101.

COPER (Conference on Psychoanalytic Education and Research) (1974), *Commission IX: Child Analysis*. New York: American Psychoanalytic Association.

Darwin, C. (1872), *The Expression of Emotions in Man and Animals*. Chicago: University of Chicago Press, 1965.

deChateau, P., & Wiberg, B. (1984), Three-year follow-up of early postpartum contact. In: *Frontiers of Infant Psychiatry*, Vol. 2, eds. J. Call, E. Galenson, & R. Tyson. New York: Basic Books, pp. 313–322.

Demos, E. V. (1982), Affect in early infancy: Physiology or psychology? *Psychoanal. Inq.*, 1:533–574.

———(1985), The elusive infant. *Psychoanal. Inq.*, 5:553–568.

Domhoff, G. (1969), But why did they sit on the king's right in the first place? *Psychoanal. Rev.*, 56:586–596.

Dowling, S. (1977), Seven infants with esophageal atresia: A developmental study. *The Psychoanalytic Study of the Child*, 32:215–256. New Haven, CT: Yale University Press.

Emde, R. N. (1980), Emotional availability: A reciprocal reward system for infants and parents with implications for prevention of psychosocial disorders. In: *Parent–Infant Relationships*, ed. P. Taylor. Orlando, FL: Grune & Stratton, pp. 87—115.

———(1981), Changing models of infancy and the nature of early development: Remodeling the foundations. *J. Amer. Psychoanal. Assn.*, 29:179–219.

———(1983), The prerepresentational self and its affective care. *The Psychoanalytic Study of the Child*, 38:165–192. New Haven, CT: Yale University Press.

———(1984), The affective self: Continuities and transformations from infancy. In: *Frontiers of Infant Psychiatry*, Vol. 2, ed. J. Call, E. Galenson, & R. Tyson. New York: Basic Books, pp. 38–54.

———(1987), Development terminable and interminable. Paper presented at the International Congress for Psychoanalysis, Montreal, Canada.

———(1988), Development terminable and interminable. *Internat. J. Psycho-Anal.*, 69:23–42.

———Gaensbauer, T. & Harmon, R. (1976), Emotional Expression in Infancy: A Biobehavioral Study. *Psychological Issues*, Monograph 37. New York: International Universities Press.

———Score, J. (1983), The rewards of infancy: Emotional availability and maternal referencing. In: *Frontiers of Infant Psychiatry*, Vol. 1, eds. J. Call, E. Galenson, & R. Tyson. New York: Basic Books.

Engel, G. (1953), *Maternal Deprivation in Young Children*. Film. Produced by J. Aubry. Distributed by New York University.

———Reichsman, F., Harway, V., & Hess, D. (1985), Monica: Infant-feeding behavior of a mother gastric fistula-fed as an infant: A 30-year longitudinal study of enduring effects. In: *Parental Influences in Health and Disease*, eds. E. Anthony & G. Pollock. Boston: Little, Brown.

Erikson, E. H. (1950), *Childhood and Society*. New York: W. W. Norton.

———(1962), Reality and actuality. *J. Amer. Psychoanal. Assn.*, 21:5–33.

Escalona, S. K. (1953), Emotional development in the first year of life. In: *Problems of Infancy and Childhood*, ed. M. J. E. Senn. New York: Josiah Macy, Jr. Foundation, pp. 11–92.

———(1963), Patterns of infantile experience and the developmental process. *The Psychoanalytic Study of the Child*, 18:197–244. New York: International Universities Press.

———(1968), *The Roots of Individuality*. Chicago: Aldine.

———Heider, G. (1959), *Prediction and Outcome: A Study of Child Development*. New York: Basic Books.

Escoll, P. (1983), The changing vistas of transference: The effect of developmental concepts on the understanding of transference. *J. Amer. Psychoanal. Assn.*, 31:699–712.

Fairbairn, W. R. D. (1954), *An Object-Relations Theory of the Personality*. New York: Basic Books.

Fantz, R. L. (1958), Pattern vision in young infants. *Psychol. Rep.*, 8:43–47.

———(1961), The origin of form perception. *Sci. Amer.*, 204:66–72.

Fraiberg, S. (1959), *The Magic Years*. New York: Scribners.

———(1977), *Insights from the Blind*. New York: Basic Books.

———ed. (1980), *Clinical Studies in Infant Mental Health: The First Year of Life*. New York: Basic Books.

Freud, A. (1936), *The Ego and the Mechanisms of Defense*. New York: International Universities Press, 1966.

———(1941), Infants without families. Reports of the Hampstead Nurseries, 1939–1945. *The Writings of Anna Freud*, Vol. 3. New York: International Universities Press, 1973.

———(1951), An experiment in group upbringing. *The Writings of Anna Freud*, Vol. 4. New York: International Universities Press, 1968, pp. 163–229.

———(1960), Discussion of Dr. John Bowlby's paper. *The Psychoanalytic Study of the Child*, 15:53–63. New York: International Universities Press.

———(1963), Assessment of childhood disturbances. *The Psychoanalytic Study of the Child*, 17:149–158. New York: International Universities Press.

————(1965), *Normality and Pathology in Childhood: Assessments of Develop-ment.* New York: International Universities Press.

————(1970), Child analysis as a subspecialty of psychoanalysis. *The Writings of Anna Freud,* Vol. 7. New York: International Universities Press, pp. 204–219.

————(1974), Introduction. *The Writings of Anna Freud,* Vol. 1. New York: International Universities Press, pp. vii–xii.

————(1976), Changes in psychoanalytic practice and experience. *Inter-nat. J. Psycho-Anal.,* 57:257–260.

————(1922–1980), *The Writings of Anna Freud,* Vols. 1–8. New York: International Universities Press.

Freud, S. (1895), A project for a scientific psychology. *Standard Edition,* 1:283–397. London: Hogarth Press, 1966.

————(1905), Three Essays on the Theory of Sexuality. *Standard Edition,* 7:125–243. London: Hogarth, Press, 1953.

————(1909), Analysis of a Phobia in a Five-Year-Old Boy. *Standard Edition,* 10:5–149. London: Hogarth Press, 1955.

————(1920a), Beyond the pleasure principle. *Standard Edition,* 18:1–64. London: Hogarth Press, 1955.

————(1920b), The psychogenesis of a case of homosexuality in a woman. *Standard Edition,* 18:145–172. London: Hogarth Press, 1955.

————(1923), The ego and the id. *Standard Edition,* 19:141–145. London: Hogarth Press, 1961.

————(1926), Inhibitions, symptoms and anxiety. *Standard Edition,* 20:77–175. London: Hogarth Press, 1959.

————(1939), Moses and Monotheism. *Standard Edition,* 23:3–137. Lon-don: Hogarth Press, 1964.

Friedman, L. (1988), *The Anatomy of Psychotherapy.* Hillsdale, NJ: Analytic Press.

Fries, M., & Woolf, P. (1953), Some hypotheses on the role of congenital activity type in personality development. *The Psychoanalytic Study of the Child,* 8:48–62. New York: International Universities Press.

Furer, M. (1967), Some developmental aspects of the superego. *Internat. J. Psycho-Anal.,* 48:277–280.

Gaensbauer, T. (1982), The differentiation of discrete affects: A case report. *The Psychoanalytic Study of the Child,* 37:29–66. New Haven CT: Yale University Press.

————(1985), The relevance of infant research for psychoanalysis. *Psy-choanal. Inq.,* 5:517–530.

Galenson, E. (1986), Some thoughts about infant psychopathology and aggressive development. *Internat. Rev. Psychoanal.,* 13:349–354.

————Fields, B. (Unpublished.)

————Roiphe, H. (1971), The impact of early sexual discovery on mood, defensive organization, and symbolization. *The Psychoanalytic Study of the Child,* 26:195–216. New York: Quadrangle.

————— ————(1974), The emergence of genital awareness during the second year of life. In: *Sex Differences in Behavior*, eds. R. C. Friedman, R. M. Richart, & R. L. Van de Wiele. New York: John Wiley, pp. 223–231.

————— ————(1976), Some suggested revisions concerning early female development. *J. Amer. Psychoanal. Assn.*, 24 (suppl.):29–57.

————— ————(1980), The preoedipal development of the boy. *J. Amer. Psychoanal. Assn.*, 28:805–827.

————Vogel, S., Blau, S., & Roiphe, H. (1975), Disturbance in sexual identity beginning at 18 months of age. *Internat. Rev. Psychoanal.*, 2:369–397.

Gedo, J. E. (1985), On the dawn of experience: The past recaptured. *Psychoanal. Inq.*, 5:601–620.

Geleerd, E. (1967), Introduction. In: *The Child Analyst at Work*, ed. E. Geleerd. New York: International Universities Press, pp. 1–14.

Glenn, J. (1978), *Child Analysis and Therapy*. New York: Jason Aronson.

Glover, E. (1931), The therapeutic effect of inexact interpretation: A contribution to the theory of suggestion. *Internat. J. Psycho-Anal.*, 12:397–411.

Goldestein, J., Freud, A., & Solnit, A. (1973), *Beyond the Best Interests of the Child*. New York: Free Press.

Green, R. (1974), *Sexual Identity Conflict in Children and Adults*. New York: Basic Books.

————Newman, L., & Stoller, R. (1972), Treatment of boyhood "transexualism": An interim report of four years' experience. *Arch. Gen. Psychiat.*, 26:213–217.

Greenacre, P. (1941), The predisposition to anxiety. In: *Trauma, Growth, and Personality*. New York: International Universities Press, 1952, pp. 27–82.

Greenson, R. (1966), A transvestite boy and a hypothesis. *Internat. J. Psycho-Anal.*, 47:396–403.

————(1968), Dis-identifying from mother: The special importance for the boy. *Internat. J. Psycho-Anal.*, 49:370–374.

Greenspan, S. (1979), Intelligence and Adaptation: An Integration of Psychoanalytic and Pragetian Developmental Psychology. *Psychol. Issues*, Monograph 47/48. New York: International Universities Press.

————(1988), Fostering emotional and social development in infants with disabilities. *Zero to Three*, 9:8–18.

Haith, M. (1977), Eye contact and face scanning in early infancy. *Sci.*, 198:853–855.

————Campos, J. (1983), Infancy and developmental psychobiology. In: *Handbook of Child Psychology*, Vol. 2, eds. M. Haith & J. Campos. New York: John Wiley.

Hampson, G. L., & Hampson, J. G. (1961), The ontogenesis of sexual behavior in man. In: *Sex and Internal Secretions*, Vol. 2, ed. W. Young. Baltimore: Williams and Wilkins, pp. 1401–1432.

Harlow, H. (1959), *The Nature and Development of Affection*. Film. Produced by University of Wisconsin at Madison. Distribution by Pennsylvania Cinema Register at Pennsylvania State University.

———(1960), *Mother Love*. Film. Produced by CBS, Inc. (same film as above with narration sound track). Distribution by Pennsylvania Cinema Register at Pennsylvania State University.

Harmon, R., Wagonfeld, S., & Emde, R. (1982), Anaclitic depression: A follow-up from infancy to puberty. *The Psychoanalytic Study of the Child*, 37:827–833. New Haven, CT: Yale University Press.

Hartmann, H. (1939), *Ego Psychology and the Problem of Adaptation*. New York: International Universities Press, 1958.

———(1950), Comments on the psychoanalytic theory of the ego. *The Psychoanalytic Study of the Child*, 5:74-96. New York: International Universities Press.

———(1952), The mutual influences in the development of ego and id. In: *Essays on Ego Psychology*. New York: International Universities Press, 1964, pp. 155–182.

———(1953), Contribution to the metapsychology of schizophrenia. *The Psychoanalytic Study of the Child*, 8:117–198. New York: International Universities Press.

———Kris, E. (1947), The genetic approach in psychoanalysis. *The Psychoanalytic Study of the Child*, 1:11–30. New York: International Universities Press.

———Loewenstein, R. (1949), Notes on the theory of aggression. *The Psychoanalytic Study of the Child*, 3/4:9–36. New York International Universities Press.

Hendrick, I. (1942), Instinct and the ego during infancy. *Psychoanal. Quart.*, 11:33–58.

Herzog, J. M. (1982), On father hunger: The father's role in the modulation of aggressive drive and fantasy. In: *Father and Child,* eds. S. Cath, A. Gurwitt, & J. Ross. Boston: Little, Brown, pp. 163–174.

———(1984), Fathers and young children: Fathering daughters and fathering sons. In: *Frontiers of Infant Psychiatry*, Vol. 2, eds. J. Call, E. Galenson, & R. Tyson. New York: Basic Books, pp. 335–342.

Izard, C. (1971), *The Face of Emotion*. New York: Appleton-Century.

Jones, E. (1955), *Sigmund Freud*, Vol. 1. London: Hogarth Press.

Kagan, J. (1984), *The Nature of the Child*. New York: Basic Books.

Khan, M. (1963), The concept of cumulative trauma. *The Psychoanalytic Study of the Child*, 18:286–306. New York: International Universities Press.

Kaplan, L. J. (1987), Discussion. *Contemp. Psychoanal.*, 23:27–44.

Kernberg, O. F. (1975), *Borderline Conditions and Pathological Narcissism*. New York: Jason Aronson.

———(1976), *Object Relations Theory and Clinical Psychoanalysis*. New York: Jason Aronson.

Klaus, M., & Kennell, J. (1976), *Maternal–Infant Bonding*. St. Louis: C. V. Mosby, 1982.

Kleeman, J. (1976), Freud's views on early female sexuality in the light of direct child observation. *J. Amer. Psychoanal. Assn.*, 24:3–27.

Klein, M. (1928), Early stages of the oedipus conflict. *The Writings of Melanie Klein*, Vol. 1. London: Hogarth Press, pp. 186–198.

———(1933), The early development of conscience in the child. *The Writings of Melanie Klein*, Vol. 1. London: Hogarth Press, pp. 248–257.

———(1958), On the development of mental functioning. *The Writings of Melanie Klein*, Vol. 3. London: Hogarth Press, 1975, pp. 236–246.

Kohlberg, L. (1966), A cognitive–developmental analysis of children's sex role concepts and attitudes. In: *The Development of Sex Differences*, ed. E. Maccoby. Stanford, CA: Stanford University Press, pp. 82–175.

———Ricks, D., & Snarey, J. (1984), Childhood Development as a Predictor of Adaptation in Adulthood. *Genetic Psychology Monographs*, 110:91–172.

Kohut, H. (1971), *The Analysis of the Self*. New York: International Universities Press.

———(1977), *The Restoration of the Self*. New York: International Universities Press.

———(1979), The two analyses of Mr. Z. *Internat. J. Psycho-Anal.*, 60:3–27.

———(1984), *How Does Analysis Cure?*, eds. A. Goldberg & P. Stepansky. Chicago: University of Chicago Press.

Korner, A. (1964), Some hypotheses regarding the significance of individual differences at birth for later development. *The Psychoanalytic Study of the Child*, 19:58–72. New York: International Universities Press.

Kretschmer, E. (1925), *Physique and Character*. New York: Harcourt, Brace.

Kris, E. (1956), The recovery of childhood memories in psychoanalysis. *The Psychoanalytic Study of the Child*, 11:54–88. New York: International Universities Press.

Langer, J. (1980), *The Origins of Logic*. New York: Academic Press.

Lebovici, S. (1983), *Le Nourisson, La Mere et le Psychanalyste. Les Interactions Precoces*. Paris: Editions du Centurion.

Leichtman, M. (1987), Developmental psychology and psychoanalysis: I. The context for a contemporary revolution in psychoanalysis. Paper presented at the American Psychoanalytic Meeting, December.

Levy, D. (1928), Finger sucking and accessory movements in early infancy. *Amer. J. Psychiat.*, 7:881–918.

Lichtenberg, J. (1981), Implications for psychoanalytic theory of research on the neonate. *Internat. Rev. Psychoanal.*, 8:35–52.

———(1983), *Psychoanalysis and Infant Research.* Hillsdale, NJ: Analytic Press.

———(1987), Infant studies and clinical work with adults. *Psychoanal. Inq.* 7:311–330.

———(1989a), *Psychoanalysis and Motivation.* Hillsdale, NJ: Analytic Press.

———(1989b), A theory of motivational–functional systems as psychic structures. *J. Amer. Psychoanal. Assn.*, 37:55–70.

Loewald, H. (1960), On the therapeutic action of psychoanalysis. *Internat. J. Psycho-Anal.*, 41:16–33.

———(1971), On motivation and instinct theory. *The Psychoanalytic Study of the Child*, 26:91–128. New York: Quadrangle.

Mahler, M. S. (1963), Thoughts about development and individuation. *The Psychoanalytic Study of the Child*, 18:307–324. New York: International Universities Press.

———(1967), On human symbiosis and the vicissitudes of individuation. *J. Amer. Psychoanal. Assn.*, 15:740–763.

———(1971), A study of the separation/individuation process and its possible application to borderline phenomena in the psychoanalytic situation. *The Psychoanalytic Study of the Child*, 26:403–424. New York Quadrangle.

———(1972a), On the first three subphases of the separation–individuation process. *Internat. J. Psycho-Anal.*, 53:333–338.

———(1972b), The rapprochement subphase of the separation–individuation process. *Psychoanal. Quart.*, 41:487–506.

———(1975), On human symbiosis and the vicissitudes of individuation. *J. Amer. Psychoanal. Assn.*, 23:740–763.

———Furer, M. (1968), *On Human Symbiosis and the Vicissitudes of Individuation.* New York: International Universities Press.

———Gosliner, B. (1955), On symbiotic child psychosis: Genetic, dynamic and restitutive aspects. *The Psychoanalytic Study of the Child*, 10:195–212. New York: International Universities Press.

———Kaplan, L. (1977), Developmental aspects in the assessment of narcissistic and so-called borderline personalities. In: *Borderline Personality Disorder: The Concept, the Syndrome, the Patient*, ed. P. Hartocollis. New York: International Universities Press, pp. 71–85.

———McDevitt, J. B. (1982), Thoughts on the emergence of the sense of the self, with particular emphasis on the body self. *J. Amer. Psychoanal. Assn.*, 30:827–848.

———Pine, F., & Bergman, A. (1975), *The Psychological Birth of the Human Infant.* New York: Basic Books.

Massie, H., & Campbell, B. (1983), The Massie–Campbell scale of mother/infant attachment indicators during stress (AIDS scale). In:

Frontiers of Infant Psychiatry, ed. J. Call, E. Galenson & R. Tyson. New York: Basic Books, pp. 394–412.

Masterson, J. (1976), *Psychotherapy of the Borderline Adult.* New York: Brunner/Mazel.

McDevitt, J. (1975), Separation/individuation and object constancy. *J. Amer. Psychoanal. Assn.,* 23:713–743.

———(1979), the role of internalization in the development of object relations during the separation/individuation phase. *J. Amer. Psychoanal. Assn.,* 27:327–343.

———(1983), The emergence of hostile aggression and its defensive and adaptive modification during the separation/individuation process. *J. Amer. Psychoanal. Assn.,* 31:273–300.

McLaughlin, J. (1978), Primary and secondary process in the context of cerebral hemisphere specialization. *Psychoanal. Quart.,* 47:273–266.

———(1981), Transference, psychic reality and countertransference. *Psychoanal. Quart.,* 50:639–644.

———(1987), The play of transference: Some reflections on enrichment in the psychoanalytic situation. *J. Amer. Psychoanal. Assn.,* 35:557–582.

Meyer, J. K., & Dupkin, C. (1985), Gender disturbance in children. An interim clinical report. *Bull. Menn. Clinic,* 59:236–269.

Middlemore, M. (1941), *The Nursing Couple.* London: Hamish Hamilton.

Mintzer, D., Als, H., Tronick, E., & Brazelton, T. (1984), Parenting an infant with a birth defect. *The Psychoanalytic Study of the Child,* 39:561–589. New Haven, CT: Yale University Press.

Money, J., & Ehrhardt, A. (1972), *Man and Woman, Boy and Girl: The Differentiation and Dimorphism of Gender Identity from Conception to Maturity.* Baltimore: Johns Hopkins University Press.

Neubauer, P. (1971), Special problems of transference and transference neurosis. In: *The Unconscious Today,* ed. M. Kanzer. New York: International Universities Press, pp. 381–455.

Novick, K., & Novick, J. (1987), The essence of masochism. *The Psychoanalytic Study of the Child,* 42:353–384. New Haven, CT: Yale University Press.

Papousek, H., & Papousek, M. (1979), The infant's fundamental adaptive response system in social interaction. In: *Orgins of the Infant Social Responsiveness,* ed. E. Thomas. Hillsdale, NJ: Lawrence Erlbaum Associates.

——— ———(1984), The evolution of parent–infant attachment: New psychobiological perspectives. In: *Frontiers of Infant Psychiatry,* Vol. 2, eds. J. Call, E. Galenson, & R. Tyson. New York: Basic Books, pp. 276–283.

Parens, H. (1979), *The Development of Aggression in Early Childhood.* New York: Jason Aronson.

———(1987), Comments made during the 18th Annual Symposium on

Child Development, Margaret S. Mahler Symposium Series, Philadelphia, May.

Piaget, J. (1924), *The Construction of Reality in the Child.* New York: Basic Books, 1954.

Provence, S. (1977), *The Challenge of Day Care.* New Haven, CT: Yale University Press.

———Lipton, R. (1962), *Infants in Institutions.* New York: International Universities Press.

Pruett, K. (1983), Infants of primary nurturing fathers. *The Psychoanalytic Study of the Child,* 38:258–280. New Haven, CT: Yale University Press.

———(1985), Oedipal configurations in young father-raised children. *The Psychoanalytic Study of the Child,* 40:435–456. New Haven, CT: Yale University Press.

Rangell, L. (1954), The psychology of poise, with a special elaboration on the psychic significance of the snout or perioral region. *Internat. J. Psycho-Anal.,* 35:313–332.

———(1955), On the psychoanalytic theory of anxiety: A statement of a unitary theory. *J. Amer. Psychoanal. Assn.,* 3:389–414.

———(1956), The borderline state and the analytic attitude. Abstracted in Robbins, L. L., Report of Panel on "The borderline case." *J. Amer. Psychoanal. Assn.,* 4:550–562.

———(1963a), The scope of intrapsychic conflict: Microscopic and macroscopic considerations. *The Psychoanalytic Study of the Child,* 18:75–102. New York: International Universities Press.

———(1963b), Structural problems in intrapsychic conflict. *The Psychoanalytic Study of the Child,* 18:103–138. New York: International Universities Press.

———(1967), Psychoanalysis, affect, and the "Human Core"–on the relationship of psychoanalysis to the behavioral sciences. *Psychoanal. Quart.,* 36:172–202.

———(1969), The intrapsychic process and its analysis—a recent line of thought and its current implications. *Internat. J. Psycho-Anal.,* 50:65–77.

———(1971), The decision-making process. A contribution from psychoanalysis. *The Psychoanalytic Study of the Child,* 26:425–452. Chicago: Quadrangle.

———(1984), Structure, somatic and psychic: The biopsychological base of infancy. In: *Frontiers of Infant Psychiatry,* Vol. 2, ed. J. Call, E. Galenson, and R. Tyson. New York: Basic Books, pp. 70–81.

———(1985), The object in psychoanalytic theory. *J. Amer. Psychoanal Assn.,* 33:301–334.

———(1986), The executive functions of the ego. An extension of the concept of ego autonomy. *The Psychoanalytic Study of the Child,* 41:1–37. New Haven, CT: Yale University Press.

———(1988), *The Human Core. The Intrapsychic Base of Behavior.* Madison, CT: International Universities Press.

Ribble, M. (1943). *The Rights of Infants.* New York: Columbia University Press.

Robertson, J. (1952), Film: A Two-Year-Old Goes to Hospital (16mm, b & w, Sound, 45 and 30 minute versions; English/French; Guide booklet). London: Tavistock Child Development Research Unit; New York: New York University Film Library.

———(1958), *Young Children in Hospitals.* New York: Basic Books.

———(1968), Film No. 2: Jane, 17 Months: In Foster Care for 10 Days (16mm, b & w, Sound, 37 minutes; Guide booklet). London: Tavistock Child Development Research Unit; New York: New York University Film Library.

———(1969), Film No. 3: John, 17 Months: For 9 Days in a Residential Nursery (16mm, b & w, Sound, 45 minutes; Guide booklet). London: Tavistock Child Development Research Unit; New York: New York University Film Library.

———(1971), Film No. 4: Thomas, 2 Years 4 Months: In Foster Care for 10 Days (16mm, b & w, Sound, 38 minutes; Guide booklet). London: Tavistock Child Development Research Unit; New York: New York University Film Library.

——— Robertson, J. (1967), Young Children in Brief Separation, Film No. 1: Kate, 2 Years 5 Months: In Foster Care for 27 Days (16mm, b & w, Sound, 33 minutes; Guide booklet). London: Tavistock Child Development Research Unit; New York: New York University Film Library.

——— ———(1971), Young children in brief separation: A fresh look. *The Psychoanalytic Study of the Child,* 26:264–315. New York: Quadrangle.

Roiphe, H., & Galenson, E. (1973), The infantile fetish. *The Psychoanalytic Study of the Child,* 28:147–166. New Haven, CT: Yale University Press.

——— ———(1981), *Infantile Origins of Sexual Identity.* New York: International Universities Press.

Sameroff, A. J., ed. (1978), *Organization and Stability of Newborn Behavior: A Commentary on the Brazelton Neonatal Behavior Assessment Scale.* Monograph 43, nos. 5–6, serial No. 177. Society for Research in Child Development.

———(1983), Developmental systems: Contexts and evolution. In: *Handbook of Child Psychology,* ed. P. Mussen. New York: John Wiley, pp. 237–294.

Sander, L. (1962), Issues in early mother–child interaction. *J. Amer. Acad. Child Psychiat.,* 1:141–166.

———(1964), Adaptive relationships in early mother–child interaction. *J. Amer. Acad. Child Psychiat.,* 3:231–264.

————(1975), Infant and caretaking environment: Investigation and conceptualization of adaptive behavior in a series of increasing complexity. In: *Explorations in Child Psychiatry*, ed. E. J. Anthony. New York: Plenum, pp. 129–166.

————(1978), Infant state regulation and the integration of action in early development. Paper presented at the First Infant Psychiatry Institute, Costa Mesa, CA, February 25.

————(1980), New knowledge about the infant from current research: Implications for psychoanalysis. *J. Amer. Psychoanal. Assn.*, 28:181–198.

————(1983), Polarity, paradox, and the organizing process in development. In: *Frontiers of Infant Psychiatry*, Vol. 2, ed. J. Call, E. Galenson, & R. Tyson. New York: Basic Books, pp. 333–346.

————(1985), Toward a logic of organization in psychobiological development. In: *Biologic Response Styles: Clinical Implications*, ed. K. Klar & L. Sieve. Washington, DC: American Psychiatric Press.

Sandler, J. (1976), Countertransference and role-responsiveness. *Internat. Rev. Psychoanal.*, 3:43–48.

————(1981), Character traits and object relationships. *Psychoanal. Quart.*, 50:694–708.

————Kennedy, H., & Tyson, R. (1975), Discussions on transference: The treatment situation and technique in child psychoanalysis. *The Psychoanalytic Study of the Child*, 30:409–442. New Haven CT: Yale University Press.

————Sandler, A-M. (1987), The past unconscious, the present unconscious and the vicissitudes of guilt. *Internat. J. Psycho-Anal.*, 68:331–342.

Scharfman, M. (1971), Transference phenomena in adolescent analysis. In: *The Unconscious Today*, ed. M. Kanzer. New York: International Universities Press, pp. 422–435.

Schlesinger, H. (1988), Case discussion and position statement. *Psychoanal. Inq.*, 8:524–534.

Schneirla, T. C. (1956), Interrelationships of the "innate" and the "acquired" in instinctual behavior. In: *L'Instinct dans le Comportement des Animaux et de l'Homme*. Paris: Massin, pp. 387–452.

————(1957), The concept of development in comparative psychology. In: *The Concept of Development: An Issue in the Study of Human Behavior*, ed. C. B. Harms. Minneapolis: University of Minneapolis Press, pp. 78–108.

Schur, M. (1960), Discussion of Dr. John Bowlby's paper. *The Psychoanalytic Study of the Child*, 15:63–84. New York: International Universities Press.

Silver, D. (1985), Prologue. *Psychoanal. Inq.*, 5:501–507.

Silverman, M. (1980), A fresh look at the case of Little Hans. In: *Freud and His Patients,* ed. M. Kanzer & J. Glenn. New York & London: Jason Aronson, pp. 95–120.

Snow, C. (1979), Talking and playing with babies. In: *Before Speech,* ed. M. Bullowa. London: Cambridge University Press, pp. 264–288.

Solnit, A. (1987), Book review of D. N. Stern: *The Interpersonal World of the Infant: A View for Psychoanalytic and Developmental Psychology. Amer. J. Psychiat.,* 144:1508–1509.

Spence, D. (1982a), Narrative truth and theoretical truth. *Psychoanal. Quart.,* 51:43–69.

———(1982b), *Narrative Truth and Historical Truth. Meaning and Interpretation in Psychoanalysis.* New York: W. W. Norton.

Sperling, M. (1963), Fetishism in children. *The Psychoanalytic Study of the Child,* 19:470–493. New York: International Universities Press.

Spitz, R. (1945a), Diacritic and coenesthetic organizations. *Psychoanal. Rev.,* 32:262–274.

———(1945b), Hospitalism: An inquiry into the genesis of psychiatric conditions in early childhood. *The Psychoanalytic Study of the Child,* 1:53–74. New York: International Universities Press.

———(1946a), Anaclitic depression: An inquiry into the genesis of psychiatric conditions in early childhood, II. *The Psychoanalytic Study of the Child,* 2:313–342.

———(1946b), Hospitalism: A follow-up report. *The Psychoanalytic Study of the Child,* 2:113–117. New York: International Universities Press.

———(1947), *Grief, a Peril in Infancy.* Film. New York Film Library.

———(1950), Anxiety in infancy: A study of its manifestations in the first year of life. *Internat. J. Psycho-Anal.,* 31:138–143.

———(1953), Aggression: Its role in the establishment of object relations. In: *Drives, Affects, Behavior,* ed. R. Lowenstein. New York: International Universities Press, pp. 126–138.

———(1957), *No and Yes: On the Genesis of Human Communication.* New York: International Universities Press.

———(1958), On the genesis of superego components. *The Psychoanalytic Study of the Child,* 18:375–404. New York: International Universities Press.

———(1959), *A Genetic Field Theory of Ego Formation: Its Implications for Pathology.* New York: International Universities Press.

———(1960), Discussion of Dr. Bowlby's paper. *The Psychoanalytic Study of the Child,* 15:85–94. New York: International Universities Press.

———(1962), Autoerotism reexamined. *The Psychoanalytic Study of the Child,* 17:283–315. New York: International Universities Press.

———(1963), Life and the dialogue. In: *Counterpoint: Libidinal Object and Subject,* ed. H. Gaskill. New York: International Universities Press, pp. 154–176.

———(1966), The evolution of dialogue. In: *Drives, Affects, Behavior,* Vol. 2, ed. M. Schur. New York: International Universities Press.

———Cobliner, W. (1965), *The First Year of Life*. New York: International Universities Press.

———Wolf, K. M. (1946), Anaclitic depression: An inquiry into the genesis of psychiatric conditions in early childhood. *The Psychoanalytic Study of the Child*, 2:313–342. New York: International Unviersities Press.

——— ———(1949), Autoerotism: Some empirical findings and hypotheses on three of its manifestations in the first year of life. *The Psychoanalytic Study of the Child*, 3/4:85–120. New York: International Universities Press.

Sroufe, L (1983), Infant caregiver attachment and patterns of adaptation in preschool: The roots of maladaption and competence. *Minnesota Symposium in Child Psychology*, ed. M. Perlmutter, 16:41–81. Hillsdale, NJ: Lawrence Erlbaum Associates.

———Fleeson, J. (1985), Attachment and the construction of relationships. In: *The Nature and Development of Relationships*, ed. W. Hartrup & Z. Rubin. Hillsdale, NJ: Lawrence Erlbaum Associates.

Stechler, C., & Halton, A. (1987), The emergence of assertion and aggression during infancy: A psychoanalytic systems approach. *J. Amer. Psychoanal. Assn.*, 35:821–838.

Stern, D. (1971), A micro-analysis of mother–infant interaction: Behaviors regulating social contact between a mother and her three-and-a-half year old twins. *J. Amer. Acad. Child Psychiat.*,10:501–517.

———(1977), *The First Relationship, Mother and Infant*. Cambridge, MA: Harvard University Press.

———(1984), Affect attunement. In: *Frontiers of Infant Psychiatry*, Vol. 2, ed. J. Call, E. Galenson, & R. Tyson. New York: Basic Books, pp. 3–14.

———(1985), *The Interpersonal World of the Infant: A View from Psychoanalysis and Developmental Psychology*. New York: Basic Books.

Stoller, R. (1968), *Sex and Gender*, Vol. 1. New York: Science House.

———(1975), *Sex and Gender*, Vol. 2. New York: Jason Aronson.

———(1976), Primary femininity. *J. Amer. Psychoanal. Assn.*, 24/5:59–78.

———(1978), Beyond gender aberrations. Treatment issues. *J. Amer. Psychoanal. Assn.*, 26:541–558.

———(1979), *Sexual Excitement: Dynamics of Erotic Life*. New York: Pantheon Books.

Stone, L. (1961), *The Psychoanalytic Situation*. New York: International Universities Press.

Thomas, A., Chess, S., & Birch, H. (1968), *Temperament and Behavior Disorders in Children*. New York & London: New York University Press.

Tomkins, S. (1962), *Affect, Imagery, Consciousness*, Vol. 1. New York: Springer.

Tronick, E., Als, M., Adamson, L., Wise, S., & Brazelton, T. (1978), The infant's response to entrapment between contradictory messages in face to face interaction. *J. Amer. Acad. Child Psychiat.*, 17:1–13.

——Gianino, A. (1986), Interactive mismatch and repair. *Zero to Three*, 6:1–6.

Valenstein, A. (1973), On attachment to painful feelings and the negative therapeutic reaction. *The Psychoanalytic Study of the Child*, 28:365–392. New Haven, CT: Yale University Press.

Weil, A. (1970), The basic core. *The Psychoanalytic Study of the Child*, 25:442–460. New York: International Universities Press.

——(1978), Maturational variations and genetic-dynamic issues. *J. Amer. Psychoanal. Assn.*, 26:461–491.

Winnicott, D. W. (1953), Transitional objects and transitional phenomena. *Collected Papers: Through Paediatrics to Psycho-Analysis*. New York: Basic books, 1958.

——(1965), *The Maturational Processes and the Facilitating Environment*. New York: International Universities Press.

——(1967), Mirror-role of mother and family in child development. In: *Playing and Reality*. New York: Basic Books, 1971, pp. 111–118.

——(1971), *Playing and Reality*. New York: Basic Books.

Wolff, P. H. (1959), Observations on newborn infants. *Psychosom. Med.*, 21:110–118.

——(1965), The development of attention in young infants. *Ann. Acad. Sci.*, 118:815–830.

——(1966), The Causes, Control, and Organization of Behavior in the Neonate. *Psychological Issues*, Vol. 1, Monograph 17. New York: International Universities Press.

——(1971), Reporter. Panel on review of psychoanalytic theory in the light of current research. *J. Amer. Psychoanal. Assn.*, 19:565–576.

——White, B. L. (1965), Visual pursuit and attention in young infants. *J. Amer. Acad. Child Psychiat.*, 4:474–484.

Zahn-Waxler, D., & Radke-Yarrow, M. (1982), The development of altruism. In: *The Development of Prosocial Behavior*, ed. M. C. Eisenberg. New York: Academic Press, pp. 109–137.

Name Index

Subject Index